THE LATINO/A AMERICAN DREAM

THE LATINO/A AMERICAN DREAM

EDITED BY SANDRA L. HANSON AND JOHN KENNETH WHITE

Texas A&M University Press
College Station

This paper meets the requirements of ANSI/NISO Z39.48-1992 (Permanence of Paper).
Binding materials have been chosen for durability.
Manufactured in the United States of America

LIBRARY OF CONGRESS CATALOGING-IN-PUBLICATION DATA

Names: Hanson, Sandra L., editor. | White, John Kenneth, 1952– editor. |
  White, John Kenneth, 1952– Whose dream?
Title: The Latino/a American dream / edited by Sandra L. Hanson and John
  Kenneth White.
Other titles: Latino American dream | Latina American dream
Description: First edition. | College Station: Texas A&M University Press,
  [2016] | Includes bibliographical references and index.
Identifiers: LCCN 2015036247| ISBN 9781623493899 (printed case: alk. paper)
  | ISBN 9781623493905 (ebook)
Subjects: LCSH: Hispanic Americans—Social conditions—21st century. |
  Hispanic American women—Social conditions—21st century. | American Dream.
Classification: LCC E184.S75 L3548 2016 | DDC 305.868/073—dc23 LC record available at
http://lccn.loc.gov/2015036247

To our students—you have provided the feedback, the questions, and the support that make our research possible.

Contents

Preface

This volume on Latino/as and the American Dream is part of a Dream sequence. Our earlier volume, *The American Dream in the 21st Century* (Temple University Press, 2011) examined the historic concept of the American Dream in the twenty-first century with a special focus on the Great Recession and the election of the first African American president. This book on Latino/as and the American Dream follows up on that volume by examining the newest immigrant group to pursue the American Dream—Latino/as. The story of the American Dream is a story of immigrants. In our earlier volume we argued that the Dream is an old Dream with roots in the American Revolution. It is a resilient Dream that continues to be a major component of American culture through times of slavery and times when women and blacks could not vote. Historian James Truslow Adams popularized the phrase "American Dream" and defined it as "that dream of a land in which life should be better and richer and fuller for every man, with opportunity for each according to ability or achievement" (Adams 1941, 404). In spite of a major recession, our earlier volume showed that most Americans retain this sense of optimism and believe in the Dream and its values of freedom and equality of opportunity. Americans often mention things such as having a good family life, having quality health care, having educational opportunities, and being able to succeed in spite of one's family background when they talk about the Dream. However, the nature of the Dream may be changing, and the idea that it is available to all who work hard is being questioned. One of the major conclusions in our look at *The American Dream in the 21st Century* was that the Dream is becoming less about wealth and more spiritual. Additionally, we concluded that there is not equity in opportunity of achieving the Dream as major divides by class, race/ethnicity, and gender continue on the American landscape.

If the story of the American Dream is a story of immigrants, then the story continues with the current immigration flow of Latino/as to the United

States. Here we ask what the Dream means to this ethnic group that will soon be the largest race/ethnic group in the United States. Is it a new Dream? Is it being achieved? Can Latino/as dream too? The current climate of fear among America's white middle class is a major theme in US media and culture. Is the Dream dead for America's white middle class in the midst of the Great Recession? Will today's youth be the first generation to not do better than their parents? Are Latino/as and the new immigrant stream taking away from the American Dream or contributing to it? How are Latino/as doing relative to African Americans—and the other racial/ethnic minority groups in the United States? In this volume a group of scholars from multiple disciplines examine the nature and complexity of the American Dream for Latino/as. If the American Dream is a story of the poor and the downtrodden rising up to success and opportunity, then Latino/as represent the new face of the American Dream and perhaps a revival of the Dream. Here we show how presidents, politics, and ongoing policy discussions are framing the dream for Latino/as. We examine the religious and community contexts that reflect the special nature of the Dream for Latino/as. The diversity among Latino/as by country of origin, immigrant status, gender, and class is explored in order to show the complexity of the Dream for Latino/as in the United States. Much of the history of the American Dream has a distinctly white cast to it. By expanding our focus to include one of America's largest ethnic (and newest immigrant) groups, we hope to provide a richer, more current and nuanced picture of the American Dream.

Reference

Adams, J. T. 1941. *The Epic of America*. Garden City, NY: Blue Ribbon Books.

Introduction

SANDRA L. HANSON AND JOHN KENNETH WHITE

Jesus Moran's parents struggled when they arrived to the United States from El Salvador. His father lost his job in construction during a wave of layoffs and now works at a car wash. His mother has been a housekeeper for 14 years for the same family. So when it came to their children, they wanted them to achieve more. "It was always kind of an unsaid thing that me and my three brothers would go to college," Moran explains. "There wasn't any pressure, but there was this mindset that we must go to college so we could avoid the struggles my parents went through." So when Moran received his college acceptance email, he took a screen shot on his smart phone and posted it on Facebook. . . . The letter said he was accepted into Harvard University. . . . But college was not the expected path for many kids living where Moran grew up. (Adney 2012)

The alarm has rung on the American Dream. Recent economic, jobs, housing, and health care crises, together with the Occupy Wall Street movement, have created considerable media attention and commentary on the state of the Dream. Much of the ongoing discussion suggests that the focus is primarily on white middle-class Americans and the concern that this group, which historically personified the achievement of the American Dream, might no longer have access to it (Acs 2012). There was little concern about the end of the Dream in past decades when race, ethnicity, class, and gender continued to structure opportunities in the United States. Americans often make the implicit assumption that although the Dream is attainable by all, it is especially reserved for the hardworking and "deserving" middle class. If others (including the poor or racial/ethnic minorities) do not achieve the American Dream, the assumption is that they did not try hard enough. Yet

1

historically the American Dream was a Dream *of* and *for* immigrants. Rising streams of Latino/a immigrants—and the reality of an American racial/ethnic demographic in which whites will no longer be the largest race/ethnic group by midcentury—have created pointed discussions about race, ethnicity, and the American way of living and dreaming. Some commentators see a threat to the Dream with a rising wave of Latino/a immigration. The notion of a zero-sum game, with competition from Latino/as reducing the chances of others to achieve the Dream, is sometimes promoted. Public opinion polls echo this fear among some sectors of the American public. Stereotypes about Latino/as involving "marginalized populations," "immigrants," and "second-language" users—as well as assumptions that the Latino/a experience is at odds with the larger US culture—are part of this current public opinion. Support of policies and programs that attempt to limit illegal immigration and benefits to illegal immigrants suggest that at least some Americans (and American media) believe that there is a tension between the quality of American life and the American Dream, on the one hand, and the new American immigrants on the other.

The authors in this volume reveal the inaccuracy of simple stereotypes as they provide a more complex picture of Latino/as, their achievements, and their Dreams in the United States. Notions of cultural integrity and agency are developed that illustrate the extensive strengths and positive attributes of Latino/a culture, as well as the work that many Latino/as are doing to resist stereotypes and succeed in spite of limitations associated with minority group status. Results from this careful analysis of the contributions, dreams, and achievements of Latino/as may come as a surprise to those who continue to see this group as a threat, a risk, and as outside of the Dream. In this chapter we present information on objective and subjective (attitudinal) indicators of achieving the American Dream for Latino/as. We also provide an overview of the goals for this volume on Latino/as and the American Dream and a preliminary discussion of some of the major issues addressed by a group of authors coming from multiple disciplines. Finally, we provide a preview of how each chapter on diverse topics, including politics, presidents, immigration, religion, race, ethnicity, nationality, and gender, helps tell a story about Latino/as and the American Dream.

The Dream: Strengths and Challenges for Latino/as

What is the American Dream for Latino/as and how do they hope to achieve it?[1] We can't assume that the American Dream means the same thing to everyone. A report by Massachusetts Mutual Life Insurance Company suggests one distinctive area involves business ownership (Massachusetts Mutual 2011). This is one of the ingredients of the Dream—Latino/as and Latino/a-owned businesses are growing at twice the rate of the national average. Latino/a business owners are unique in their heavy emphasis on family and community as a major reason for entrepreneurship and achieving the Dream. The study also found that Latino/a business owners are struggling and not doing enough planning and investment management. Challenges are greatest for those Latino/as with less education and English language skills. Research reports like this are important for providing insight into unique strengths and challenges for Latino/as who are reaching for the Dream. They are also important in providing specific recommendations for empowering Latino/a business owners with tools that will make the achievement of their American Dream more likely.

The report on business ownership among Latino/as brings up the larger issue of the achievements and contributions of Latino/as in the United States. Latino/as participate in and contribute to the American Dream. Latino/as make major contributions to the US economy vis-à-vis job creation and economic growth (Gonzalez 2011). They are not just a "swing" vote (Cisneros and Rosales 2009). For some time now, Latino/as have represented a success story in the United States and are part of a rising middle class (Chavez 1997b; Cisneros and Rosales 2009). Although the rise in the Latino/a population in the United States is often thought of as being associated with an increase in unauthorized immigrants, the entrance of many *legal* Latino/a citizens into the middle class is the larger, more precise, reality (Pachon 2009). The Latino/a presence in the United States is representative of much of what we associate with the American Dream: youth, value on hard work, ambition to succeed, and commitment to family/community. Latino/as constitute a major strength and resource for the United States. Many Latino/as and their ancestors are not newcomers and were essential in building America's economy and culture (Cisneros and Rosales 2009). The young Latino/a demographic impacting the US population and fueling a population growth is striking, especially when compared to the population decline typical of demographic trajectories in other industrialized countries (for example, Japan, France, Italy, Germany) (Cisneros and Rosales 2009).

Objective Indicators of the Dream for Latino/as

Our discussion of Latino/as and the American Dream can benefit from recent figures on education, occupations, income, housing, and health insurance. How are Latino/as doing on these indicators of status and well-being that are considered part of the American Dream? How do these statistics compare to other race/ethnic groups? The chapters in this volume consider aspects of this answer in more detail, but here we provide some demographic context using 2010 Census data from a recent report on Latino/as published by the Pew Research Center (Motel 2012). With regard to *education*, Latino/as are over-represented among those adults with less than a ninth grade education (for example, 22 percent for Hispanics, 2 percent for non-Hispanic whites, and 5.1 percent for African Americans). This figure is much lower, however, for native-born Latino/as (8 percent). Residential and school segregation, together with schools characterized by tracking, low resources, few mentoring opportunities, lack of cultural sensitivity in schools, educators and curriculum, and a shortage of qualified teachers, present challenges to high school completion for Latino/as (Yosso 2006; Fry 2008; Rochin and Mello 2007; Crespo-Sancho 2009; Rierson 2006; Contreras 2011). Some have shown an increase in segregation of Latino/a youth in the US education system (Fry 2008). Latino/as are underrepresented among adults with a college degree (for example, 13 percent for Hispanics, 31 percent for non-Hispanic whites, and 18 percent for African Americans). But the college enrollment gap is narrowing (Fry 2010). Education scholars have observed that community colleges and Hispanic-serving institutions play a major role in college attainment (McGlynn 1999; DiMaria 2006; Brown 2009). Among native-born Latino/a adults, 17 percent have a college degree. High school dropout rates are relatively high for Latino/as if foreign born are included (8.2 percent). When only native-born Latino/as are considered, these rates are lower than for other minority groups (for example, they are 5.8 percent for Hispanics and 6.2 percent for African Americans). Comparisons with the 2000 census data show considerable progress on this indicator of education, with the dropout rate declining from 12.2 percent to 5.8 percent for native-born Hispanics. Latino/as are, however, less likely than other racial/ethnic minorities to get a GED if they drop out of high school (Fry 2010). The increasing level of educational attainment for Latino/as in the United States is no doubt related to a demand for Latino/a professionals in markets that are increasingly Latino/a dominated (DiMaria 2006).

Occupational achievement data for 2010 show that Latino/as are underrepresented in higher-status occupations and overrepresented in lower-status occupations. For example, in 2010, 7 percent of Latino/as were employed in management occupations and 2 percent of Latino/as were employed in science and engineering occupations. These figures were 15 percent and 9 percent for non-Hispanic whites. They were 9 percent and 2 percent for African Americans. When only native-born Latino/as are considered, 9 percent of this group is in management occupations and 3 percent in science and engineering. On the other end of the occupational spectrum, 9 percent of Latino/as are in food preparation/serving occupations and 9 percent in cleaning and maintenance (as compared to 5 percent and 3 percent for whites and 7 percent and 6 percent for African Americans). When only native-born Latino/as are considered, the figures are less high, with 7 percent in food preparation/serving and 5 percent in cleaning and maintenance.

Personal earning data for 2010 reveal a lower average for Latino/as ($20,000) than for whites ($31,000), African Americans ($24,700), or Asian Americans ($34,000). This is true even when considering native-born Latino/as ($22,700). When looking at *household income*, 25 percent of Latino/as (24 percent of native born) are in the lowest quintile. This figure is lower for non-Hispanic whites (17 percent) and higher for African Americans (33 percent). When considering the highest quintile, Latino/as (12 percent of total and 15 percent of native born) again fare better than African Americans (10 percent) but less well than non-Hispanic whites (22 percent). *Poverty* data also provide insight into how Latino/as are doing on achieving the American Dream. Here we see that Latino/as (25 percent) and African Americans (27 percent) had a poverty rate over twice the poverty rate for non-Hispanic whites (11 percent) in 2010. On this indicator, there was little difference between foreign-born and native-born Latino/as.

Health insurance and *housing* are two final indicators that Americans think of when considering the American Dream. Latino/as are by far the largest group without health insurance. Almost one-third of Latino/as are without health insurance, as compared to 11 percent of non-Hispanic whites and 19 percent of African Americans. Over half of foreign-born Latino/as are without health insurance. This figure is 19 percent for native-born Latino/as. When considering housing, 2010 census data show that the percent "owner-occupied" for Latino/as, non-Hispanic whites, and African Americans is 47 percent, 73 percent, and 45 percent respectively. Among native-born Latino/as the figure is 50 percent.

Attitudes toward the American Dream—Latino/as

The data for US Latino/as on a broad range of issues from education to income and housing show progress for Latino/as but also continuing race/ethnic inequality. The authors in this volume examine the nature and sources of the ongoing racism in a society that is not "postracial" and that does not yet allow full equality of opportunity in achieving the American Dream. Recent public opinion polls suggest that Americans are aware of these inequalities.

When asked about who has a better chance to get ahead in today's society—Hispanic people or white people—52 percent said white people; only 36 percent said both had an equal chance.[2] Results from the same public opinion survey show men and women slightly disagree as to whether minorities can get ahead: 34 percent for women and 38 percent for men. One of the goals of this volume is to show the complex intersection between race/ethnicity and gender in understanding Latino/as and the American Dream.

Data on demographics also reveal a complex relationship between the two largest race/ethnic minority groups in the United States. Latino/as are doing better on some measures (for example, housing) and African Americans are doing better on others (for example, college degrees). When asked who has a better chance of getting ahead in today's society, black people or Hispanic people, a majority (59 percent) reported that they had an equal chance. However, 23 percent said "Black" over "Hispanic" and only 14 percent said "Hispanic" over "Black."[3] The authors in this volume offer insights into the comparative experiences of Latino/as and African Americans in their race to achieve the American Dream.

Like other race/ethnic groups that immigrated to the United States, there is considerable evidence that Latino/as believe in the American Dream and its promise of upward mobility. Some who have looked at belief in the American Dream across race/ethnic groups find that Latino/as stand out for their optimism (Cohen-Marks and Stout 2011). Like earlier immigrant groups, they place a high value on education, working hard, and success in careers (Pew 2009). Latino/a youth are similarly optimistic about their futures. Like Latino/as in general, they value education, hard work, and career success. These values persist in spite of challenges involving poverty, higher than average high school dropout rates, and high exposure to gangs (Pew 2009). The authors in this volume examine these attitudes and consider them in light of stereotypes that see Latino/a and white-ethnic US cultures as being at odds, with some viewing the Latino/a culture as representing a threat to the American Dream.

Organizations and Movement toward the Dream—Latino/as

To the extent that there has been progress for Latino/as, credit must be given to organizations like the United Farm Workers Union, ASPIRA, the Southwest Voter Registration Project, the National Leadership Institute, the National Council of La Raza, the Cuban National Forum, the League of United Latino/a American Citizens, and the US Hispanic Chamber of Commerce, to name a few (Cisneros and Rosales 2009). The legal, education, and community work of these organizations has contributed to gains in educational attainment among Latino/as. These organizations have also helped fuel an increase in mobility by Latino/as into the middle class that is often disguised by general population data for Latino/as regarding occupation and earnings (Pachon 2009). Sociologists often speak of status quo, elites, and inequality. They also speak of social movements, resistance, and social change. A discussion of the American Dream for Latino/as sets the stage for insights and understanding of these ongoing dialectics involving status quo and social change.

Diversity among Latino/as

Figures on objective measures of the American Dream for Latino/as as a whole are helpful, but there is considerable diversity among Latino/as on these measures as well as on other attitudes and experiences. Much of the diversity is associated with variation on factors such as ethnic national- ity, race, immigration experience, foreign-born status, and generation. For example, 17 percent of native-born Latino/as have a college degree, but only 10 percent of foreign-born Latino/as possess one. It is difficult to make gen- eralizations about Latino/as' achievements and Dreams, given the diversity in the countries that they (or their ancestors) emigrated from. In 2010, more than six out of ten Latino/as in the United States identified themselves as being of Mexican origin. The other largest Latino/a groups—Puerto Rican, Cuban, Salvadoran, Dominican, Guatemalan, Colombian, Honduran, Ecua- doran, and Peruvian—make up over 25 percent of the US Latino/a popula- tion (Lopez and Dockterman 2011). These groups vary in geographic loca- tion and have unique motivations, immigration experiences, and adaptations (Portes and Fernández-Kelly 2008; Pew 2007). For example, Latino/as who identify as being of Mexican origin have a poverty rate that is higher than the average rate for the United States. Those who identify as having Cuban origins have a rate of poverty that is similar to that of the overall US popula- tion (Pew 2007). The issue of racial variation across Latino/as is related to but also distinct from ethnic nationality. Although past work on race and ethnicity traditionally saw these as two separate concepts, race scholars are increasingly acknowledging the ways in which they intersect (for example, Frank, Akresh, and Lu 2010; Cobas, Duany, and Feagin 2009; Feliciano and Robnett 2014). Some even argue that Latino/as are a distinct category that does not fit into the race or ethnic categories often used (Feliciano and Robnett 2014). As our thinking about multiple race and ethnic statuses pro- gresses, we will hopefully become better at understanding measurement of these concepts. It wasn't until the 2000 census that respondents could identify multiple races and ethnic statuses. Race and ethnicity are difficult, complex concepts that have historically changed in meaning. The diversity of Latino/a experience is better understood in the context of Latino/as' multiracial and ethnic identities. Issues of language for Latino/as who have English as a second language are also important for understanding achievement experiences in the United States (Pew 2009; Fry 2008). Importantly, any research on US Latino/as should acknowledge that many have historic roots and indigenous status in the southwestern United States. Additionally, there is diversity in migrations with some Latino/a immigrants being labor immigrants (Mexicans and Central Americans), some refugees (Cubans and the Nicaraguans, Salvadorans, and Guatemalans during the 1980s), and some contemporary immigrants being professionals from Puerto Rico and much of South America (Portes and Rumbaut 2014). The implications of these diverse experiences are considered by the authors of this volume as they judge the social, political, economic, and cultural aspects of the American Dream for Latino/as in the United States. Just as some have noted that Latino/as have become American "the Latino/a way" (Jacoby 2009), we reveal how Latino/as are evaluating and achieving the American Dream "the Latino/a way."

The History and Emerging Nature of the Dream

The American Dream is as old as the country itself. It involves values that are resilient and timeless: life, liberty, and the pursuit of happiness. For some, it has come to mean material wealth. Looking back from our recent experiences in the Great Recession, we see that American culture has been hijacked to some degree by an emphasis on individual material gain and excess. The media and corporate America are major actors in focusing on a Dream that involves spending, accumulation, and wealth. But recent public opinion polls show that a majority believes the American Dream is more about spiritual happiness (for them and their family) than about material goods (Hanson and Zogby 2010). As the authors in this volume explore the ideas and experiences of Latino/as and the American Dream, the reader will be reminded of the values of freedom, liberty, and equality of opportunity—as well as the focus on family and community—that were involved in early inceptions of the American Dream. These values represent the core of today's Latino/a Dream and possibly a revival of the original meaning of the Dream.

Some have argued that it is during difficult times—like the Great Recession of the late 2000s—that we *especially* need the Dream. Sociologist Barry Glassner argues (in Seelye 2009) that individuals want to hold on to their dreams when times are hard. Even though the prospects of achieving the American

Dream are slim during hard times, the promise remains. Some have observed this phenomenon during the Great Recession with a reinvigoration of the American Dream (Seelye 2009). Yet many questions remain. Do we still see our diversity (with current groups of non-European immigrants) as a source of growth and strength? Is the American Dream dying or is it being revived? Historically, the American Dream survived slavery; times when women and blacks couldn't vote; and continued race, gender, and class discrimination. Will it survive this era of economic challenge and demographic change? Will it survive for the privileged as well as the less privileged? Do Latino/as believe in the American Dream despite not having had full access to opportunities and success? Will their journey toward achieving the American Dream be a distinct one blending Latino/a culture and values with success in mainstream America?

Age, Generation, and the Dream for Latino/as

Sociologists have historically noted the importance of age and generational experiences in understanding social issues. Age and generation are relevant to understanding Latino/as and the American Dream, since it is the attitudes of today's young generation toward upward mobility, race/ethnicity, immigration, and opportunity that will play a significant role in the future. It is these young people that will be heading US institutions and forming future policy. Pollster John Zogby sees a unique attitude toward the American Dream among the nation's youth and refers to them as the "first global" generation (Zogby 2011). According to Zogby there is a change in emphasis toward a new dream that is "not mine, not yours, but ours" and has implications for issues involving race/ethnicity, inequality, and getting ahead.

This new dream is important since one of the most significant aspects of the US Latino/a population is its youth. Latino/as are the youngest and fastest-growing population in the United States. Almost one-quarter of US youth are Latino/a (Childstats 2012). The median age for Latino/as and non-Hispanic whites in the United States is twenty-seven and forty-two, respectively (Murphy et al. 2014). And these Latino/a youth have distinctive characteristics. A majority of them are US citizens *and* live with both parents (Murphy et al. 2014). These young Latino/as are getting new opportunities for mobility in part because of the efforts made by their parents. Demographers Ren Farley and William Frey have discovered considerable progress between first- and second-generation Latino/as (Alba and Nee 2003). Many from earlier generations worked multiple jobs as gardeners, janitors, and housekeepers in order to assure a better life for their children (Carbajal and Medina 2008). How does the idea of the American Dream and access to it vary across generations with distinct characteristics? Implications of age and generation for the multiple aspects of the American Dream are explored by the authors in this volume as they consider public opinion about the American Dream and the politics, history, complexity, and reality of the American Dream for Latino/as.

Presidents, Politics, and the Dream for Latino/as

The American Dream is intertwined with presidents and politics. From the Fourteenth Amendment to literacy tests and debates over various immigration statutes, there has been an ongoing process involving presidents, politics, and legislation that has affected the dreams of US immigrants and their children. Thus the American Dream for Latino/as has a deeply rooted history in US politics and is constantly evolving as the policy debates surrounding the DREAM act and immigration reform intensify. Given their rising presence in the United States, Latino/as have increasing political power. During the recent 2012 presidential campaign both Democrats and Republicans courted Latino/a voters. This volume considers the American Dream for Latino/as from the lens of the politics of immigration and thus the politics of the Dream for immigrants to the United States.

Goals of This Volume

This volume seeks to examine the attitudes and experiences of Latino/as in their quest for the American Dream. The questions that motivate the research involve the intersections of race, ethnicity, and the American Dream. How do Latino/as view the American Dream? Does this view represent and revive earlier versions of the Dream based on community, family, hard work, youth, and hope? Has the recent economic downturn affected their hopes of achieving the Dream? What about recent immigrants? What about Latina women? How much success have Latino/as (across gender, ethnic, generation, and immigrant statuses) had in achieving the American Dream and how does this compare to other racial minorities? Do other non-Latino/a groups see opportunities and fair access to the Dream for Latino/as? Do they see Latino/as as a threat to the Dream? What about the political and legal system? What is the message that Democrats and Republicans are giving to Latino/as? In sum, the major questions that motivate this volume involve queries focusing on what we can learn about the American Dream from a focus on Latino/as. The chapters authored by a diverse group of social scientists contribute to the ongoing dialogue on the complex historical and contemporary experiences with assimilation, multiculturalism, and the Dream for US Latino/as.

This book seeks to provide a sociological, political, and historical framework for thinking about opportunity systems among US Latino/as. Latino/as are the fastest growing racial/ethnic minority group in the United States. Growth in the Latino/a population in the United States between 2000 (when they represented 13 percent of the population) and 2010 (when they represented 16 percent) contributed to over one-half of the growth in the US population over that period (Humes, Jones, and Ramirez 2011). In spite of this significant presence, we tend to know less about Latino/as than other racial/ethnic minorities (Pew 2009, 2010). When minorities are considered in social science examinations of inequality, mobility, and achievement, it is often African Americans who are the focus (Rochin and Mello 2007). Stereotypes about Latino/as involving "marginalized populations," "immigrants," and "second-language" users—as well as assumptions that the Latino/a experience is at odds with the larger US culture—have undoubtedly contributed to a neglect of this group in research on achievement and the "American" dream (Rochin and Mello 2007). Cultural images often present Latino/as as the "dregs" of society, and expectations for their participation in the dream are low (Chavez 1997a). When researchers and commentators focus on Latino/as, often they highlight their problems and limitations—not resources and assets (Gandara and Contreras 2009). Federal agencies and social scientists are only now beginning to provide more extensive and accurate data on Latino/as. Recently, the *Washington Post* (Morello and Lazo 2012) included a story that covered the efforts of a number of US cities (including Baltimore) that are courting Latino/as after experiencing decades of population loss. Latino/as are revitalizing the same communities that were once inhabited by European immigrants—including Greeks, Italians, and Poles. This volume looks at how Latino/as are revitalizing the American Dream in ways that resonate with earlier race/ethnic groups and in other ways that are unique and distinctive. The authors also consider areas in which the American Dream is slow to be realized given racial stereotypes and racist structures that limit opportunities.

The paucity of information on the large and growing US Latino/a population is a primary motivation for this volume. A critical part of the story on Latino/as and the American Dream will be told in their voice and from their perspective. The Pew Hispanic Center is one of the organizations that are providing key data in this area. A recent report looked at labels about Latino/as and Latino/as' own view of their identity (Taylor et al. 2012). Results reveal that Latino/as do not see themselves as having one Latino/a culture but many different cultures. They do not identify with the racial categories used in the United States. They feel that their group has done at least as well as other racial/ethnic minorities. A majority finds that life is better in the United States than in their family's country of origin, but the United States is not necessarily seen as better than their family's country of origin. The issue of a good life is a real concern for many Latino/as. Pew Hispanic data show that a majority feel that the recent economic downturn has hit them harder than other groups (Taylor et al. 2012), and housing is one of their key areas of concern (Lopez, Livingston, and Kochhar 2009).

Chapters include a variety of historical and contemporary data on the quantity and quality of opportunity, mobility, and achievement experiences for Latino/as in the United States. Some of the complexities of the American Dream will be explored by analyzing public opinion data. Insights from a perspective that considers parties, election periods, and legislation from the perspective of both Latino/as and the political-legal system are included. The researchers provide considerable insight into the different directions that Republicans and Democrats have taken and the significant impact that Latino/as will have on the 2016 presidential election. Implications of diverse legislation and policies (such as the DREAM Act) and laws that seek to identify, prosecute, and deport illegal immigrants are examined. The potential of a family-oriented and Catholic-affiliated Latino/a culture for reinvigorating an American Dream that historically was focused on religious commitment, community, equality of opportunity, and freedom will be considered. A diverse group of respected experts in race, ethnicity, gender, politics, social class, immigration, and public opinion tell the story of Latino/as, America, and the Dream. As previously noted, much of the history of the American Dream has a distinctly white cast to it. By expanding our focus to include one of America's largest ethnic and newest immigrant groups, we hope to provide a richer, more nuanced picture of the American Dream.

Chapters in the Volume

We have argued that the American Dream for Latino/as is deeply rooted in presidents and politics. The next two chapters in the volume look at political aspects of the Dream for Latino/as. In his chapter on "Whose Dream? US Presidents, Hispanics, and the Struggle for the American Future," John Kenneth White describes how presidents have used the American Dream to advance the idea of equality for immigrants. He examines the stories and myths presidents have used and their historic relevance to today's immigration debate. In his chapter on "DREAM-ing the American Dream: The Struggle to Enact the DREAM Act," Matthew Green describes the legislative history of the DREAM Act, legislation that grants legal status and in-state tuition to young undocumented residents of the United States. He examines the critical role that activists, public opinion, and political elites—as well as widespread belief in the American Dream—play in making immigration policy at the state and national level.

Immigration experiences are a critical factor for Latino/as and their search for the American Dream. In the chapter by Daniel Martínez, Jeremy Slack, Alex E. Chávez, and Scott Whiteford ("'The American Dream': Walking toward and Deporting It"), the authors examine a new and unprecedented data set based on surveys and in-depth interviews with recently repatriated Mexican migrants. The authors ask what role the search for the "American Dream" plays in explaining the reasons for Mexican deportees' future crossing intentions.

Two chapters in the volume look at a number of issues involving race/ethnicity and the American Dream for Latino/as. We have suggested that a large part of the diversity in Latino/a experiences is associated with ethnic nationality. Enrique S. Pumar ("Hispanics and the American Dream: Lessons from the Experiences of Hispanics across Nationalities Residing in Washington, DC") uses national data and unique qualitative data from Latino/as in Washington, DC, to examine the complexities of the American Dream. In his work on ethnic nationality and the Dream, Pumar argues that structural factors such as level of national development in an immigrant's country of origin are important for understanding the success of Latino/a immigrants. In his chapter on "The Color of the Dream: Latino/as, African Americans, and the American Dream," Steven A. Tuch notes the radical changes in the racial and ethnic composition of twenty-first-century America. He examines attitudes of the two major race/ethnic groups in the United States (Latino/as and African Americans) toward achievement and the Dream in the context of the potential for threat and competition in their quest for the Dream.

Given the importance of religion for the American Dream, the volume includes two chapters looking at issues related to religion and the Dream for Latino/as. Maria Mazzenga and Todd Scribner ("From the Margins to the Center: The US Catholic Bishops, Latino/as, and the American Dream in the Twentieth Century") use data from the archival record of the Bishops' Conference of the United States to trace evolving attitudes and practices of the formal hierarchy of the Catholic Church toward Latino/a Catholic immigrants and their implications for Latino/as and the American Dream. In their chapter on "Changing for the Dream? Latino/a Religious Change and Socioeconomic Success," Jessica Hamar Martínez and Phillip Connor use new data from the

Pew Research Center to examine how Latino/as of different religious groups experience the American Dream and how religious affiliation (and religious switching) is related to the American Dream for an ethnic group that has been historically Catholic.

It is impossible to examine race/ethnic effects on achievement and the Dream in the American landscape without considering the intersection of race/ethnicity and gender. In her chapter on "Latino/a, American, Dream: Men, Women," Sandra L. Hanson argues that discussions of Latino/as often refer to Latino/as as a group, without attention to distinct experiences of Latino/a men and women. She uses a number of recent public opinion polls to examine the extent to which Latino/a men and women share in their Dreams and the extent to which their experiences and Dreams are not interchangeable.

The volume ends with a statement of the major conclusions from a group of scholars representing multiple disciplines examining the nature and complexity of the American Dream for Latino/as. If the story of the American Dream is a story of immigrants, then the story continues with the current immigration flow of Latino/as to the United States.

Notes

1. The terms "Hispanic" or "Latino/a" refer to persons who trace their origin or descent to Mexico, Puerto Rico, Cuba, Spanish-speaking Central and South American countries, and other Spanish cultures. Origin involves the heritage, nationality group, lineage, or country of the person or the person's parents (or ancestors) before their immigration to the United States. People who identify their origin as Hispanic or Latino/a may be of any race (US Bureau of the Census 2008). In this volume the authors use both terms "Hispanic" and "Latino/a." A majority of Hispanics/Latino/as does not have a preference for the term "Hispanic" or "Latino/a" (Taylor et al. 2012). Some authors in the volume use the term "Latino/a". Unless otherwise noted, all terms used here refer to both men and women.

2. Data accessed through ipoll of Roper Center Public Opinion Archives. Survey was conducted by CBS News/New York Times in July 2011 on a national sample of adults.

3. Data accessed through ipoll, public opinion archives of the Roper Center. Survey was conducted by CBS News/New York Times in March 2011 on a national sample of adults.

References

Acs, G. 2012. "Downward Mobility from the Middle Class: Waking Up from the American Dream." A Research Report. Washington, DC: Pew Charitable Trusts.

Adney, I. 2012. "Our American Dream: Son of El Salvadoran Immigrants Heads to Harvard." Accessed on January 16, 2015, at http://Latinofoxnews.com/Latino//community/2012/08/14/Our-american-dream-son-el-salvadoran-immigrants-heads-to-harvard/.

Alba, R., and V. Nee. 2003. *Remaking the American Mainstream: Assimilation and Contemporary Immigration*. Cambridge, MA: Harvard University Press.

Brown, S. E. 2009. "Making the Next Generation Our Greatest Resource." In *Latinos and the Nation's Future*, edited by H. G. Cisneros, 83–100. Houston: Arte Público Press.

Carbajal, F., and H. Medina. 2008. *Building the Latino Future: Success Stories for the Next Generation*. Hoboken, NJ: Wiley.

Chavez, L. 1997a. "Hispanics and the American Dream." *Education Digest* 62 (6): 57–60.

———. 1997b. "Hispanics Pursue the American Dream." *USA Today* 126: 22–25.

Childstats. 2012. "America's Children in Brief." Accessed on December 20, 2011, at http://www.childstats.gov/pdf/ac2012/ac_12.pdf.

Cisneros, H. G., and J. Rosales, eds. 2009. *Latinos and the Nation's Future*. Houston, TX: Arte Público Press.

Cobas, J. A., J. Duany, and J. R. Feagin, eds. 2009. *How the United States Racializes Latinos: White Hegemony and Its Consequences*. Boulder, CO: Paradigm.

Cohen-Marks, A., and C. Stout. 2011. "Can the American Dream Survive the New Multiethnic America? Evidence from Los Angeles." *Sociological Forum* 26 (4): 824–45.

Contreras, F. 2011. *Achieving Equity for Latino Students: Exploring the Pathway to Higher Education through Public Policy*. New York: Teachers College Press.

Crespo-Sancho, C. 2009. "Migration in the Age of Globalization: Transnationalism, Identity, Social Class, and Education of Latino Families." PhD diss., State University of New York at Buffalo, ProQuest Dissertations and Theses.

DiMaria, F. 2006. "Latinos and the American Dream—Some Still Wait." *Hispanic Outlook in Higher Education* 17: 26–28.

Federal Interagency Forum on Child and Family Statistics. 2012. "American Children in Brief: Key National Indicators of Well-Being, 2012." Accessed on June 10, 2013, at http://www.childstats.gov/.

Feliciano, C., and B. Robnett. 2014. "How External Racial Classifications Shape Latino Dating Choices." *Du Bois Review* 11 (2): 295–328.

Frank, R., I. Redstone Akresh, and B. Lu. 2010. "Latino Immigrants and the U.S. Racial Order: How and Where Do They Fit In?" *American Sociological Review* 75: 378–401.

Fry, R. 2008. How Far Behind in Math and Reading Are English Language Learners? Pew Hispanic Center.

———. 2010. *Latinos and the 2010 Census.* Accessed on May 15, 2013, at http://www.pewhispanic.org/files/reports/121.pdf.

Gandara, P., and F. Contreras. 2009. *The Latino Education Crisis: The Consequences of Failed Social Policies.* Cambridge, MA: Harvard University Press.

Gonzalez, C. 2011. "Renewing the American Dream: Hispanics' Share of the American Dream." Accessed on May 22, 2012, at http://www.whitehouse.ogv/blog/2011/10/11/nrewing-american-Dream-hispanics-share-americandream.

Hanson, S. L., and J. K. White. 2011. *The American Dream in the 21st Century.* Philadelphia: Temple University Press.

Hanson, S. L., and J. Zogby. 2010. "The Polls-Trends: Attitudes about the American Dream." *Public Opinion Quarterly* 74: 551–84.

Humes, K. R., N. A. Jones, and R. R. Ramirez. 2011. "Overview of Race and Hispanic Origin: 2010." Accessed on November 17, 2010 at http://www.census.gov/prod/cen2010/briefs/c2010br-02.pdf.

Jacoby, T. 2009. "Becoming American—The Latino Way." In *Latinos and the Nation's Future*, edited by H. G. Cisneros, 41–70. Houston: Arte Público Press.

Lopez, M. H., G. Livingston, and R. Kochhar. 2009. "Hispanics and the Economic Downturn: Housing Woes and Remittance Cuts." Accessed on October 29, 2011, at http://www.pewhispanic.org/2009/01/08/hispanics-and-the-economic-downturn-housing-woes-and-remittance-cuts/.

Lopez, M. H., and D. Dockterman. 2011. "U.S. Hispanic Country of Origin Counts for Nation, Top 30 Metropolitan Areas." Accessed on February 17, 2015, at http://www.pewhispanic.org/2011/05/26/us-hispanic-country-of-origin-counts-for-nation-top-30-metropolitan-areas/.

Massachusetts Mutual Financial Group. 2011. "The Pursuit of the American Dream: The Fiscal Practices of Today's Hispanic Business Owners." Springfield: Massachusetts Mutual Financial Group.

McGlynn, A. P. 1999. "Community Colleges: Improving the Future for Hispanic Americans: The Role of Community Colleges." *Hispanic Outlook in Higher Education* 9: 23–23.

Morello, C., and L. Lazo. 2012. "Baltimore Puts Out Welcome Mat for Immigrants, Hoping To Stop Population Decline." Accessed on August 29, 2011, at http://www.washingtonpost.com/local/baltimore-puts-out-welcome-mat-for-immigrants-hoping-to-stop-population-decline/2012/07/24/gJQA4WEk7W_story.html.

Motel, S. 2012. "Statistical Portrait of Hispanics in the United States, 2010." Accessed on October 29, 2011, at http://www.pewhispanic.org/2012/02/21/statistical-portrait-of-hispanics-in-the-united-states-2010/.

Murphy, D., L. Guzman, and A. Torres. 2014. "Hispanic Children: Gaining Ground, Looking Forward." Washington, DC: Childtrends. Publication # 2014-38.

Pachon, H. P. 2009. "Increasing Hispanic Mobility into the Middle Class: An Overview." In *Latinos and the Nation's Future*, edited by H. G. Cisneros, 57–70. Houston: Arte Público Press.

Pew Hispanic Center. 2007. Country of Origin Profiles. Accessed on January 12, 2010, at http://pewhispanic.org/data/origins.

———. 2009. *Between Two Worlds: How Young Latinos Come of Age in America*. Accessed on January 12, 2010, at http://pewhispanic.org/reports/report.php?ReportID=117.

———. 2010. *Statistical Portrait of Hispanics in the United States, 2008*. Washington, DC.

Portes, A., and P. Fernández-Kelly. 2008. "No Margin for Error: Educational and Occupational Achievement among Disadvantaged Children of Immigrants." *ANNALS of the American Academy of Political and Social Science* 620 (1): 12–36.

Portes, A., and R. Rumbaut. 2014. *Immigrant America: A Portrait*. 4th ed. Oakland: University of California Press.

Rierson, S. L. 2006. "'I Was Born Here but I'm Not an American': Understanding the United States History Curriculum through the Eyes of Latino Students." PhD diss., Ohio State University, ProQuest Dissertations and Theses.

Rochin, R. I., and S. F. Mello. 2007. "Latinos in Science: Trends and Opportunities." *Journal of Hispanic Higher Education* 6: 305–55.

Seelye, K. C. 2009. "What Happens to the American Dream in a Recession?" Accessed on March 10, 2012, at http://www.nytimes.com/2009/05/08/us/08dreampoll.html?_r=0.

Taylor, P., M. H. Lopez, J. Martinez, and G. Velasco. 2012. "When Labels Don't Fit: Hispanics and Their Views of Identity." Accessed on June 10, 2013, at http://www.pewhispanic.org/2012/04/04/when-labels-dont-fit-hispanics-and-their-views-of-identity/.

Yosso, T. J. 2006. *Critical Race Counterstories along the Chicana/Chicano Educational Pipeline*. New York: Routledge.

Zogby, J. 2011. "Want Meets Necessity in the New American Dream." In *The American Dream in the 21st Century*, edited by S. L. Hanson and J. K. White, 105–16. Philadelphia: Temple University Press.

Whose Dream?

US Presidents, Hispanics, and the Struggle for the American Future

JOHN KENNETH WHITE

It's a complex fate being an American.

Henry James, novelist and
American expatriate (1843–1916)

Addressing the nation on the need for immigration reform following the 2014 midterm elections, Barack Obama reaffirmed his faith in the American Dream and the contributions immigrants—even those who come to the United States without documentation—make toward its continued fulfillment. Stating his case for immigration reform, Obama cited Astrid Silva as a person who is adding her story to the countless others who compose the American Dream:

> Astrid was brought to America when she was four years old. Her only possessions were a cross, her doll, and the frilly dress she had on. When she started school, she didn't speak any English. She caught up to other kids by reading newspapers and watching PBS, and she became a good student. Her father worked in landscaping. Her mom cleaned other people's homes. They wouldn't let Astrid apply to a technology magnet school, not because they didn't love her, but because they were afraid the paperwork would out her as an undocumented immigrant—so she applied behind their back and got in. Still, she mostly lived in the shadows—until her grandmother, who visited every year from Mexico, passed away, and she couldn't travel to the funeral without risk of being found out and deported. It was around that time she decided to begin advocating for herself and others like her, and today, Astrid Silva is a college student working on her third degree. (Obama 2014a)

Successful stories, like Astrid Silva's, embody the allure of the American Dream and have a profound hold on presidential audiences. This chapter describes how presidents from both major parties have personally embodied the American Dream and used it to evoke both emotion and support. Such appeals are hardly new. Historian James Truslow Adams—the one who coined the phrase "American Dream"—once wrote that John Quincy Adams believed his country "stood for opportunity, the chance to grow into something bigger and finer, as bigger and finer appealed to him" (Adams 1941, 174). Presidential appeals to striving Americans who, like President Adams, dream of things "bigger and finer" have particular resonance in today's politics when the number of Hispanic arrivals in the United States has reached record highs. The chapter describes how presidents have continued to appeal to Hispanic immigrants using the American Dream as a catch-all appeal, even as a politics of resentment has produced a backlash—largely within the Tea Party wing of the Republican Party—that has somewhat blunted the effectiveness of such appeals.

Like their immigrant predecessors, newly arrived Hispanics show an overwhelming appreciation for the American Dream and its promise of future success, as Obama acknowledged in his televised address:

> Over the past few years, I have seen the determination of immigrant fathers who worked two or three jobs without taking a dime from the government, and at risk any moment of losing it all, just to build a better life for their kids. . . . These people—our neighbors, our classmates, our friends—they did not come here in search of a free ride or an easy life. They came to work, and study, and serve in our military, and above all, contribute to America's success. (Obama 2014a)

The desire to be "something more" has not only instilled a faith in the ongoing success of the American Dream but also a strong sense of nationalism. Among foreign-born Americans who have become US citizens, 71 percent said a "major reason" for choosing citizenship was "to show a commitment and pride in being an American" (Public Agenda Foundation 2009). Indeed, among all races and ethnic groups, the American Dream is suffused with meaning. One 2014 poll found 61 percent of Hispanics, 63 percent of whites, and 53 percent of African Americans agree that the American Dream "has meaning to you personally" (*Washington Post*/Miller Center 2013). Frenchman Clotaire Rapaille captured the romantic aspects surrounding the American Dream, saying: "The inner life of America is not a place—Canada is a place. Maybe the best place in the world. But if you are Canadian and you have a dream, you leave. Why? Because America is not a place. It is a dream" (Hitt 2000, 74).

As Rapaille indicates, becoming an American means more than simply inhabiting US soil. It requires an almost rigid adherence to three key values contained in the American Dream: (1) a celebration of freedom, (2) the enthronement of the individual and a strong emphasis on individual rights, and (3) a firm belief in equality of opportunity. In his 2014 State of the Union address, Barack Obama cited these principles as the glue keeping a politically divided union together: "What I believe unites the people of this nation, regardless of race or region or party, young or old, rich or poor, is the simple profound belief in opportunity for all—the notion that if you work hard and take responsibility, you can get ahead" (Obama 2014b). Obama's view commands a decisive majority: 62 percent believe that if individuals work hard, "they can still achieve the American Dream of making a decent living, owning a home, and sending their children to college" (Fox News 2013).

Barack Obama's reaffirmation of the American Dream is nothing new. As a presidential candidate in 2008, he published a book titled *The Audacity of Hope: Thoughts on Reclaiming the American Dream*. In it, he maintained that the "classic immigrant story . . . of ambition and adaptation, hard work and education, assimilation and upward mobility . . . [is playing itself out] in hyperdrive. As beneficiaries of a nation more tolerant and more worldly than the one immigrants faced generations ago, a nation that has come to revere its immigrant myth, [immigrants] are more confident in their place here, more assertive of their rights" (Obama 2006, 260). Obama's comments stood in sharp contrast to his 2012 opponent, former Massachusetts governor Mitt Romney, who argued that undocumented immigrants should "self-deport" (Republican Debate Transcript 2012). Not surprisingly, Obama beat Romney by a margin of 50 percent to 42 percent among all voters as the candidate who would do the better job of "helping people achieve the American Dream" (Fox News 2012). Hispanics, in particular, resonated to Obama's message of inclusion and recoiled at Romney's "self-deportation" remark by giving Obama an overwhelming 71 percent of their votes (Edison Research 2012).

Barack Obama is hardly the first president to pay homage to the American creed of unlimited opportunity. At a 1983 news conference, Ronald Reagan declared: "What I want to see above all is that this country remains a country where someone can always get rich. That's the thing that we have and that must be preserved" (Reagan 1983). Three years later, Reagan told a nationally televised audience: "Think for a moment how special it is to be an American. Can we doubt that only a Divine Providence placed this land, this land of freedom, here as a refuge for all those people in the world who yearn to breathe free?" (Reagan and Reagan 1986). Reagan's successor, George H. W. Bush, cited his own story as illustrative of an American Dream that was transformed into a tangible reality:

> [Barbara Bush and I] moved to west Texas forty years ago. The war was over, and we wanted to get out and make it on our own. Those were exciting days. Lived in a little shotgun house, one room for the three of us. Worked in the oil business, started my own.
>
> In time we had six children. Moved from the shotgun to a duplex apartment to a house. Lived the dream—high school football on Friday night, Little League, neighborhood barbecue. (Bush 1988)

Four years later Bill Clinton promised to make his story of climbing the heights a reality for those yet to come: "Somewhere at this very moment, a child is being born in America. . . . Let it be our cause to see that child has a chance to live to the fullest of her God-given capacities. . . . Let it be our cause that we give this child a country that is coming together, not coming apart, a country of boundless hopes and endless dreams, a country that once again lifts its people and inspires the world" (Clinton 1992). As president, Clinton continually reiterated his faith in the American Dream: "The American Dream that we were all raised on is a simple but powerful one—if you work hard and play by the rules, you should be given a chance to go as far as your God-given ability will take you" (Huntington 2004, 70). Running for president in 2000, George W. Bush frequently invoked the motto posted on a billboard in his hometown of Midland, Texas: "The sky's the limit" (Gormley 2001, 81).

This uniquely American belief in the Protestant ethic of hard work—and the success that surely derives from it—forms an integral part of our national identity. The Frenchman Michel Chevalier, who visited the United States in the 1830s, commented:

> The manners and customs are those of a working, busy society. A man who has no profession and—which is nearly the same thing—who is not married enjoys little consideration; he who is an active and useful member of society, who contributes his share to augment the national wealth and increase the numbers of the population, he only is looked upon with

respect and favor. The American is brought up with the idea that he will have some particular occupation and that if he is active and intelligent he will make his fortune. He has no conception of living without a profession, even when his family is rich. The habits of life are those of an exclusively working people. From the moment he gets up, the American is at his work, and he is absorbed in it till the hour of sleep. Even mealtime is not for him a period of relaxation. It is only a disagreeable interruption of business which he cuts short as much as possible. (Huntington 2004, 71–72)

While Americans have left the farms of Michel Chevalier's nineteenth century for the World Wide Web of Barack Obama's twenty-first, their penchant for (and belief in) the value of hard work remains undiminished: 65 percent assert that people can get ahead if they are willing to work hard, and 68 percent believe hard work and the American Dream go hand in hand (*Washington Post*/Miller Center 2013). Building on these beliefs, presidents love to tell stories of hard work leading to lasting achievements. In his 2014 State of the Union address, Obama described how Estiven Rodriguez "couldn't speak a word of English when he moved to New York City at age nine." Less than a decade later, Rodriguez "led a march of his classmates—through a crowd of cheering parents and neighbors—from their high school to the post office, where they mailed off their college applications." Recently, Obama reported, "this son of a factory worker just found out that he's going to college this fall" (Obama 2014b).

Rodriguez's story is hardly unique. Today, half of all Hispanics residing in the United States are first generation, and many have their own success stories. One such involves first-generation immigrant Jorge Garcia and his wife, Sara, who traveled to the United States in 1996 from Cochabamba, Bolivia, to Falls Church, Virginia, with their two young daughters then aged eleven and twelve. No one knew English, although the young girls assimilated into their new school and quickly learned the language. In 2013, after years of paying thousands of dollars to become permanent residents, both Jorge and Sara were sworn in as US citizens—promising (as all newcomers do) to renounce fidelity to foreign princes, defend the US Constitution, and bear arms on behalf of the United States. After the ceremony, an emotional Sara Garcia remembered: "I thought to myself that now I have everything I want. I am an American citizen, both my daughters are professionals and their future is ahead of them. What more could I ask of life?" (Constable and Clement 2014, A-1). As US Supreme Court justice Anthony Kennedy once wrote, "The history of the United States is in part made of the stories, talents, and lasting contributions of those who crossed oceans and deserts to come here" (Kennedy 2012). Today the Garcia story is just one of millions that compose the American story of hard work and personal success that make the American Dream a reality for many.

Given so many such stories as the Garcias', it is hardly surprising that when asked to define the American Dream, Hispanics, whites, and African Americans are united in their responses. Majorities agree that the dream means doing better than their parents, owning a home, having the freedom of choice in living one's life, obtaining a college education, receiving rewards for hard work, balancing work and family life, and being able to become wealthy (see table 1). In five of these six categories, Hispanics are even more fervent followers of the American Dream than whites or African Americans. No wonder stories of Hispanic successes—whether told either by US presidents or their fellow citizens—have such a powerful resonance.

Perceptions of the American Dream by Race and Ethnicity, 2013
Percent who say this is "very much" what they understand the American Dream means

	Hispanics	Whites	African Americans
To do better than one's parents did	68	50	60
To own a home	68	62	54
To have freedom of choice in how to live one's life	67	79	63
To be able to get a college education	64	50	48
To be rewarded for hard work	64	71	53
To have the ability to balance work and family life	58	57	56

Source: *Washington Post*/Miller Center poll, September 6–12, 2013. Reported in Pamela Constable and Scott Clement, "Despite Hurdles, Hispanics Cling Tightly to American Dream," *Washington Post*, January 31, 2014, A-1.

Stories that validate the values cited in table 1 create an atmosphere of optimism that permeates American political thought. One oft-stated axiom of US politics is that it is the most optimistic candidate who wins the presidency. Even in tough times, Americans expect their presidents to offer hope, not gloom. In the midst of the Vietnam War, race riots in US cities, and a youth rebellion, Richard Nixon told cheering delegates to the 1968 Republican National Convention that his life story was a uniquely American one that could serve as a lesson to others:

I see [a] child tonight. He hears the train go by at night and he dreams of far away places where he'd like to go. It seems like an impossible dream. But he is helped on his journey through life. A father who had to go to work before he finished the sixth grade, sacrificed everything he had so that his sons could go to college. A gentle, Quaker mother, with a passionate concern for peace, quietly wept when he went to war, but she understood why he had to go. A great teacher, a remarkable football coach, an inspirational minister encouraged him on his way. A courageous wife and loyal children stood by him in victory and also defeat. And in his chosen profession of politics, first there were scores, then hundreds, then thousands, and finally millions [who] worked for his success. And tonight he stands before you—nominated for President of the United States of America. You can see why I believe so deeply in the American Dream. (Nixon 1968)

Decades later facing certain death from Alzheimer's disease, Ronald Reagan wrote a farewell letter to his fellow citizens that did not dwell on the devastating news, but was filled with hope for his beloved country: "When the Lord calls me home, whenever that may be, I will leave the greatest love for this country of ours and eternal optimism for its future. I now begin the journey that will lead me into the sunset of my life. I know that for America there will always be a bright dawn ahead" (Reagan 1994). Indeed, US presidents in times of both national and personal calamities are expected to be optimistic cheerleaders—regaling audiences with American Dream success stories from which their listeners can take inspiration.

If optimism is a characteristic of presidential rhetoric, it is not surprising that the American Dream is infused with it. It is worth remembering that the term "American Dream" was popularized in 1931 by historian James Truslow Adams in a book titled *The Epic of America* (Adams 1941). Written during the Great Depression at a time when the stock market had lost 75 percent of its 1929 value, national income had been cut in half, exports were at their lowest levels since 1904, and more than 600,000 properties had been foreclosed, Adams described "that dream of a land in which life should be better and richer and fuller for every man, with opportunity for each according to ability or achievement" (Alter 2006, 148). Two years later Franklin D. Roosevelt brought to the presidency a jaunty sense of optimism, telling a frightened country at his 1933 inaugural: "This great Nation will endure as it has endured, will revive and will prosper" (Roosevelt 1933).

At its core, the American Dream represents a state of mind—that is, an enduring optimism given to a people who might be tempted to succumb to the travails of adversity, but who, instead, repeatedly rise from the ashes to build a great nation. In the late 1950s, researchers Lloyd Free and Hadley Cantril discovered that when survey respondents were given a picture of a ladder with eleven rungs numbered zero to ten—with ten representing "the best possible life for you as you describe it" and zero "the worst"—people often placed themselves toward the lower end of the scale five years earlier, and saw themselves headed for its upper reaches in five years hence (Ladd 1999, 112–13). Americans are almost genetically optimistic, even during punishing times. Jorge Garcia, the aforementioned immigrant who recently obtained citizenship, described a difficult life in the United States that saw him receive taunts about his Hispanic heritage, fall victim to a greedy landlord who charged $700 a month for an apartment with no furniture, a time when he fell ill and could not work for six months, and a daughter taking a part-time job to make up for lost wages. Through it all, Garcia persevered, remembering: "It was hard. Everything I have endured was all so my girls could succeed in America" (Constable and Clement 2014, A-1).

And succeed they did. One is the finance manager for an international firm and is engaged to be married; another is studying for a doctorate in physical therapy (ibid). Certainly, Jorge and Sara Garcia can relate to their offspring a message of perseverance and eventual success. For them, the American Dream is a tangible reality. But not everyone is celebrating the Garcia success story and those like it.

From Dreamers to Fanatics

Not surprisingly, devout believers in a "we-can-do-anything" American Dream can easily wander into the world of fanaticism. Englishman G. K. Chesterton once remarked that the United States is "a nation with the soul of a church" (Huntington 2004, 48). To Chesterton, the American church is characterized by a rigid orthodoxy. Seeking entrance to the United States during the Red Scare in 1920, Chesterton found himself being asked by the American consulate, "Are you an anarchist?" and "Are you in favor of subverting the government of the United States by force?" To these queries, Chesterton was tempted to answer, "I prefer to answer that question at the end of my tour and not the beginning" (Chesterton 1922, 4).

This tendency to turn ideological devotion to the American Dream into fanaticism is nothing new. As longshoreman-turned-philosopher Eric Hoffer once wrote, "All mass movements . . . breed fanaticism, enthusiasm, fervent hope, hatred, and intolerance; all of them are capable of releasing a powerful flow of activity in certain departments of life; all of them demand blind faith and single-hearted allegiance" (Hoffer 1951, xi). During the Cold War, the phrase "McCarthyism" was coined to describe the meandering into the fanatical world of anticommunism. Hundreds were summoned before the US Congress to profess their faith in the American ideology, and to name names of those who supposedly did not. In 1978, historian Garry Wills wrote that in the United States one must adopt the American Dream "wholeheartedly, proclaim it, prove one's devotion to it" (Wills 1978, xxii).

Indeed, the expectation that all must subscribe to a commonly held acceptance of the utility of the American Dream produces its own linguistic fanaticism. As historian Daniel Boorstin once noted, "Who would think of using the word 'un-Italian' or 'un-French' as we use the word 'un-American?'" (Boorstin 1953, 14). Political scientist Louis Hartz echoes Boorstin, saying, "When one's ultimate values are accepted wherever one turns, the absolute language of self-evidence comes easily enough" (Hartz 1955, 58). Indeed, our evangelical-like advancement of the "American Way of Life" has taken on missionary proportions. John Winthrop, the British colonial governor of the Massachusetts Bay Colony, described that Puritan-dominated settlement as "a city on a hill [and] the eyes of all people are upon us" (Winthrop 1630). In the nineteenth century, Herman Melville compared Americans to the biblical tribes of Israel, calling them "the peculiar chosen people, the Israel of our time" (quoted in Cronin 1980, 161). Today, the phrase "American Exceptionalism" is used to refer to this idea of a nation set apart from all others (see Lipset 1996). Political scientist Benedict Anderson once remarked that nations are "imagined communities," and the American Dream is firmly embedded into our collective imaginations that we are a special people set apart from all others (Huntington 2004, 22).

Can Hispanics Dream, Too?

But is the American Dream so firmly implanted in our imaginations that it becomes the exclusive preserve of a white majority that sees its status threatened by millions of Hispanic immigrants? Some years ago the novelist Henry James exclaimed, "It's a complex fate being an American" (quoted in Shirer 1985, 15). Part of that complexity revolves around a centuries-old debate as to whether newcomers are "American enough" to deserve full citizenship. Yale Law School professor Peter Schuck writes, "If citizenship is anything, it is membership in a political community with a more or less distinctive political identity—a set of public values about governance and law that are very widely shared by those within it" (Huntington 2004, 214).

Throughout the centuries Americans have had to decide who gets to belong to this special community and who should be excluded. For example, during the early twentieth century, the question arose whether newly arrived immigrants from eastern, central, and southern Europe were "American enough." Could these foreign-tongued Catholics and Jews assimilate into US life and culture, learn English, and become full-fledged Americans? In 1924, a Republican-controlled Congress and White House responded to a public outcry over opening the borders to these mostly European migrants and closed them. The congressional vote was overwhelming: 306–58 in the House, and 69–9 in the Senate (Shlaes 2013, 287). President Calvin Coolidge declared, "I am convinced that our present economic and social conditions warrant a limitation of those to be admitted" (ibid., 268). But *The Providence Visitor*—the official newspaper of the Catholic diocese of Providence, Rhode Island—disagreed with Coolidge and decried the "fangs" in the new law as "a sop to labor, balm to the prejudiced, and the first practical measure proclaiming an ascendancy of the Anglo-Saxon race" (quoted in White 1983, 8). It later fell to Coolidge's successor, Franklin D. Roosevelt, to remind his fellow citizens "that all of us, you and I especially, are descended from immigrants and revolutionists" (Huntington 2004, 38). But FDR's plea did not always fall on receptive ears. During the 1930s, George Kennan, who later authored the US strategy of containment during the Cold War, confided that he was discomfited by the egalitarian, multiracial immigrant society the United States had become: "The overflow of the entire world has seeped into a great territory and has drowned out the heritage of my fathers." Half a century later, Kennan believed that the United States would be a better country if it stopped immigration altogether and sterilized any male who had more than two children (Ignatieff 2014, 20).

The immigration debate was renewed in 1965 when President Lyndon B. Johnson signed into law the Hart-Celler Act. This statute followed on the heels of the Civil Rights Act of 1964, which prohibited discrimination against minorities—especially African Americans—and the Voting Rights Act of 1965, which allowed African Americans to register to vote in the South under federal protection. The Hart-Celler Act abolished the quotas imposed in the Immigration Act of 1924, and forbade their use based on national origin. Until then, just three countries supplied 70 percent of all US immigrants—a fact that President Johnson described as "un-American" (Johnson 1965). Vice

President Hubert H. Humphrey captured the spirit behind the law: "We must in 1965 remove all elements in our immigration law which suggest that there are second-class people. . . . We want to bring our immigration law into line with the spirit of the Civil Rights Act of 1964" (Hajnal and Lee 2011, 8). At the bill signing at the foot of New York's historic Statue of Liberty, Johnson declared that the bill "corrects a cruel and enduring wrong in the conduct of the American nation. . . . [F]rom this day forth those wishing to immigrate to America shall be admitted on the basis of their skills and their close relationship to those already here" (Johnson 1965). At the same time, Johnson declared that it is not "revolutionary," adding: "It does not affect the lives of millions. It will not reshape the structure of our daily lives, or really add importantly to either our wealth or our power" (ibid).

Johnson's claim that the statute would have little effect could not have been more wrong. Instead it made possible an immense Hispanic influx, as refugees fled from dictatorships, economic hardships, and natural calamities. Indeed, the sheer volume of immigrants exceeded the European migration that spurred passage of the 1924 law. Speaking at the 1998 commencement exercises at Portland State University, Bill Clinton cast his eye toward the impending new century and saw a "third great revolution"—one as powerful as the American Revolution, which gave birth to the democratic ideas of the eighteenth and nineteenth centuries, and as imposing as the civil rights and women's rights revolutions that broadened the definition of personal liberties in the late twentieth. According to Clinton, this gathering revolution was being manned by an army of immigrants, many of them Hispanic: "Today, largely because of immigration, there is no majority race in Hawaii or Houston or New York City. Within five years there will be no majority race in our largest state, California. In a little more than fifty years, there will be no majority race in the United States" (Clinton 1998).

The facts bear out Clinton's argument. Consider: when Richard M. Nixon took the presidential oath in 1969, there were approximately 9.6 million foreign born residing in the United States. Forty-four years later, when Barack Obama raised his hand to repeat the same oath, the number of foreign born had grown to 41.7 million (Williams 2006, 33; Preston 2013). Viewed from another perspective, during the 1970s approximately 400,000 persons entered the United States on an annual basis; a decade later, 800,000; and by the end of the twentieth century, more than 1,000,000 (Huntington 2004, 196). Today, there are more immigrants living in California (10.2 million) than there are people residing in *all* of Michigan (9.9 million) ("New Americans in California").

This demographic transformation has given rise to a renewed debate over immigration policy that has roiled presidential politics. During their competitive run for the Republican nomination in 1980, George H. W. Bush and Ronald Reagan were asked whether undocumented aliens should be allowed to attend public schools for free, or whether their parents should pay for their education. Both were open to solving the immigration problem in a humane manner:

> Bush: I'd like to see something done about labor needs and human needs that that problem wouldn't come up. Today, if those people are here, I would reluctantly say that they get whatever society is giving to their neighbors. But the problem has to be solved. The problem has to be solved. If we make illegal sometimes the labor I'd like to see legal, we're doing two things: we're creating a whole society of really honorable, decent, family-loving people that are in violation of the law and, secondly, we're exacerbating relations with Mexico. The answer to your question is much more fundamental than whether they attend Houston schools it seems to me. If they're living here, I don't want to see a group of six, seven, and eight-year-old kids living here totally uneducated and made to feel that they're living outside the law. Let's address ourselves to the fundamentals. These are good people, strong people. Part of my family is Mexican-American. [Applause]

> Reagan: I think the time has come that the United States and our neighbor to the south [Mexico] should have a better relationship than we've ever had. And I think we haven't been sensitive enough to our size and our power. There's a problem of 40 to 50 percent unemployment [in Mexico]. Now this cannot continue without the possibility arising with regard to Cuba and what it is [doing] stirring up of [sic] trouble below the border. We could have a very hostile and strange neighbor on our border. Rather than talking about putting up a fence, why don't we work out some recognition of our mutual problems, make it possible for them to come here legally with a work permit, and then while working and earning here, they pay taxes here, and when they want to go back, they can go back. Open the border both ways by understanding their problems. (Reagan-Bush 1980)

But in the decades since Reagan and Bush agreed on both the problem and the solution, hostility toward Hispanic immigrants increased. In 1994, Californians ratified Proposition 187, which banned all state spending on illegal immigrants and required police to report suspected illegals to the state Department of Justice and the US Immigration Service. The backlash prompted Alfredo Alvarez, a legal immigrant from Honduras, to seek US citizenship, saying: "I love this country, but I feel unwanted. I feel like unless I am a true American, the government could one day knock on my door and tell me, 'Alfredo, go back to Honduras!'" (Booth 1996, A-1). These sentiments were commonplace in polls taken up to 2006: 83 percent wanted federal authorities to crack down on noncitizens by using fingerprinting and random interviewing (Opinion Dynamics 2004); 81 percent believed illegal immigration was out of control (Gallup Poll 2006c); 74 percent agreed it was either "extremely important" or "very important" to halt the flow of illegal immigrants (Gallup Poll 2006a); and 66 percent said illegal immigrants cost taxpayers too much (Gallup Poll 2006b).

Whose Country?

A major reason behind the anti-immigrant stance was the recoloring of the American face from white to some shade of bronze. In 2010, the US Census Bureau reported a Hispanic population that totaled 50.5 million people, and that grew four times faster than the rest of the US population during the previous decade (US Census Bureau 2011b). Today, Hispanics are the nation's number one minority group and outnumber blacks, who stand at 38.9 million (US Census Bureau 2011a). Most significantly, 75 percent of Hispanics are concentrated in eight key states that determine presidential elections: California, Texas, Florida, New York, Illinois, Arizona, New Jersey, and Colorado (Ennis, Rios-Vargas, and Albert 2011, 5). Added to this is the fact that Hispanics are the nation's youngest major racial or ethnic group—making their voices crucial in presidential contests for decades to come (Pew Research Hispanic Trends Project 2013). The fast-growing rise of Hispanics (and other racial minorities) points to an inevitable reality: By midcentury, whites will be the nation's *new minority* with Hispanics approaching 29 percent of the total population—up from their current 16 percent (Passel and Cohn 2008; Roberts 2008; Taylor and Cohn 2012; and Ennis, Rios-Vargas, and Albert 2010, 2).

This infusion of Hispanics has produced a powerful political backlash. Campaigning for president in 2000, Patrick J. Buchanan was approached by voters who collectively said, "Pat, we're losing the country we grew up in" (Buchanan 2002, 1). Fourteen years later, many Republicans still feel the same way. Democratic pollster Stanley Greenberg and his partner, former Clinton strategist James Carville, found that while moderate Republicans supported immigration reform, evangelicals and Tea Party members (who compose 70 percent of the GOP base) are firmly opposed. A 2013 focus group of Republicans captured the strong anti-immigrant sentiments that are deeply felt within the GOP:

> Don't come here and make me speak your language. Don't fly your flag. You're on American soil. You're American. You come to our country, you need to learn our language. Why should I put "press 1" if I want to speak in English? You know, everything—every politically correct machine out there says, "Press 1 for English. Press 2 for Spanish." (Evangelical man, Roanoke)

> There's so much of the electorate in those groups that Democrats are going to take every time because they've been on the rolls of the government their entire lives. They don't know better. (Tea Party man, Raleigh) (Greenberg and Carville 2014)

These sentiments were amplified by the Great Recession that began in 2007. When George W. Bush left the White House in 2009, he was the first two-term president since Woodrow Wilson to have left the average household with less income than when he became president. Barack Obama may be the second (Will 2014, A-19). Increased unemployment and heightened economic insecurities continue to pose a threat to the American Dream. A 2014 poll found 68 percent think people who work hard have a difficult time maintaining their standard of living and cannot get ahead, 85 percent say that when it comes to advancing there are different rules for the well connected and the wealthy, 80 percent believe it requires more effort to get ahead today than in the past, and 78 percent think the next generation will require even more effort to advance. In addition, 60 percent of white Americans and 53 percent of Latino/as believe government policies shut out the middle class (Marist College Institute for Public Opinion 2014). No wonder that 59 percent believe that the American Dream "has become impossible for most people to achieve" (CNN/Opinion Research Corporation, 2014b).

These numbers belie the usual optimism that is historically associated with the American Dream, and they have created opportunities for aspiring politicians who want to stir up the political waters. Lou Barletta is one. In 2006, the then-Republican mayor of Hazelton, Pennsylvania, sponsored legislation that would fine landlords $1,000 for every illegal tenant (Goodnough 2006, A-12). Barletta later won a seat in the US House of Representatives on an anti-immigrant platform, even though the federal courts later struck down the local law he helped enact. As a member of Congress, Barletta claims he can save not just one town but also an entire nation from "terrorists and drug dealers" (Kamen 2014, A-17).

Not to be outdone, Barletta's fellow Republican, Iowa congressman Steve Kings, gave voice to anti-Hispanic prejudices and opposed legislation granting citizenship to undocumented immigrant minors, saying: "For everyone who's a valedictorian, there's a 100 out there that weigh 130 pounds, and they've got calves the size of cantaloupes because they're hauling 75 pounds of marijuana across the desert. Those people would be legalized with the same act" (Huffington Post 2013). Republican leaders John Boehner and Eric Cantor denounced King, with Boehner calling him an "asshole" (Kludt 2014). California Democratic congressman Raul Ruiz spoke for many on his side of the aisle, describing King's remarks as "a disgrace to this institution . . . unacceptable and just plain wrong on so many levels." King continued to defend himself, telling an Iowa radio station: "We have people that are mules, that are drug mules, that are hauling drugs across the border and you can tell by their physical characteristics what they've been doing for months, going through the desert with 75 pounds of drugs on their back. And if those who advocate for the Dream Act, if they choose to characterize this about valedictorians, I gave them a different image that we need to be thinking about, because we just simply can't be passing legislation looking only at one component of what would be millions of people" (Siddiqui 2013).

Beginning in the 1990s, several anti-immigration measures won approval on state ballots. As mentioned, in 1994, Californians easily ratified Proposition 187, which banned all state spending on illegal immigrants and required police to report suspected illegals to the state Department of Justice and the US Immigration Service. At the time, California television sets flickered with pictures of illegal Mexicans swarming across the border as an announcer intoned, "They just keep coming" (Barone and Ujifusa 1997, 81). Sixty-nine percent of white voters supported Proposition 187; 69 percent of Hispanics disapproved (Ladd 1995, 124). A decade later, 56 percent of Arizonans supported Proposition 200—a law that required proof of citizenship in order to vote and receive public benefits. Phoenix mayor Phil Gordon decried the measure as creating "the equivalent of a police state" (Crawford, Diz, and Wingett 2004, 1). But Arizona did not stop there, passing a 2010 law that allowed police officers to ask for citizenship papers based on "probable cause" that someone "has committed any public offense that makes the person removable from the United States." This could happen even during a routine motor violation, or if a person was detained for some other offense. Although the law was later amended to prohibit discrimination based on race, color, or national origin, the US Supreme Court struck down its important provisions in 2012—including the requirement that immigrants carry papers verifying their citizenship, a proviso that allowed police officers to arrest someone for suspicion of being an illegal immigrant, and a third provision that made it a crime for an undocumented alien to hold a job in the state (*Arizona v. United States* 2012).

The backlash against Hispanic immigrants became so great that some social commentators questioned whether the newcomers had a greater loyalty to their birthplaces than to their newly adopted homeland. Foremost among these was political scientist Samuel P. Huntington, who described Hispanic immigrants as "sojourners"—coming to the United States to work for a few years and later returning home (Huntington 2000, 5). For Huntington, Hispanics posed an immediate threat to the commonly held values of US citizens and undermined their sense of national identity: "Some societies, confronted with serious challenges to their existence, are also able to postpone their demise and halt disintegration, by renewing their sense of national identity, their national purpose, and the cultural values they have in common. America did this after September 11. The challenge they face in the first years of the third millennium is whether they can continue to do this if they are not under attack" (Huntington 2004, 12).

Hispanics felt the sting. Some claimed that after years of residing in the United States they no longer felt comfortable. Olga Contreras Martinez was twelve years old when she and her family entered the United States illegally from Mexico. Contreras migrated to Florida to pick fruits and vegetables and later moved to Georgia, where she became a high school teacher. Despite having obtained a college degree and US citizenship, Contreras Martinez did not feel welcome in her adopted state: "I call it home, but I know I'm not welcome in my own home. Maybe that feeling of home will be something that will always be missing for me" (Swarns 2006).

The Future Catches Up

While the backlash against immigrants remains a short-term viable political strategy for some, it is neither a route to the presidency nor a long-term plan for political survival. Already, there is evidence to suggest that anti-immigrant sentiments are waning. A 2013 survey found 49 percent agreed with the statement, "Immigrants today strengthen our country because of their hard work and talents"; only 40 percent believe immigrants "are a burden on our country because they take our jobs, housing, and health care" (Pew Research Center for the People and the Press/*USA Today* 2014). Similarly, another poll found 48 percent saying "immigration helps the United States more than it hurts it," while 42 percent thought it hurt more than it helps (NBC News/*Wall Street Journal* 2014). One reason for the changed attitudes is the slowing of immigration, which is at a forty-year low (Will 2014, A-19). Moreover, those who are here are becoming more assimilated into American society—even if their legal status is uncertain. For example, 35 percent of illegal immigrants own their own homes (ibid). Pollster Stanley Greenberg believes that the United States has "passed some tipping point on scale, density, and familiarity" with immigrants (Williams 2014).

Both George W. Bush and Barack Obama realize that a flourishing future is predicated upon an accommodation by all to an increased Hispanic presence. In 2001, Bush became the first president to utter a few Spanish words before a joint session of Congress. Pleading for support of his domestic agenda, Bush told lawmakers: "Juntos podemos [Together we can]" (Bush 2001). A few months later, he paid tribute to the Mexican holiday Cinco de Mayo by becoming the first president to broadcast his weekly radio address in both English and Spanish (Allen 2001, A-7). Later that year, the White House website was modified to include Spanish translations of the administration's press briefings, biographies of the president and first lady, and Bush's radio addresses (Cohn 2004, A-1). Accepting renomination at the Republican National Convention in 2004, Bush referred to his signature "No Child Left Behind" education reform, saying: "No dejaremos a ningún niño atrás!" ["We will leave no child behind!"] (Bush 2004).

Bush backed these symbolic gestures by proposing policy changes designed to benefit Hispanics and foster a Republican realignment that would renew the GOP majority. In May 2006, he endorsed an overhaul of the nation's immigration laws, pleading with recalcitrant House Republicans to forego their misgivings and embrace a multicultural future: "I believe that illegal immigrants who have roots in our country and want to stay should have to pay a meaningful penalty for breaking the law, to pay their taxes, to learn English, and to work in a job for a number of years. People who meet these conditions should be able to apply for citizenship, but approval would not be automatic, and they will have to wait in line behind those who played by the rules and followed the law. What I've just described is not amnesty; it is a way for those who have broken the law to pay their debt to society, and demonstrate the character that makes a good citizen" (Bush 2006).

Following his reelection in 2012, Barack Obama continued to support legislation that would reform US immigration laws and grant legal status to undocumented aliens. In 2013, the US Senate approved a measure that offered a pathway to citizenship to undocumented immigrants if they passed a background check, learned English, paid taxes and a fine. After the Senate vote, Obama declared, "We have a unique opportunity to fix our broken system in a way that upholds our traditions as a nation of laws and a nation of immigrants. We just need Congress to finish the job" (Office of the Press Secretary 2013). But the Republican-controlled House stymied the bill, and the bill died in Congress. As Hispanic deportations continued, with nearly two million illegal immigrants sent from the United States during Obama's years in office, the head of the National Council of La Raza derided Obama as the "deporter-in-chief" and demanded more be done to protect undocumented families.

That something turned out to be Obama's signature on executive orders that allowed certain undocumented immigrants to remain in the United States under the following conditions: (1) has resided in the United States for more than five years; (2) has children who are American citizens or legal residents; (3) passes a criminal background check; and (4) pays a "fair share" of taxes (Obama 2014a). On the other hand, Obama's offer did not apply to those who came to the United States more recently; it does not grant citizenship to illegals; and it does not offer a guarantee that those who are undocumented could stay in the United States permanently, since any executive order could be overridden either by the courts or by a future president. Still, the offer buoyed Hispanic support for Obama. Immediately after the president's address, 68 percent of Hispanics said they strongly supported the executive actions, with another 21 percent saying they "somewhat supported" the move. In addition, 80 percent of Latino/as opposed Republican moves to defund the executive orders, and 74 percent objected to filing a lawsuit to stop the president from acting. Ben Monterroso, executive director of Mi Familia Vota, an organization dedicated to boosting Latino/a voter turnout, said shortly after Obama's speech: "This is the most united Latino voters have been on any issue during the Obama years. We will make sure that our community learns how to apply for the new program. We will make sure they know who is trying to block it. And we will take those names to the voters in 2016" (Planas 2014).

Whether Obama and the Democrats can maintain the overwhelming support they have received from Hispanics may be in doubt, as Republicans try to blunt the opposition's advantage in the 2016 presidential contest by potentially nominating a Hispanic candidate for president or vice president, or by placing Jeb Bush, who is married to a Hispanic, at the top of the ticket. But what is not in doubt is that the changing political demography of the United States is catching up to the present. A recent survey found 53 percent agreeing that illegal immigrants should stay in the United States and apply for citizenship; an additional 16 percent would allow undocumented aliens to stay, but would not grant them citizenship (CBS News/*New York Times* 2014). In 2014, 50 percent said it was either "extremely important" or "very important" that Congress pass "significant new immigration legislation this year"—another instance of congressional failure (Pew Research Center 2014). Moreover, 54 percent wanted the federal government to stop its focus on deportations and develop a plan for legal residency; only 41 percent wanted more deportations—something that would be ameliorated if Obama's executive orders were to be translated into actual legislation (CNN/Opinion Research Corporation 2014b). And as for those illegals who have been in the United States for a number of years, hold a job, pay taxes, and learn English, 81 percent want them to stay and apply for citizenship (which is not possible under Obama's executive actions) (ibid.). The voters also have a message for both parties: 47 percent want the Republican Party to "do more to address the needs and concerns of Hispanic voters," and 38 percent say the same about the Democrats (CBS News/*New York Times* 2014).

In reforming US immigration laws nearly half a century ago, Lyndon Johnson spoke of the contributions made by immigrants to the American story:

> Our beautiful America was built by a nation of strangers. From a hundred different places or more they have poured forth into an empty land, joining and blending in one mighty and irresistible tide.
>
> This land flourished because it was fed from so many sources— because it was nourished by so many cultures and traditions and peoples.
>
> And from this experience, almost unique in the history of nations, has come America's attitude toward the rest of the world. We, because of what we are, feel safer and stronger in a world as varied as the people who make it up—a world where no country rules another and all countries can deal with the basic problems of human dignity and deal with those problems in their own way. (Johnson 1965)

These words continue to echo among the immigrants already here and those who still wish to come. At the heart of Johnson's rhetoric is the promise that the American Dream still holds true for those entering our harbors or crossing our deserts. Hispanics, as this chapter has showed, are no exception. Despite the failures of our two most recent presidents to enact immigration reform, a failure caused by worries among some already here that Hispanics are not truly American, the data show that Hispanics believe fervently in the American Dream and its promise of a better life. While Americans continue to espouse the core values that shape the American Dream—namely, freedom, equality of opportunity, and individual rights—and elect presidents whose promises are to make good on these values, there are moments in American history, as this chapter has shown, when these values are turned on their heads. Newcomers, such as Hispanics, are sometimes subjected to criticism that they are not American enough. Such criticism has prevented the enactment of immigration reform, as proposed by Presidents George W. Bush and Barack Obama, forcing Obama to take unilateral action to the howls of Republican opposition. One suspects that whatever the decision of the courts on this issue, the need for immigration reform, and the advocates of it—including future presidents—will use the power of the American Dream in their speeches to evoke both emotion and support for such measures. The debate over immigration reform, like the squabbles of yesteryear, will eventually be brought to a close, which is what happened for a time when Lyndon Johnson signed the 1965 immigration law.

Until that happens, the debate as to whether Hispanics can assimilate into American life and subscribe to the deeply held American values of freedom, equality of opportunity, and individual rights, which form the core of American political thought, will continue. But it is a debate that year by year is coming to a close. As this chapter has shown, Hispanics are thoroughly American in thought and deed. It is only American politics that needs to catch up to this fact.

References

Adams, J. T. 1941. *The Epic of America.* Garden City, NY: Blue Ribbon Books.
Allen, M. 2001. "Bush: Respect Mexican Immigrants." *Washington Post*, May 6.
Alter, J. 2006. *The Defining Moment: FDR's Hundred Days and the Triumph of Hope.* New York: Simon and Schuster.
Arizona v. United States. 2012. No-11-182. Decided June 25.

Associated Press/National Opinion Research Center. 2013. Poll. December 12–16.

Barone, M., and G. Ujifusa. 1997. *The Almanac of American Politics, 1996.* Washington, DC: National Journal.

Boorstin, D. 1953. *The Genius of American Politics.* Chicago: University of Chicago Press.

Booth, W. 1996. "In a Rush, New Citizens Register Their Political Interest." *Washington Post,* September 26.

Buchanan, P. J. 2002. *The Death of the West: How Dying Populations and Immigrant Invasions Imperil Our Country and Civilization.* New York: St. Martin's Press.

Bush, G. H. W. 1988. Acceptance Speech. Republican National Convention. New Orleans, Louisiana, August 18.

Bush, G.W. 2001. Address to Congress. Washington, DC, February 27.

———. 2004. Acceptance Speech. Republican National Convention. New York, New York, September 2.

———. 2006. Address to the Nation on Immigration Reform. Washington, DC, May 15.

CBS News/*New York Times.* 2014. Poll. February 19–23.

Chesterton, G. K. 1922. *What I Saw in America.* New York: Dodd, Mead.

Clinton, B. 1992. Acceptance Speech. Democratic National Convention. New York, New York, July 17.

———. 1998. "Remarks by the President at Portland State University Commencement." Portland, Oregon, June 13.

CNN/Opinion Research Corporation. 2014a. Poll A. January 31–February 2.

———. 2014b. Poll B. May 29–June 1.

Cohn, D'V. 2004. "Area Immigration Booming: Census Finds Steady Flow Despite Economy, 9/11." *Washington Post,* November 23.

Constable, P., and S. Clement. 2014. "Despite Hurdles, Hispanics Cling Tightly to American Dream." *Washington Post,* January 31.

Crawford, A., E. Diaz, and Y. Wingett. 2004. "Initiative Raises Questions." *Arizona Republic,* November 4.

Cronin, T. E. 1980. *The State of the Presidency.* Boston: Little, Brown.

Edison Research. 2012. Exit poll. November 6.

Ennis, S. R., M. Rios-Vargas, and N. G. Albert. 2011. "The Hispanic Population: 2010." US Census Bureau press release, September 29.

Fox News. 2012. Poll. October 28–30.

———. 2013. Poll. December 14–16.

Gallup Poll. 2006a. May 5–7.

———. 2006b. June 8–25.

———. 2006c. "Bush's Speech on Immigration Policy Closely Follows Public Opinion." Press release, May 17.

Goodnough, A. 2006. "A Florida Mayor Turns to an Immigration Curb to Fix a Fading City." *New York Times*, July 10.

Gormley, B. 2001. *President George W. Bush: Our Forty-Third President.* New York: Aladdin Paperbacks.

Greenberg, S. and J. Carville. 2014. "Inside the GOP: Why Boehner Is Halting Immigration Reform." *National Memo, Democracy Corps*, February 2.

Hajnal, Z. L., and T. Lee. 2011. *Why Americans Don't Join the Party: Race Immigration and the Failure (of Political Parties) to Engage the Electorate.* Princeton, NJ: Princeton University Press.

Hartz, L. 1955. *The Liberal Tradition in America.* New York: Harcourt Brace Jovanovich.

Hitt, J. 2000. "Does the Smell of Coffee Brewing Remind You of Your Mother?" *New York Times Magazine*, May 7.

Hoffer, E. 1951. *The True Believer.* New York: Harper and Row.

Huffington Post. 2013. "Steve King: Most Dreamers Are Hauling 75 Pounds of Marijuana across the Desert." July 23.

Huntington, S. P. 2000. "Reconsidering Immigration: Is Mexico a Special Case?" *Center for Immigration Studies Backgrounder.* November.

———. 2004. *Who Are We? The Challenges to America's National Identity.* New York: Simon and Schuster.

Ignatieff, M. 2014. "America's Melancholic Hero." *New York Review of Books*, March 6.

Johnson, L. B. 1965. Remarks at the Signing of the Immigration Bill. Liberty Island, New York, October 3.

Kamen, A. 2014. "Border Focus Still Intact." *Washington Post*, March 5.

Kennedy, A. 2012. *Arizona v. U.S.* Majority Opinion.

Kludt, T. 2014. "Boehner Thought Steve King Was an 'Asshole' for 'Cantaloupes' Comment." *Talking Points Memo*, January 17.

Ladd, E. C. 1995. *America at the Polls, 1994.* Storrs, CT: Roper Center for Public Opinion Research.

——— 1999. *The Ladd Report.* New York: Free Press.

Lipset, S. M. 1996. *American Exceptionalism: A Double-Edged Sword.* New York: W. W. Norton.

Marist College Institute for Public Opinion. 2014. "McClatch-Marist Poll: Is the American Dream Still Attainable?" Press release, February 14.

NBC News/*Wall Street Journal.* 2014. Poll. December 10–14.

"New Americans in California." 2013. Immigration Policy Center. May.

Nixon, R. 1968. Acceptance Speech. Republican National Convention. Miami Beach, Florida, August 8.

Obama, B. 2006. *The Audacity of Hope: Thoughts on Reclaiming the American Dream.* New York: Crown.

———. 2014a. Remarks by the President in Address to the Nation on Immigration. Washington, DC, November 20.

———. 2014b. State of the Union Address. Washington, DC, January 28.

Office of the Press Secretary. 2013. "Statement by President Obama on Senate Passage of Immigration Reform." The White House. Washington, DC, June 27.

Opinion Dynamics. 2004. Poll. April 6–7.

Passel, J. S., and D'V. Cohn. 2008. "U.S. Population Projections: 2005–2050." Pew Research Center Report. February 11.

Pew Research Center. 2014. Poll. February 14–23.

Pew Research Center for the People and the Press/*USA Today.* 2014. Poll. January 15–19.

Pew Research Hispanic Trends Project. 2013. February 13. See http://www.pewhispanic.org/2013/02/15/hispanic-population-trends/ph_13–01–23_ss_hispanics6/. Accessed February 27, 2014.

Planas, R. 2014. "Latino Voters Overwhelmingly Back Obama's Executive Action on Immigration: Poll." *Huffington Post.* November 24. http://www.huffingtonpost.com/2014/11/24/poll-obama-immigration-latinos_n_6213212.html. Accessed February 23, 2015.

Preston, J. 2013. "Number of Illegal Immigrants in U.S. May Be on Rise Again, Estimates Say." *New York Times,* September 23.

Public Agenda Foundation. 2009. Poll. April 23–June 7. Sample: National foreign-born adults.

Reagan, R. 1983. News Conference. Washington, DC, June 28.

———. 1994. Farewell Letter. November 5.

Reagan, R., and N. Reagan. 1986. Remarks by the President and First Lady in a National Television Address on Drug Abuse and Prevention. Washington, DC, September 14.

Reagan-Bush Republican Presidential Debate. 1980. Houston, Texas. April 23. See http://www.youtube.com/watch?v=lx9cciy8w. Accessed March 7, 2014.

Republican Debate Transcript. 2012. Tampa, Florida. January 23.

Roberts, S. 2008. "A Generation Away, Minorities May Become the Majority in U.S." *New York Times,* August 14.

Roosevelt, F. D. 1933. Inaugural Address. Washington, DC, March 4.

Shirer, W. L. 1985. *Twentieth Century Journey*. Vol. 1, *The Start, 1904–1930*. New York: Bantam Books.

Shlaes, Amity. 2013. *Coolidge*. New York: Harper Perennial.

Siddiqui, S. 2013. "Steve King Blasted over Dreamers Remark by Congressional Hispanic Caucus." *Huffington Post*, July 24.

Swarns, R. L. 2006. "In Georgia, Newest Immigrants Unsettle an Old Sense of Place." *New York Times*, August 4.

Taylor, P., and D'V. Cohn. 2012. "A Milestone En Route to a Majority Minority Nation." Pew Research Social and Demographic Trends. Press release, November 7.

US Census Bureau. 2011a. "2010 Census Shows Black Population Has Highest Concentration in the South." Press release, September 29.

———. 2011b. "2010 Census Shows Nation's Hispanic Population Grew Four Times Faster Than Total U.S. Population." Press release, May 26.

Washington Post/Miller Center. 2013. Poll. September 6–12.

White, J. K. 1983. *The Fractured Electorate: Political Parties and Social Change in Southern New England*. Hanover, NH: University Press of New England.

Will, G. F. 2014. "Warming to Immigration Reform." *Washington Post*, February 14.

Williams, F. 2014. "Gay Rights Can Unlock Immigration Reform." *Bloomberg*, February 11.

Williams, K. M. 2006. *Mark One or More: Civil Rights in Multiracial America*. Ann Arbor: University of Michigan Press.

Wills, G. 1978. *Inventing America*. New York: Vintage Books.

Winthrop, J. 1630. "We Shall Be as a City upon a Hill." Sermon: "A Model of Christian Charity." March.

DREAM-ing the American Dream

The Struggle to Enact the DREAM Act

MATTHEW GREEN

The American Dream—the belief that any citizen of the United States can achieve his or her goals with dedication and hard work—entices millions of people to come to the United States. But the American reality is that a substantial portion of those millions cannot become US citizens. This conflict between the ideal and the real is a source of profound frustration for the many foreign born who wish to live in America or who do so without US citizenship. It also explains why immigration is one of the country's thorniest public policy issues: while Americans are proud of their nation's immigrant heritage, they also acknowledge the pragmatic need for—and some, out of fear and hostility, demand—limits on who can become part of that heritage.[1]

To navigate these competing impulses and make new laws governing who can come to the United States and the benefits they may receive is no easy feat. Witness the effort to revise the nation's immigration laws that started in the early 2000s, an effort that, as of the summer of 2015, remained unsuccessful. Yet despite the stubbornly elusive goal of enacting major immigration reform, one specific proposal did make some headway: the DREAM Act. First introduced in the US Congress in 2001, the DREAM Act would allow undocumented residents of the United States[2] who had been brought to the country as minors to obtain some degree of legal status, and also make it easier for undocumented youth to receive in-state tuition at public universities. Although the DREAM Act had still not become federal law by the end of 2014, members of both political parties had endorsed it, the US Senate had passed an immigration bill that included DREAM Act provisions, and over a dozen states had extended in-state tuition rates to their own undocumented residents.

Passage of a nationwide DREAM Act has been a major goal for hundreds of thousands of young people who came to America as children, most commonly from Latin America, and who have coveted a college education and US citizenship. They understandably see citizenship and a university degree as central to achieving the American Dream. One recent poll, for instance, found that while half of whites believed "very much" that college education has meaning for the American Dream, 64 percent of Latino/as believed so (Constable and Clement 2014).

For those young people, the long (and, as of this writing, unfinished) legislative path that the federal DREAM Act has followed over the past dozen years has undoubtedly been frustrating. Yet it is remarkable that an idea once widely derided as an unjust reward to lawbreakers has become acceptable to many legislators from both political parties. Explaining this dramatic shift in attitude, and the adoption of certain DREAM Act provisions in a number of states, is the purpose of this chapter. I begin by outlining John Kingdon's model of agenda setting, which explains how a proposal can become part of the legislative agenda and gain support among elected leaders. After briefly reviewing the history of immigration policy in the United States, I apply Kingdon's model to the story of the DREAM Act from the initial push behind it in the early 2000s to its partial, but by no means complete, success at state and national levels of government by the mid-2010s. That story also highlights the reasons that policy change often happens more readily at the state versus the federal level and underscores the political potency of the concept of the American Dream, not only to those hoping to become American citizens but also to Americans themselves.

How Policy Agendas Are Made

Political scientists have proposed various and often competing theoretical models to predict when major new national laws are enacted. Some models emphasize the importance of elections bringing new parties to power; others concentrate on how the media, interest groups, and citizens raise awareness of issues that demand governmental solutions; others stress the particular policy-making power of Congress, the president, or the courts; and others highlight strategic relationships among influential political actors. Alas, there is no clear consensus among scholars about which of these models is best.[3] Furthermore, behind every policy issue is a unique constellation of lobbying groups, electoral coalitions, economic interests, legal frameworks, and cultural values that shape and drive it. Immigration is no exception; economic conditions, labor rights, attitudes toward cultural assimilation and ethnic diversity, and international law all contribute to the nature of America's immigration laws and the ability to alter them.

Nonetheless, some theories of US policy making—specifically, theories of agenda setting—offer important insights into why ideas for new laws arise and become salient regardless of whether those laws are approved. Of particular value for understanding how the DREAM Act transformed from a fringe issue to one with bipartisan endorsement in Congress is the model of agenda setting John Kingdon proposed in his landmark 1984 book *Agendas, Alternatives, and Public Policies.*[4]

According to Kingdon, two "streams" determine whether an issue becomes part of Congress's agenda. The *problem stream* represents the emergence of some condition that demands action, perhaps because it is contrary to universal beliefs or is identified as such by an entrepreneurial politician or other person of influence. The other stream is the *political stream*, which includes political changes (like new voter attitudes, dramatic elections, or emerging interest groups) that oblige key policy players to acknowledge that an issue is important. A favorable flow and direction of these streams creates a *policy window*: a chance for "visible participants" in the policy-making process who have agenda-setting power (like members of Congress or the president) to bring particular issues forward (Kingdon 1984, 206–8, 210, 212–15).

Once a policy window opens, the next stage of policy making is the proposal of specific alternatives to the status quo. According to Kingdon, a policy idea rises to the level of serious consideration if it is carried by a third stream: the *policy stream*, or the "primeval soup" in which competing proposals merge and collide until those considered the most feasible come to the fore. This stream is also aided by "hidden participants" in policy making, like government staff and think-tank specialists, who wield considerable influence and expertise in drafting laws (Kingdon 1984, 209–10).

Political entrepreneurs are especially important for the agenda-setting process. They help set the national agenda by highlighting some problems over others, garner maximum attention and support for particular policy proposals, and "couple" the three streams when a policy window opens (Kingdon 1984, 214–15). They are also essential for getting a proposed alternative enacted, in particular one (like the DREAM Act) that offers voting citizens relatively few immediate or tangible benefits.[5] Given that Americans have competing, and to some degree contradictory, attitudes toward immigration, entrepreneurs are critical for framing immigration-related issues and spinning "policy narratives" that endorse a certain goal. "Hortatory language" that makes immigrants appear sympathetic and "deserving" is, in the words of political scientist Lina Newton, "crucial to crafting immigration policy" that would grant them citizenship or other benefits (Newton 2008, 3, 18).[6] More generally, as one pair of scholars put it, "images . . . are an integral part of the political battle" over policy (Baumgartner and Jones 1993, 28).

A proposal is not guaranteed to become law just because it joins the national policy agenda. In particular, there is an inherent status quo policy bias that results from multiple veto points within the national government, including a bicameral Congress, the rules of the US Senate that require a 60-vote supermajority to overcome filibusters, the president's veto pen, and the power of the courts to overturn laws (Grossmann 2014, 5).[7] At the same time, the nation's federalist system gives states substantial governing authority and the incentive and opportunity to innovate. Put together, these twin features of American governance tend to discourage major legislative action at the national level but encourage it at the state level, even on matters, like immigration, that are ostensibly under the sole purview of Washington.

Before looking at how these elements—streams, windows, policy-making participants, entrepreneurs, status quo bias, and federalism—help explain the growing popularity of the DREAM Act (if not immigration reform more generally), and how that popularity has so far translated to new laws at the state but not the national level of government, it is worth briefly reviewing the history of immigration policy in the United States. That history reveals how (relatively) recently the United States began imposing restrictions on immigration, when Latino/a immigration emerged as a particular concern, and how American immigration law has swung between more lenient and more punitive approaches.

Immigration Policy and Latino/a Immigration before 2001

The history of immigration policy in the United States is a long and complex one; only a brief summary can be offered here.[8] Until the late nineteenth century, the United States had no national laws limiting immigrants by number or origin, and immigration rules were seen as the responsibility of state governments. In 1875, however, the Supreme Court ruled that the federal government had the sole authority to regulate immigration, and Congress eventually took the lead on immigration policy. In 1882, it approved the Immigration Act, which established a head tax on each immigrant and prohibited admission of "any convict, lunatic, idiot, or any person unable to take care of himself or herself without becoming a public charge." The same year it also passed legislation sharply reducing the number of Chinese allowed into the country, in response to their use as substitute laborers and reflective of widely held racial prejudices against them (Smith 1997, 357–63; Tichenor 2002, 68, 106–8). Then, in 1921, Congress imposed the first-ever numerical limits on future immigration from all nations; three years later, lowered quotas drastically reduced the number of foreign born entering the United States. These limits were structured such that emigration from non-European countries to the United States would be far more difficult than from Western Europe or the Americas (Gimpel and Edwards 1999, 94–95).

Although this quota-based immigration policy lasted for over four decades, as time went on a changing domestic and international political environment made it "increasingly difficult to defend." Many saw it as "arbitrary and discriminatory" and, in the early years of the Cold War, impeding the country's ability to serve as sanctuary to those fleeing communist regimes (Gimpel and Edwards 1999, 99). In 1965, federal law was changed so that the right to immigrate would be determined by personal skills, profession, family ties to American citizens, and danger of persecution (Gimpel and Edwards 1999, 100–109).[9] Penalizing some immigrants over others based solely on where they happened to be born seemed to be a thing of the past.

Meanwhile, federal law notwithstanding, America's unique geography made it easier for certain foreign nationals to come to the United States. For instance, though immigration from Europe surged in the late 1800s and early 1900s, so too did immigration from neighboring Canada (Gibson and Jung 2006, table 4). After 1900, Mexico became a new and growing source of immigrants, thanks not only to its proximity to the United States but also to lobbying efforts against more restrictive immigration rules by railroad and agriculture companies that relied on south-of-the-border laborers. Mexicans were further encouraged to immigrate to the United States (albeit only as temporary laborers) through the Bracero guest-worker program, which operated from 1942 until 1964 (Gimpel and Edwards 1999, 96–97; Newton 2008, 27).

As the number of emigrants from Mexico to the United States resumed its upward trajectory following the Great Depression, concerns about immigrants crossing the southern border illegally began appearing in the public sphere (Passel, Cohn, and Gonzalez-Barrera 2012, 19). In 1951, president Harry Truman asked Congress to halt the inflow of what he and others at the time called "wetbacks," and a number of bills were introduced over the years to tighten security along the southern border or penalize companies that employed non-US citizens (Gimpel and Edwards 1999, 97). The term *illegal* became "the primary marker of the Mexican in the United States" (Newton

2008, 21). Worries about southern migrants grew more intense when Latino/a immigration expanded after 1970, made up of not only Mexicans but also Central and South Americans and people fleeing Fidel Castro's Cuba (Gibson and Jung 2006, table 4; Passel, Cohn, and Gonzalez-Barrera 2012, 19–20). One poll from 1986 found that three-quarters of those surveyed believed that foreign immigration "somewhat" or "severely" threatened "the future of the American Dream" (*Wall Street Journal*, American Dream Poll, October 1986, USROPER.86DRM.R18N).

Legislative efforts to curtail the inflow of southern immigrants and alleviate fears about the violation of immigration laws fell short. In 1986, Congress passed a major comprehensive immigration law that combined legal amnesty for undocumented workers with new, unprecedented sanctions against employers of workers lacking legal documentation, but the sanctions proved too weak to discourage such employers (Gimpel and Edwards 1999, 169–80; Newton 2008, 5). Americans again grew hostile to immigration, and in the early 1990s nearly two-thirds of those surveyed believed that it should be decreased (see figure 1). In 1996, President Bill Clinton signed a more stringent immigration bill into law, one that (among other things) made it difficult for states to give collegiate financial assistance to undocumented immigrants on the basis of in-state residency (Bruno and Kuenzi 2007; Tichenor 2002, 280–85). Yet the booming American economy created a major demand for semiskilled and unskilled labor that could be readily met by workers coming from other countries (Aguilar 2001; Schmitt 2001). In 2000, 770,000 Mexicans arrived in the United States, a new peak, and by that year people born in Latin America made up an absolute majority of all foreign-born US residents for the first time (Gibson and Jung 2006, table 2; Passel, Cohn, and Gonzalez-Barrera 2012, 17). Whereas less than 1.5 percent of the US population consisted of undocumented workers in 1990, that percentage had more than doubled by 2000, with more than eight million unauthorized residents estimated to be living within the United States (see figure 2).

Although one might expect that these numbers would press Congress into cracking down even more severely on illegal immigration, the political environment suggested instead a shift away from punitive approaches. Americans' hostility to immigration was starting to subside; by the fall of 2000, a Gallup survey showed that for the first time in decades, more people believed that immigration levels should be preserved than reduced (see figure 1). The eligible Latino/a voting population had also been growing since the early 1990s, and polls showed that Latino/as tended to look with disfavor at laws that penalized immigrants, legal or otherwise (Tichenor 2002, 285–86).

Figure 1

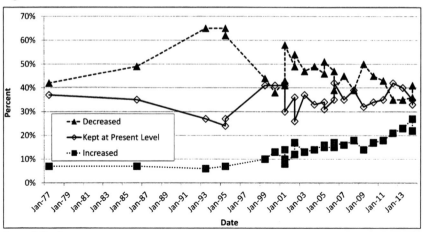

Source: Gallup Surveys.

Figure 2

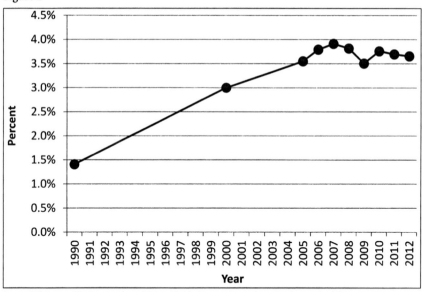

Source: US Census. The increase from 2009 to 2010 is due to a change in estimation methodology.

Accordingly, Congress began taking more charitable approaches toward dealing with illegal immigration and Latino/a immigrants specifically. In 1997 it granted Social Security benefits to some immigrants who had previously been denied them, and in 2000 it approved legislation that allowed certain families to reunite when one family member was undocumented and another was not (Schmitt 2001; Tichenor 2002, 287). Congress was further encouraged to take this direction when George W. Bush was narrowly elected president in

2000. A bilingual former governor of a state with one of the largest Hispanic populations in the country, Bush garnered 35 percent of the Latino/a vote, fourteen points higher than the previous GOP presidential nominee and a larger share than that received by any Republican presidential candidate since Ronald Reagan.[10]

Given these changing circumstances, the political ground seemed fertile for action on legislation that might offer benefits to noncitizens, particularly Latino/as, with a sympathetic story to tell. It was in this environment that a new idea came to the forefront: granting affordable education and citizenship for undocumented immigrants who had been brought to the United States as children.

The Story of the DREAM Act

The chronicle of how the DREAM Act went from a single initiative to a broadly supported policy proposal, partially adopted in nearly a score of states, involves many players and a variety of events both in and outside of government. In the following narrative I divide the history of the act into four eras: its initial appearance in Congress and the circumstances leading to it (1990s–2002); multiple attempts to pass the act under the George W. Bush administration, with some success in the Senate and in a number of states (2003–8); efforts by President Barack Obama and congressional Democrats to enact the DREAM Act (2009–12); and finally, its endorsement by members of both political parties in Congress and its passage in the Senate (for a second time) as part of an omnibus immigration reform bill that failed to become law (2013–14).[11]

1. An Idea Emerges and Takes Root (1990s–2002)

The massive wave of Latino/a immigrants to the United States in the 1970s and 1980s included many families with young children, including thousands who had entered the country illegally. As these children grew older, attended elementary school, and reached high school age, they presented a significant social problem. A college degree was increasingly seen as the prerequisite to a successful career, and by the late 1990s well over 60 percent of US high school graduates went on to college (Bureau of Labor Statistics 2000). But without the right to pay in-state tuition or the ability to get federal loans— not to mention lacking citizenship—undocumented youth faced almost insurmountable obstacles to going to college and getting a job, creating the very real possibility of "a permanent underclass" of American Latino/a youth (Parr 2012, 483). A problem stream had emerged.

That problem stream initially ran against a strong opposing political current. As noted previously, public sentiment in the 1990s leaned strongly against immigration and "illegals" getting citizenship or educational benefits. In 1994, California voters passed Proposition 187, which, among other things, denied children who were noncitizens the right to attend public school. Politicians, putting their fingers to the political wind, took note. Two years later, the US House of Representatives passed an immigration bill that would allow other states to do the same. Although a federal court later effectively nullified Proposition 187, and the House bill never became law, the political environment was clearly hostile to the idea of government-subsidized education to undocumented youth (Olivas 2009, 1761–63).

Political rhetoric at the time also tended to frame undocumented residents and immigrants, including the young, as lawbreakers rather than people in need of aid. Supporters of the House bill frequently employed a "zero-sum narrative" in which immigrant youth were depicted as unfairly taking opportunities from American citizens. Even immigrant advocates, by insisting that uneducated, undocumented residents were in greater danger of relying on welfare or breaking the law, were unintentionally labeling them with a "criminal alien stigma" (Newton 2008, 106, 108–10, 134).

But currents began to shift in the latter half of the 1990s as American attitudes toward immigration changed and the Latino/a population continued to grow. Reporters started writing compassionate stories about bright young college-age Latino/as unable to get a higher education.[12] States with large or fast-growing numbers of undocumented Latino/a residents, while not able to grant them citizenship, could offer greater leniency for those seeking college admittance and even find ways to circumvent the 1996 federal restrictions on postsecondary education benefits for undocumented state residents. In 2000, the university system in Georgia (where the population of Hispanics, primarily Mexican immigrants, had doubled in a decade) started allowing undocumented individuals to be admitted. In May 2001, Texas passed a new law granting in-state tuition breaks to unauthorized immigrants, and other states, including California (in 2001), Utah (in 2002), and New York (in 2002) soon followed (Bixler 2000, 2001; Bixler and Salzer 2000; Dyer 1999; Gamboa 2002; National Conference of State Legislatures 2013; Solis 2002; Suggs 1999).[13]

This state-level activity suggested that the political stream was moving with, not against, the problem stream. And that political stream began to trickle up from the state to national level as leaders of both political parties realized that their parties' future success depended on the ability to court the vote of Latino/as—who, surveys showed, were as a group far more open to increasing immigration than other ethnic groups (for example, Moore 2005).

In the 107th Congress (2001–2), some half-dozen bills were introduced to address the citizenship status of immigrant youth and (in all but one bill) overturn the 1996 ban on in-state university tuition to undocumented immigrants (see table 1).[14] One proposal in particular, however, gained considerable legislative traction: the "Development, Relief and Education for Alien Minors Act," or DREAM Act.[15] Introduced by Republican senator Orrin Hatch (UT), the bill not only repealed the 1996 restrictions on giving in-state college benefits to noncitizens but also allowed certain undocumented residents to remain in the United States while attending college and, upon graduation and maintaining a clean criminal record, apply for permanent legal residency in the United States.

The bill had several advantages over other, similar legislative proposals. For one thing, the bill's sponsor was the top Republican on the Senate Judiciary Committee, which had jurisdiction over the measure. Another advantage was its name: a savvy acronym that evoked the American Dream and the aspirations of immigrants. In addition, by narrowly focusing on one subset of undocumented residents—young people who wanted to better themselves—the DREAM Act made it possible for reporters to write stories that humanized those who would benefit, emphasizing their civic virtues rather than their potential for criminal behavior. They included stories like those of "Sam," a young polio victim and an A student, born in Vietnam, who "loves pizza . . . and the Red Sox" and dreamed of going to college; and Pablo Flores, who graduated at the top of his class at a high school in Los Angeles and wanted to attend UCLA. As one leader of the opposition to the DREAM Act admitted, "you feel badly for these kids, obviously" (Florio 2002; McMahon 2002).

One other advantage of Hatch's DREAM Act was that it quickly acquired grassroots support, often a key component of success in the political stream. Some of the young people who would directly benefit from the act started organizing on its behalf, adopting a moniker ("DREAMers") that further evoked American idealism. Remarkably, they did so despite the risk of deportation; one small group, for example, bravely spoke at a news conference on Capitol Hill in July 2002 (Gamboa 2002).

Given these advantages, as well as the favorable political climate, the chances of the measure's enactment seemed good. Nonetheless, the DREAM Act did not become law before Congress adjourned because a crisis event shut the bill's window of opportunity. The September 11, 2001, terror-

Table 1. Summary of Congressional Action Related to Financial Aid and Immigration Status of College-Bound Unauthorized Immigrants, 2001–14

Congress (Years)	DREAM-Related Bills Introduced (Sponsor, Party)	House Action	Senate Action
107th (2001–2)	S. 1291 (Hatch, R) S. 1265 (Durbin, D) H.R. 1563 (Jackson-Lee, D) H.R. 1582 (Gutierrez, D) H.R. 1918 (Cannon, R) H.R. 5600 (Gephardt, D)	None	Judiciary Committee approves S. 1291 (as amended)
108th (2003–4)	S. 1545 (Hatch, R) H.R. 84 (Jackson-Lee, D) H.R. 1684 (Cannon, R) H.R. 1830 (Jackson-Lee, D) H.R. 3271 (Gephardt, D)	None	Judiciary Committee approves education bill (S. 8), which includes DREAM provisions from S. 1291, and S. 1545 (as amended)
109th (2005–6)	S. 2075 (Durbin, D) H.R. 5131 (Diaz-Balart, R)	None (it approves an immigration bill with no DREAM provisions)	Senate approves Comprehensive Immigration Reform Act (S. 2611) which includes text from S. 2075
110th (2007–8)	S. 774 (Durbin, D) S. 2205 (Durbin, D) H.R. 1275 (Berman, D) H.R. 1221 (Gillmor, R) H.R. 1645 (Gutierrez, D)	None	Senate fails to invoke cloture on Comprehensive Immigration Reform Act (S. 1348), which includes DREAM provisions; broad immigration reform bill (S. 1639), which includes DREAM provisions; and S. 2205
111th (2009–10)	S. 729 (Durbin, D) S. 3827 (Durbin, D) S. 3962 (Durbin, D) S. 3963 (Durbin, D) S. 3992 (Durbin, D) H.R. 1751 (Berman, D) H.R. 6327 (Djou, R) H.R. 6497 (Berman, D)	House approves judicial procedure bill (H.R. 5281), which includes text from H.R. 6497	Senate fails to invoke cloture on defense authorization bill (S. 3454), which includes DREAM provisions; DREAM language in H.R. 5281; and S. 3992
112th (2011–12)	S. 952 (Durbin, D) H.R. 1842 (Berman, D) H.R. 3823 (Rivera, R)	None	None
113th (2013–14)	S. 1943 (Murray, D) S. 2954 (Harkin, D) H.R. 15 (comprehensive immigration reform) (Garcia, D) H.R. 3921 (Polis, D)	None	Senate approves comprehensive immigration reform bill (S. 744), which includes DREAM provisions

Sources: Barron 2011; Bruno 2012; Bruno and Kuenzi 2007; Olivas 2012; Wasem 2013

ist attacks, which were mounted by foreign terrorists who had entered the country legally (including one who did so on a student visa), quickly soured the public on the cause (see figure 1). Opponents of the DREAM Act now found a more receptive audience to their argument that the proposal unfairly gave scarce spots in public universities to noncitizens and "rewards those who knowingly and willingly violate immigration laws" (Tabor 2012, 487).[16] Those opponents included vocal and influential groups like the Federation for American Immigration Reform and the Center for Immigration Studies (Florio 2002; Gamboa 2002). They also included an outspoken congressman, Tom Tancredo (R-CO), who went so far as to openly urge the deportation of an undocumented Colorado youth who had sought a college degree (Solis 2002). Although the Senate Judiciary Committee still managed to approve the DREAM Act in June 2002, it never reached the Senate floor.

2. FURTHER PROGRESS, NEW ROADBLOCKS (2003–8)

Experienced lawmakers know that it can take time to get a bill turned into a law. Despite the closure of the policy window for the DREAM Act in late 2001, the problem stream's relentless flow, powered by the ever-growing number of undocumented immigrants seeking a college education, could not be ignored.

Both states and the federal government responded. In the 108th Congress (2003–4), five bills related to tuition breaks and/or citizenship paths for would-be college students were introduced (table 1). The Senate Judiciary Committee also took action, approving both a DREAM Act bill introduced by Senator Hatch and a bigger education bill (S. 8) that included DREAM Act provisions. Meanwhile, more states considered the problem of college accessibility and affordability for undocumented youth. By mid-2003 bills had been introduced in nearly two dozen state legislatures to provide in-state tuition to undocumented students, and by the end of the following year four states had adopted them: Illinois, Kansas, Oklahoma, and Washington (National Conference of State Legislatures 2013; Scavongelli 2003). Young undocumented immigrants also continued to lobby for the legislation even though they were "exposing themselves to the risk of deportation in the process" (Kong 2003).[17]

Congress failed to pass a DREAM bill before it adjourned in 2004, yet new developments in presidential politics suggested a reopening of the policy window for not only the DREAM Act but also immigration reform more broadly. President Bush was reelected with an impressive 44 percent of the Latino/a vote, nearly ten percentage points higher than he had received four years before.[18] In addition, Bush quickly emerged as an important visible participant in the immigration debate, endorsing a comprehensive fix to the nation's immigration laws to address both border security and the fate of the nation's many undocumented residents (West 2013).

In spite of this, the political environment was less amenable to the DREAM Act than it first appeared. Bills were introduced in the legislatures of Arizona, North Carolina, and Virginia to explicitly ban tuition benefits for undocumented immigrants (Scavongelli 2003). Legal challenges were filed against the in-state tuition laws of California, Texas, and New York, though they ultimately proved unsuccessful (Olivas 2009, 1765–68). Opinion polls showed that a plurality of Americans believed immigration rates were too high and needed to be cut (see figure 1). Furthermore, the Republican Party, which controlled both Congress and the White House, was becoming divided internally over the issue of immigration.

As a result, not only did the DREAM Act fail to become law, but it also seemed that greater stringency, not leniency, was the most likely direction of any new immigration policy. True, the DREAM Act reached a new milestone—passage in one of the chambers of Congress—when the Senate approved a broad immigration reform bill in 2006 (S. 2611) that contained DREAM Act language (table 1). But the House had already passed a bill of its own that emphasized border enforcement and deportation and had no citizenship pathway for undocumented immigrants. The only immigration bill President Bush signed into law in the 109th Congress (2005–6) authorized a new seven-hundred-mile fence along the southern border (Bruno 2012; Wasem 2013, 3–4, 10, 21). While New Mexico and Nebraska joined the ranks of states offering in-state tuition to the undocumented, Arizona earned national headlines after it gave local law enforcement the power to enforce immigration laws, and the state adopted a ballot proposition in 2006 that banned financial aid and in-state tuition rates for undocumented residents (Cannato 2012; National Conference of State Legislatures 2013).

The Democratic Party, which had come out more strongly for immigration reform and was less divided on the matter than the GOP, won control of Congress in 2006. Five DREAM-related measures were introduced in the following (110th) Congress, all but one by Democrats (table 1). But increased partisan conflict in Congress, coupled with rising Republican grassroots opposition to creating pathways to citizenship for undocumented immigrants, meant that the political stream was now pushing against adoption of the DREAM Act (Olivas 2009; Rothenberg 2007; Stanton and Billings 2007). In June 2007, Senate Democrats tried to pass an immigration bill (S. 1348) that was similar to the one that had passed the Senate in 2006 (and which included the text of the DREAM Act) but they failed to get the necessary three-fifths of senators to invoke cloture (that is, end a threatened filibuster). Another effort the following month to pass a different immigration reform bill (S. 1639), which contained a modified version of the DREAM Act, was abandoned for the same reason. And in October 2007 the Senate was unable to get the necessary three-fifths vote to invoke cloture and bring S. 2205, a DREAM Act bill introduced by senator Dick Durbin (D-IL) but opposed by President Bush, to the floor (Barron 2011, 633–34; Wasem 2013, 4–5, 26).[19]

Once again, not a single DREAM bill managed to become federal law. Furthermore, by the end of 2008, Colorado, Georgia, and South Carolina had joined the ranks of states that either explicitly banned noncitizen residents from paying in-state university tuitions or kept them from attending public universities at all.

3. Obama and Congressional Democrats Give It a Go (2009–12)
Amid the wreckage of comprehensive immigration reform in late 2008, supportive lawmakers and grassroots activists tried more piecemeal, incremental approaches to addressing various immigration problem streams, including the plight of undocumented college-eligible youth. As in 2004, the election results of 2008 seemed to bode well for advocates of immigration reform. Democrats not only kept control of Congress but also had a filibuster-proof, sixty-seat majority in the Senate and could also count on a new partisan ally in the White House, Barack Obama. More importantly, Obama had called for new national immigration policy on the presidential campaign trail, pointedly contrasting himself with his opponent, senator John McCain of Arizona, who, though originally an advocate of comprehensive reform, had endorsed tougher control over the US-Mexico border while downplaying benefits or citizenship for those in the country illegally—a sign that the GOP was becoming steadily less lenient toward undocumented residents.

Eight DREAM bills, a record number, were introduced between January 2009 and December 2010 (table 1). Five of the eight were sponsored by Senator Durbin, an early advocate for the DREAM Act who had surfaced as its principal legislative backer in the Senate when Republicans became increasingly reluctant to endorse it (Barron 2011). Meanwhile, young DREAMers garnered headlines by continuing to press publicly in favor of reform. The Immigrant Youth Justice League, formed in 2009, launched protests and demonstrations to draw attention to the concerns of undocumented youth. In 2010, four students who were not US citizens walked from Florida to DC to raise awareness of the DREAM Act, while another five occupied the Arizona office of Senator

McCain in "the first act of civil disobedience practiced by undocumented students which exposed them to arrest and deportation" (Galindo 2012, 590; Montgomery 2010).

Supporters of the DREAM Act would yet again be disappointed—not by a crisis, as in 2001, or by divisions within the governing party, as in 2005–6, but by the decision of Democrats to give greater priority to health care reform. Immigration had also become an increasingly partisan issue, with congressional Republicans opposed to expanding citizenship opportunities while Democrats were in favor, and political conflict killed most attempts to pass immigration bills, including the DREAM Act. Senate Democratic leaders included DREAM language in a defense authorization bill (S. 3454), but the bill was blocked by Senate Republicans from coming to a vote in September 2010. Three months later, the House for the first time approved language as part of another bill that had DREAM Act provisions; it allowed those with military service, as well as those completing at least two years of college, the right to apply for citizenship. But that came after an election that showed Republicans would be taking back control of Congress, and Senate Republicans saw no reason to cooperate with Democrats to pass the House bill. Despite last minute lobbying by immigration activists, Catholic bishops, and others, the measure failed to overcome a Senate filibuster (Bruno 2012; Pattison 2010).[20]

In the next Congress (the 112th, 2011 12) three DREAM bills were introduced (table 1), but none of them saw any action in either the House or Senate. Congress seemed less likely than ever to pass immigration reform, especially with the election of a large new class of conservative, limited-government Republicans to the House of Representatives in 2010. In a major victory for DREAMers, the Obama White House did announce in June 2012 the Deferred Action for Childhood Arrivals (DACA), which temporarily deferred deportation proceedings for certain undocumented residents who had been brought to the United States as children, were in (or had graduated from) school or were honorably discharged from the military, and had no criminal record (Wong et al. 2013).[21] But the year before, the Republican state government of Alabama had passed a measure that put limits on unauthorized immigrants seeking to enroll in state colleges, while the GOP-led government of Indiana prohibited undocumented residents from receiving in-state tuition rates at state schools (National Conference of State Legislatures 2013). Despite polls showing majority support for giving citizenship to young people if they went to college or joined the military,[22] the policy window for the DREAM Act, and immigration reform more generally, seemed to have been shuttered tight.

4. An Emerging, If Limited, Consensus (2013–14)

Given that the 2012 elections did not change who was in the White House, nor which party controlled the House (Republicans) or the Senate (Democrats), it appeared that the odds of enacting immigration legislation were no better than before. But the elections did give the Republican Party two important reasons to revisit its strong stance against citizenship pathways for, or benefits to, the undocumented. First, the percentage of Latino/as who voted in the 2012 elections was, while low (10 percent), higher than the previous two presidential cycles. Second, a meager 27 percent of Latino/as voted for the GOP's presidential candidate, Mitt Romney—a figure that helped Obama eke out a win in critical swing states like Florida, Nevada, and Colorado (Lopez and Taylor 2012; West 2013).

Lawmakers tend to believe that elections carry a message (Mayhew 1974, 71). And although Hispanics' voting preferences may vary by issue, income, and country of origin, Romney's aggregate loss of Latino/a support, which conservative columnist Michael Gerson called "a frightening portent," could be easily interpreted as a referendum on his (and his party's) position on immigration (Gerson 2014).[23] In December 2011, Romney had told one voter that he opposed the DREAM Act, and his entreaty for immigrants without citizenship status to "self-deport" garnered considerable attention. His tough anti-illegal immigration stand helped position him well among conservative primary voters, but it clearly proved damaging among Latino/a voters. By contrast, in his January 2012 State of the Union address Obama explicitly called for passage of legislation to halt the deportation of young undocumented residents, and his administration's DACA program was revealed five months later (White House 2012).[24]

If Republicans wanted to remain viable over the long term as a national party, it seemed they would need to change their tune on immigration.[25] Democrats could not be complacent either. DACA proved to be quite popular, with more than half a million individuals applying for deferred action on deportation within a year of its announcement. The program did not have the force of law, however, and it could be quickly repealed by a less-amenable successor to Obama (Constable 2014; Wong et al. 2013). In April 2012, a group of high-powered Latino/a campaign contributors told the president at a fund-raiser that Hispanics were "angered" Obama had "not worked harder to pass the Dream Act" (Stolberg 2013).

Promising signs appeared that comprehensive immigration reform could become law in the next (113th) Congress. The Senate voted for a major reform bill in mid-2013, and some prominent House Republicans, including Paul

Ryan (WI) and Speaker John Boehner (OH), openly endorsed taking some substantive action on immigration reform, perhaps even establishing an avenue for certain undocumented residents to earn legal status (Eldridge 2014; Korecki 2013; Nakamura and Kane 2014). In a mid-2013 survey, a whopping 83 percent of Latino/as said they would be disappointed (and 61 percent said they would be angry) if the House failed to ratify legislation that gave undocumented immigrants some means of earning citizenship status (Cohen and Balz 2013).

For the DREAM Act specifically, the 2012 elections brought about a remarkable and encouraging development: for the very first time, its provisions were embraced by the leaders of the Republican as well as the Democratic Party. Although the term DREAM was "a taboo word in the Republican Conference," House majority leader Eric Cantor announced he would be developing a GOP measure that, according to one report, "would provide a pathway to citizenship for young immigrants." "People expect that there should be fairness for children who came to this country illegally but through no fault of their own," Speaker Boehner told the press in July 2013 (Fuller 2013).

There were additional reasons for DREAM Act advocates to be optimistic. Immigrant rights activists continued to organize and mobilize; one group even began a hunger strike in front of the Capitol in late 2013 to encourage House action on comprehensive reform. Media stories about the benefits of DACA and the aspirations of young would-be citizens continued to appear (for example, Constable 2014), and public opinion remained solidly in favor of the provisions of the DREAM Act and a way for undocumented immigrants to become legal residents, if not citizens (Constable and Boorstein 2014). In fact, the climate seemed so favorable that some supporters of the DREAM Act, most notably President Obama, argued that the act itself was no longer enough. "In 2010, they [undocumented children] would have welcomed this," one immigrant rights activist said, but now insisted that only a broad reform bill that addressed the needs of all undocumented residents would suffice (Nakamura 2013).

As it turned out, the current of the political stream was not running entirely one way. The GOP's conservative base seemed unlikely to embrace what it could construe as unjustified amnesty for lawbreakers. The Senate did pass a reform bill with the DREAM Act included, but in an opinion survey taken shortly thereafter, over 60 percent of Republicans expressed opposition to the measure (Cohen and Balz 2013), and House Republicans were hesitant to lend their votes for legislation that might anger their core constituents. The government shutdown of October 2013 distracted Washington from immigration matters, and when the GOP came out as the decisive loser of the shutdown, many assumed the party would find repellent any legislation that was desired by President Obama—even if a number of Republicans, whether out of personal preferences or for political purposes, saw passage of the DREAM Act and immigration reform as beneficial. Momentum for immigration legislation in the House died altogether when Majority Leader Cantor was defeated in a primary in June 2014 by a rival who had campaigned heavily against immigration reform. It served as another example of how incumbent legislators broadly interpret the meaning of individual elections, for within three weeks Speaker Boehner declared that the House would not consider immigration reform in that Congress (Dennis 2014).

Despite the disappointing outcome, DREAM Act advocates could look outside of Congress for some signs of progress. Obama continued to support the DREAM Act and, in a controversial move after the November elections, used his executive authority to limit the deportation of millions of undocumented immigrants. By early April 2014 a record nineteen states had allowed at least some of their undocumented residents to pay in-state tuition for public universities—including one, Maryland, which was the first to approve it by popular referendum (Anderson and Lazo 2012).[26]

Conclusion

The description of the American Dream proffered by the author James Truslow Adams perhaps best sums up why US citizenship and a college degree matter so much to young undocumented residents of the United States. The Dream, he wrote in the early 1930s, is one "of social order in which each man and each woman shall be able to attain to the fullest stature of which they are innately capable, and be recognized by others for what they are, regardless of the fortuitous circumstances of birth or position" (Adams 1931). In today's society, if one has neither citizenship nor a college education, it is all but impossible to "attain to the fullest stature" one's goals or "be recognized" for one's character and achievements.

The continuing story of the DREAM Act is one in which this acceptance, even embrace, of the American Dream compelled lawmakers and undocumented youth to fight for legislative relief. It is also one that highlights the core elements of policy making at the national level: entrepreneurs in and out of government, political and policy streams, and policy windows. Unfortunately for DREAM Act advocates, often those streams turned unfavorable and the window of opportunity closed as other issues, like terrorism and health care, became a higher priority.

The story of the DREAM Act also emphasizes three significant features of American politics in particular. First, American political parties tend to be diverse and heterogeneous when compared with their compatriots in other democracies, and this diversity often lends itself to significant divisions within them. Immigration traditionally has split both parties, but the issue has proven far more divisive to the GOP in recent years. That division proved fatal to immigration reform and the DREAM Act specifically when Republicans controlled the White House and both chambers of Congress in the early 2000s, and also in 2010–14 when the party held the reins of power in just the House of Representatives.

Second, the multiple veto points that exist within the national government make it difficult to enact new federal laws, especially during periods of sharp partisan conflict. When in the majority, House Republicans, disagreeing with their Senate counterparts on the necessity of new pathways to citizenship for undocumented immigrants, have been able to use their power to block immigration bills, including the DREAM Act. Senate Republicans have similarly exploited the minority-empowering rules of their chamber to thwart Democratic efforts to enact DREAM legislation. More generally, these veto points contribute to an inherent status quo bias in American public policy that challenges any effort to pass major legislative measures, let alone controversial ones. This helps explain why, despite strong favorable currents of the problem stream and political stream at times, the federal DREAM Act has been in legislative limbo for over a dozen years.

Third, American federalism and the separation of powers offer alternative avenues to make policy. Even though Congress has often proved too divided—either between parties, within parties, or between chambers—to pass immigration reform, DREAM advocates have made some headway with a more amenable executive branch, while the number of states that have granted expanded educational opportunities to undocumented college-bound youth has been remarkable.

As of this writing, it is difficult to predict when or even if comprehensive immigration reform, not to mention the DREAM Act, will become law. A federal DREAM Act has come closest to enactment when it has been included in larger bills, and it is reasonable to expect that its best chance for success will come as part of a bigger legislative package—most likely a broad, comprehensive immigration reform measure that most agree is long overdue.[27] If history is any guide, such a reform measure will need the support of all major players in Washington: the president, legislative leaders, interest groups, and members of both parties in the House and Senate (Grossmann 2014, 88–89). Such support seemed even less likely after the GOP won control of the Senate in November 2014, and when President Obama announced shortly thereafter that he would expand the DACA program and refrain from deporting millions of non-US citizens, infuriating congressional Republicans. Nonetheless, though the number of unauthorized immigrants in the United States has leveled off (figure 2), the pressure on both political parties to fix what most agree is a broken immigration system remains significant, and the fact that Republicans and Democrats have endorsed some version of the DREAM Act is an especially encouraging sign. It may ultimately take increased grassroots pressure, positive media coverage, and elections that bring new leaders to Washington for the players that matter to unite around a proposal that can become law. Until then, DREAMers will undoubtedly keep pressing for legislative action that brings them closer to achieving the American Dream.

Acknowledgments

Thanks to Chris Darnton, James Gimpel, Cecilia Levin, Yuval Levin, and James McCann for suggestions and comments and Gregory Collins for helpful research assistance.

Notes

1. Many others have pointed out this apparent contradiction, or at least dichotomy, of American attitudes toward immigration (e.g., Newton 2008, 1; Tichenor 2002, 289–90).

2. Although I use the term in this chapter, Lina Newton points out that the term "undocumented" is something of a misnomer, since some immigrants residing in the United States illegally do technically possess documents, albeit illegitimate ones (Newton 2008, ix).

3. For an excellent summary of the competing schools of thought regarding when national policy proposals are most likely to be approved, see Grossmann (2014, chap. 1).

4. Grossmann (2014) argues that Kingdon's model overstates the correlation between an item getting on Congress's agenda and that item becoming law. Grossmann's critique, while persuasive, does not negate the power of Kingdon's theory to explain why Congress might consider and debate proposals regardless of whether they become law.

5. For more on the role of entrepreneurs in congressional lawmaking, see Arnold (1990).

6. For an example of how framing has been used successfully to enact policy, see Graetz and Shapiro (2006).

7. As Daniel Tichenor observes, the location of these veto points can vary over time, as can countervailing "institutional opportunity points" to make policy (Tichenor 2002, 29–34).

8. For more on the history of immigration legislation in the United States, see Higham (1955) and Tichenor (2002).

9. The law did impose caps on immigration from each hemisphere (Gimpel and Edwards 1999, 108; Tichenor 2002, 215–16).

10. On the importance of "immigrant enfranchisement" more generally as the impetus for lenient immigration laws, see Tichenor (2002, chap. 9).

11. For more detailed legislative histories of the DREAM Act through 2010, see Barron (2011) and Olivas (2010, 2012).

12. Media coverage and elite rhetoric may have had an impact on how citizens perceived the desirability of the DREAM Act. See, e.g., Druckman, Peterson, and Slothuus (2013).

13. California, for instance, circumvented the prohibition by granting their tuition discount to all high school graduates, regardless of citizenship status (Bunis and Canto 2002).

14. Some of the bills (such as H.R. 5600) did not overturn the 1996 ban on in-state tuition. For a detailed explanation of the differences among these bills in the 107th and 108th congresses, see Bruno and Kuenzi (2007).

15. A companion measure was introduced in the House by one of Hatch's Republican colleagues from Utah, Chris Cannon, in May 2001 (Bruno and Kuenzi 2007; Del Muro 2002).

16. See also Barron (2011, 638–47), and Bruno (2013, 11) for a summary of arguments for and against the DREAM Act.

17. For more on grassroots activism by would-be DREAM Act recipients, see Nicholls (2013).

18. For more on the reasons behind Latino/a support for Bush, see Abrajano, Alvarez, and Nagler (2008).

19. Durbin also considered amending the defense authorization bill (S. 2919) in mid-2007 with DREAM Act language.

20. Some of these failures could be attributed to the majority Democrats' decision to bring immigration legislation to a vote without consultation with the minority, daring their opponents to reject popular initiatives and face voters' wrath rather than seeking common ground.

21. DACA was called "DREAM Act-lite" by some (Grant 2012).

22. Between December 2010 and September 2012, various polls showed between 54 percent and 70 percent of those surveyed supporting such legislation. See, e.g., Gallup Poll (USGALLUP.10DEC03.R01H), December 3–6, 2010, and various surveys by the Public Religion Research Institute, August 2011–September 2012.

23. Abrajano, Alvarez, and Nagler (2008, 369–70) offer a short summary of the literature on the complexities of Hispanic voting participation and preferences. For more on the factors that mobilize Latino/as politically, see Ramirez (2013).

24. Perhaps not coincidentally, a poll in January 2012 found that almost 70 percent of registered Latino/a voters would support a candidate who endorsed the DREAM Act (Univision News/Latino Decisions National Latino Poll [USLD.12HISP1.R30], January 24, 2012, http://faculty.washington.edu/mbarreto/ld/jan_national.html, accessed December 4, 2013).

25. One study suggested that the majority of both unauthorized Latino/a immigrants and legal permanent Latino/a residents were unattached to either party, giving Republicans a chance to win their votes (Pantoja 2013).

26. The states included California, Colorado, Connecticut, Hawai'i, Illinois, Kansas, Maryland, Michigan, Minnesota, Nebraska, New Mexico, New Jersey, New York, Oklahoma, Oregon, Rhode Island, Texas, Utah, and Washington (National Conference of State Legislatures 2013). Some states did so through legislative action, others via other paths, such as decisions by universities themselves. Virginia joined the list later in April when its attorney general unilaterally granted in-state tuition for some of the state's undocumented residents (Vozzella and Constable 2014).

27. For more on the likelihood that the DREAM Act passes as part of an omnibus immigration bill, see Olivas (2009).

References

Abrajano, Marisa A., R. Michael Alvarez, and Jonathan Nagler. 2008. "The Hispanic Vote in the 2004 Presidential Election: Insecurity and Moral Concerns." *Journal of Politics* 70 (2): 368–82.

Adams, James Truslow. 1931. *The Epic of America.* Boston: Little, Brown.

Aguilar, Louis. 2001. "Bush Nominee's Admission Underscores Surging Number of Illegal Workers." *Denver Post*, January 9.

Anderson, Nick, and Luz Lazo. 2012. "Maryland Voters Approve 'Dream Act' Law." *Washington Post*, November 6.

Arnold, R. Douglas. 1990. *The Logic of Congressional Action.* New Haven, CT: Yale University Press.

Barron, Elisha. 2011. "The Development, Relief, and Education for Alien Minors (DREAM) Act." *Harvard Journal on Legislation* 48 (2): 623–55.

Baumgartner, Frank R., and Bryan D. Jones. 1993. *Agendas and Instability in American Politics.* Chicago: University of Chicago Press.

Bixler, Mark. 2000. "Hispanics Forecast to Outnumber Blacks." *Atlanta Journal and Constitution*, January 13.

———. 2001. "U.S.-Mexico Changes Will Affect Georgia." *Atlanta Journal and Constitution*, February 15.

Bixler, Mark, and James Salzer. 2000. "Georgia Colleges Open to All Immigrants." *Atlanta Journal and Constitution*, November 2.

Bruno, Andorra. 2012. "Unauthorized Alien Students: Issues and 'DREAM Act' Legislation." CRS Report, June 19, Report No. RL-33863.

Bruno, Andorra, and Jeffrey J. Kuenzi. 2007. "Unauthorized Alien Students: Legislation in the 107th and 108th Congresses." CRS Report, January 17.

Bunis, Dena, and Minerva Canto. 2002. "Bill Would Give Nation Immigrant Tuition Law." *Orange County Register*, July 17.

Bureau of Labor Statistics. 2000. "Decline in College Enrollment Rate." TED: The Editor's Desk, May 18. http://www.bls.gov/opub/ted/2000/may/wk3/art04.htm, accessed December 4, 2013.

Cannato, Vincent J. 2012. "Our Evolving Immigration Policy." *National Affairs*, fall.

Cohen, Jon, and Dan Balz. 2013. "Conflicting Desires Pull at GOP on Border Issues." *Washington Post*, July 24.

Constable, Pamela. 2014. "A Fresh Start toward the Future." *Washington Post*, April 7.

Constable, Pamela, and Michelle Boorstein. 2014. "Most Want Illegal Immigrants to Have Ability to Become U.S. Citizens." *Washington Post*, June 10.

Constable, Pamela, and Scott Clement. 2014. "Despite Hurdles, Hispanics Cling Tightly to American Dream." *Washington Post*, January 31.

Del Muro, Mike. 2002. "Panel OKs In-State Tuition Bill for Undocumented Immigrants." *Salt Lake Tribune*, June 22.

Dennis, Steven T. 2014. "Immigration Bill Officially Dead." *Roll Call*, June 30.

Druckman, James N., Erik Peterson, and Rune Slothuus. 2013. "How Elite Partisan Polarization Affects Public Opinion Formation." *American Political Science Review* 107 (1): 57–79.

Dyer, Jim. 1999. "The Dreams of Rigo Nunez." *Atlanta Journal and Constitution*, January 24.

Eldridge, David. 2014. "Immigration Overhaul Shows Signs of Life in GOP." *Roll Call*, April 28.

Florio, Gwen. 2002. "College Dreams Face Harsh Reality." *Denver Post*, October 20.

Fuller, Matt. 2013. "Boehner Wants 'Fairness' for Young Immigrants." *Roll Call*, July 18.

Galindo, René. 2012. "Undocumented and Unafraid: The DREAM Act 5 and the Public Disclosure of Undocumented Status as a Political Act." *Urban Review* 44 (5): 589–611.

Gamboa, Suzanne. 2002. "Students Rally for In-State College Tuition, Legalization Bill." *Associated Press*, July 17.

Gerson, Michael. 2014. "The GOP Tries Good Will." *Washington Post*, February 4.

Gibson, Campbell, and Kay Jung. 2006. *Historical Census Statistics on the Foreign-Born Population of the United States: 1850–2000*. Working Paper No. 81. http://www.census.gov/population/www/documentation/twps0081/twps0081.html, accessed June 18, 2014.

Gimpel, James G., and James R. Edwards Jr. 1999. *The Congressional Politics of Immigration Reform*. Boston: Allyn and Bacon.

Graetz, Michael J., and Ian Shapiro. 2006. *Death by a Thousand Cuts: The Fight over Taxing Inherited Wealth*. Princeton, NJ: Princeton University Press.

Grant, David. 2012. "DREAM Act-lite." *Christian Science Monitor*, September 14.

Grossmann, Matt. 2014. *Artists of the Possible: Governing Networks and American Policy Change since 1945*. New York: Oxford University Press.

Higham, John. 1955. *Strangers in the Land: Patterns of American Nativism, 1860–1925*. New Brunswick, NJ: Rutgers University Press.

Jones, Bryan D., Heather Larsen-Price, and John Wilkerson. 2009. "Representation and American Governing Institutions." *Journal of Politics* 71 (1): 277–90.

Kingdon, John W. 1984. *Agendas, Alternatives, and Public Policies*. Boston: Little, Brown.

Kong, Deborah. 2003. "Undocumented Students Rallying for Legislation Discover a New Voice." *Associated Press*, December 1.

Korecki, Natasha. 2013. "U.S. Representatives Luis Gutierrez, Paul Ryan Team Up to Push for Immigration Reform." *Chicago Sun-Times*, May 24.

Lopez, Mark Hugo, and Paul Taylor. 2012. "Latino Voters in the 2012 Election." Pew Research Hispanic Center, November 7.

Mayhew, David R. 1974. *Congress: The Electoral Connection*. New Haven, CT: Yale University Press.

McMahon, Susan. 2002. "Illegal Immigrants' Dream: Residency, Then College." *Lowell Sun*, July 17.

Montgomery, David. 2010. "For Immigration, Students Take Toughest Course: Action." *Washington Post*, May 1.

Moore, David W. 2005. "Public Ambivalent about New Immigrants." Gallup News Service, July 7. http://www.gallup.com/poll/17206/public-ambivalent-about-new-immigrants.aspx, accessed December 4, 2013.

Nakamura, David. 2013. "Immigrant Children Are New Flash Point." *Washington Post*, August 13.

Nakamura, David, and Paul Kane. 2014. "House Republicans Say They Are Open to Legal Status for Illegal Immigrants." *Washington Post*, January 31.

National Conference of State Legislatures. 2013. "Undocumented Student Tuition: State Action." http://www.ncsl.org/research/education/undocumented-student-tuition-state-action.aspx, accessed December 4, 2013.

Newton, Lina. 2008. *Illegal, Alien, or Immigrant: The Politics of Immigration Reform*. New York: New York University Press.

Nicholls, Walter J. 2013. *The DREAMers: How the Undocumented Youth Movement Transformed the Immigrant Rights Debate*. Stanford, CA: Stanford University Press.

Olivas, Michael A. 2009. "The Political Economy of the Dream Act and the Legislative Process: A Case Study of Comprehensive Immigration Reform." *Wayne Law Review* 55 (4): 1757–810.

———. 2012. *No Undocumented Child Left Behind:* Plyer v. Doe *and the Education of Undocumented Schoolchildren*. New York: New York University Press.

Pantoja, Adrian. 2013. "Latino Non-Citizens Are Neither Democrats nor Republicans." Latino Decisions blog, July 11. http://www.latinodecisions.com/blog/2013/07/11/latino-non-citizens-are-neither-democrats-nor-republicans/, accessed December 4, 2013.

Parr, Andrew J. 2012. "Higher Education and Immigration Status: Point." In *Debates on U.S. Immigration*, edited by Judith Gans, Elaine M. Replogle, and Daniel J. Tichenor, 478–90. Los Angeles: Sage.

Passel, Jeffrey S., D'Vera Cohn, and Ana Gonzalez-Barrera. 2012. "Net Migration from Mexico Falls to Zero—and Perhaps Less." Washington, DC: Pew Research Center, April 23.

Pattison, Mark. 2010. "After DREAM Act Failure, Advocates Remain Determined." *National Catholic Reporter*, December 20.

Ramirez, Ricardo. 2013. *Mobilizing Opportunities: The Evolving Latino Electorate and the Future of American Politics*. Charlottesville: University of Virginia Press.

Rothenberg, Stuart. 2007. "Immigration Reform Legislation Still Faces an Uphill Battle." *Roll Call*, May 24.

Scavongelli, Sara. 2003. "States Weigh Tuition Breaks for Illegal Immigrants." *Stateline.org*, June 23.

Schmitt, Eric. 2001. "Chavez's Withdrawal Reopens Immigration Issue." *Contra Costa Times*, January 14.

Shortle, Allyson F. 2013. "Public Opinion and the Path to Immigration Reform." *Extensions* (Summer): 16–20.

Smith, Rogers M. 1997. *Civic Ideals: Conflicting Visions of Citizenship in U.S. History*. New Haven, CT: Yale University Press.

Solis, Dianne. 2002. "Push to Deport Family Stirs Debate on College Tuition Breaks." *Dallas Morning News*, October 3.

Stanton, John, and Erin P. Billings. 2007. "Reid Set to Move Border Bill." *Roll Call*, May 10.

Stolberg, Sheryl Gay. 2013. "Latinos Gain Political Muscle, and Fund-Raisers Show How." *New York Times*, March 7.

Suggs, Ernie. 1999. "Task Force: Hispanics Need Access at Colleges." *Atlanta Journal and Constitution*, June 10.

Tabor, Matthew K. 2012. "Higher Education and Immigration Status: Counterpoint." In *Debates on U.S. Immigration*, edited by Judith Gans, Elaine M. Replogle, and Daniel J. Tichenor, 478–90. Los Angeles: Sage.

Tichenor, Daniel J. 2002. *Dividing Lines: The Politics of Immigration Control in America*. Princeton, NJ: Princeton University Press.

Vozzella, Laura, and Pamela Constable. 2014. "Va. AG Rules on 'Dreamer' Tuition." *Washington Post*, April 30.

Wasem, Ruth Ellen. 2013. "Brief History of Comprehensive Immigration Reform Efforts in the 109th and 110th Congresses to Inform Policy Discussions in the 113th Congress." *Congressional Research Service*, February 27, Report No. R-42980.

West, Darrell M. 2013. "How the Politics of Immigration Reform Have Changed." *Brookings Institution*, February 5.

White House. 2012. Remarks by the President in State of the Union Speech, January 24. http://www.whitehouse.gov/the-press-office/2012/01/24/remarks-president-state-union-address, accessed December 4, 2013.

Wong, Tom K., Angela S. García, Marisa Abrajano, David FitzGerald, Karthick Ramakrishnan, and Sally Le. 2013. *Undocumented No More: A Nationwide Analysis of Deferred Action for Childhood Arrivals, or DACA.* Center for American Progress, Washington, DC. http://www.american progress.org/wp-content/uploads/2013/09/DACAReportCC-2-1.pdf, accessed December 4, 2013.

"The American Dream"

Walking toward and Deporting It

Daniel E. Martínez, Jeremy Slack, Alex E. Chávez, and Scott Whiteford

Introduction

Cristina, a thirty-nine-year-old woman from the Mexican state of Guana-juato, was apprehended in South Texas after successfully crossing the Rio Bravo on an inflatable raft and spending the better part of a day walking through the desert trying to avoid detection by US authorities. She was traveling with a *coyote* (human smuggler) she agreed to pay $2,000 to take her across the border. Cristina was on her way to San Antonio, Texas, not only in search of work, but also to be reunited with her husband who was living and working there. Although she has tried crossing the border three times, Cristina has never successfully made it to the United States. Our research team spoke with her the same day she was deported back to Mexico after having spent several weeks in a detention facility. When asked what she was going to do next, she seemed uncertain, perhaps even somewhat confused after the whole experience of being apprehended, processed, detained, and returned to Mexico. "I really don't know, I'm scared that they'll catch me again and give me more detention time. Besides, I need to wait and see what my husband says, to see if I go back home [to Guanajuato], or if I try [the crossing] again. If it were up to me I wouldn't do it again, it'd be better for me to go home" (interviewed on August 9, 2011). Hundreds of miles from her hometown in Guanajuato, and actually closer to San Antonio, Cristina must decide her next move while attempting to navigate a border town that is not only completely unfamiliar to her but also recently plagued by drug-trafficking-related violence. And apart from this material reality, another conceptual reality equally looms as she simultaneously edges closer to and farther away from multiple places—indeed, where is home?

Deportation is the lowest point in the unauthorized migration journey. Thousands of deportees arrive by bus to Mexican border towns every day, often unsure of where they are and what their next move may be. For many caught at the border in this state of limbo, the search for the "American Dream" quickly turns into "*la pesadilla Americana*" or the "American Nightmare." For people who attempted to cross for the first time, walking toward a vague notion of prosperity and the possibilities that a future in the United States may hold, the decision to try another crossing may seem too physically dangerous or difficult. For those who have spent years working in the United States, bought property, and started a family, returning to a life in Mexico becomes even more financially and socially costly.

Using a grounded and critical framework—one that places migrant subjectivity at the center of the discussion—we ask: What role does the continued search for the American Dream play in explaining the reasons for Mexican deportees' future crossing intentions postdeportation? Does the search for the American Dream still seem to matter for people who have spent time living and working in the United States before being deported? Or do other more proximate social factors, such as the intimacy of one's home or family in the United States, help to explain repeat crossing intentions among this group? How does the experience of being apprehended and processed through the US Department of Homeland Security's recently adopted Consequences Delivery System (CDS) affect future migration intentions, and what are the impacts of increased border and immigration enforcement? We address these questions by drawing on the second wave of the Migrant Border Crossing Study (MBCS), a new and unprecedented data set (n = 1,110) based on surveys and in-depth interviews with recently repatriated Mexican migrants. Personal accounts are provided alongside discourse analysis in order to provide a more direct and storied approach to this rich set of data.

A primary objective of the MBCS was to ascertain the most recent migration experience and future crossing intentions of unauthorized Mexican migrants, which relate to the search for the American Dream, although that precise wording was not explicitly mentioned in the research questions. Instead, we specifically asked respondents to discuss why they initially left their hometowns. We inquired as to whether or not they intended on crossing the border again following their most recent deportation and invited them to expand on their response to this question in greater detail. These open-ended responses can be used to better understand how, if at all, the notion of the American Dream shapes people's crossing intentions in an era of increased border and immigration enforcement. Better still, these revealing responses shed light on migrant conceptions of family and home that help understand how they assign particular meanings to their migrations in ways that go beyond, if not altogether escape, hegemonic notions of the American Dream. While we indeed encountered responses such as "*para sacar la familia adelante* (to get my family ahead)," "*para buscar el 'sueño Americano'* (in search of the American Dream)" and "*para una vida mejor* (for a better life)" as common reasons for leaving one's hometown in Mexico, and to a lesser extent, cited as motives for wanting to attempt a postdeportation border crossing, many respondents also noted increased punitive penalties associated with unauthorized migration, issues of racial/ethnic discrimination, difficulty of navigating day-to-day life being undocumented, and a weak US economy as reasons for *not* wanting to attempt a repeat crossing. In this way, migrants identify—and therefore implicitly critique—the political economies in which they are positioned and amid which they have carved out lives and meaningful relationships in the United States. Beyond facile narratives of the American Dream, migrants speak to how the everyday pressures and challenges of undocumented life unfold beneath the dehumanizing restrictions of the state and moreover with regard to how multiple places and the people in them have come to matter, have become connected, and the challenges of maintaining those ties. Overall, open- and closed-ended survey questions from the MBCS shed light on the contexts of people's future crossing intentions postdeportation and how these intentions fit within the discourse of desire for a better life juxtaposed with fear stemming from the deportation experience.

LANGUAGE, MIGRANT PERSONHOOD, AND THE AMERICAN DREAM

Our research draws upon literature in linguistic anthropology, particularly recent works that contextualize transnational migrants' ways of speaking about their migration in relation to the political economies in which their lives are positioned (Eisenlohr 2006; Farr 2006; Mendoza-Denton 2008; Dick 2010a, 2011a). Some of this work makes use of Mikhail Bakhtin's ([1935] 1981) concept of the chronotope as an optic with which to explore the interdependent temporal and spatial dimensions that contour narrative constructions of migrant personhood (Bakhtin [1935] 1981, 425–26). The work of Hilary Parsons Dick is especially helpful in conceptualizing relevant links between transnational mobility, systems of power, and migrant ways of speaking (Dick 2010b, 106; 2011a, 228).

In both her ethnographic explorations and assessments of the literature focused on social disparities produced through language, Dick attends to the relationship between chronotopes generated at the level of nation-states and by migrants themselves, both of which are populated by corresponding social personae who foot subjectivities across time and space. One such chronotope, for our purposes, is the prevailing ideology of the "American Dream"—a framing that configures social membership in the space of the US nation-state with adherence to an aspirational/forward-looking ethic grounded in civic duty, hard work, and a broadly conceived "American Creed" of enterprise (the pursuit of happiness) that assures success in the future. The "American Dream," Hanson and White note, is a "state of mind" containing a sense of optimism that drives people and nation to continue to move forward (2011, 3). In this way, the American Dream is a forceful chronotopic framing that compels persons toward future action, often conceived in terms of physical movement to a new locale where fresh opportunities are available. Its meanings are of promise, hope, and reliable ambition that rest on the geographic and symbolic existence of an American "imagined community" of hardworking, self-reliant, enterprising, and autonomous subjects who make the best of limitless opportunities.

And while the chant of America as a "nation of immigrants" is routinely mobilized to inscribe this purported essence of the nation-state onto the ideal-typical industrious "rational actor" (the immigrant who takes full advantage of the unfettered opportunity abundantly available to all), the imagined subject at the center of the American experiment, as such, represents a specific "ethnonational lineage"—white Europeans (Dick 2011a, 231). Linguistic representations of the "American Dream" and "nation of immigrants" construct a racial formation that equates citizenship with "whiteness" and "illegality" with race, such that persons of color are forever assumed to lack the juridical, social, and cultural capital that would afford them the entitlements of membership in the nation-state. This point resonates with Patrick Eisenlohr's (2006) work on the competing transnational and local imaginings of Mauritian nationhood between Indo-Mauritians and the indigenous ethnic Creole community, respectively. There, the cultural politics of "Little India"—as he so terms the Mauritian national imaginary—illustrate the central and symbolic role language plays in building opposing ideological constructions of nationhood in which individuals who lack ties to officialized ancestral cultures and languages with "origins elsewhere" are pushed to the periphery (Eisenlohr 2006, 7). Drawn also along ethnoracial lines, a comparison can be made between the tensions Eisenlohr describes and similar racializing practices articulated in things like "English Only" movements, which promote notions of cultural and racial homogeneity.

THE FALLACY OF ASSIMILATION, UPWARD MOBILITY, AND THE
AMERICAN DREAM

While scholars have dispelled the notion of straight-line assimilation in favor of a more segmented process (Portes and Zhou 1993; Waters 1999; Portes and Rumbaut 2001; Alba and Nee 2003; Kasinitz 2004), there seems to remain a misconception among the general public that the American Dream is synonymous with cultural assimilation into the dominant mainstream, which in turn is rewarded with upward social mobility into US middle-class status. It is not uncommon to hear accounts from members of dominant society describing how their distant relatives arrived in the United States from Europe, abandoned their native language, left their cultural or ethnic identity by the wayside, and pulled themselves up by their proverbial bootstraps to achieve the "American Dream" to ultimately become "American." As cited by Dixson and Rousseau (2005), Delgado notes that in these types of stories, the dominant group tells a narrative intended to "remind it of its identity in relation to outgroups and provide a form of shared reality in which its own superior position is seen as natural" (Delgado 1989, 240). In American society, individual-level agency and responsibility, however skewed, prevail over the importance of social structure and a sociohistoric context in explicating social and economic disparities.

The perpetuation of these historically misinformed family histories and the popular ethos of the American Dream centered on assimilation and achieving middle-class status are problematic for a number of reasons. First, they run counter to research noting that European immigrants were able to successfully integrate culturally into dominant mainstream US society only when the boundaries of "whiteness" expanded to include groups previously seen as "non-white," including Poles, Italians, Russians, and other southern and eastern Europeans (Alba and Nee 2003). Yet other scholars have convincingly argued that "the categorization of SEEs [southern and eastern European immigrants] as nonwhite was neither widely recognized nor institutionalized" (Fox and Guglielmo 2012, 365; also see Guglielmo 2004). The authors go on to state that "the boundary between whites and Mexicans appeared simultaneously bright and blurred" (Fox and Guglielmo 2012, 366), further calling into question whether traditional assimilation models of the twentieth century apply to racialized new post-1965 immigrants.

Second, and dovetailing with our first point, this understanding of the American Dream underplays the racialized sociohistoric contexts that have contributed to Native Americans, African Americans, Latino/as, and Asian Americans—many of which can trace their ties to this country back further than most European Americans—occupying the status of "second-class citizens." Omi and Winant (1994) have detailed these processes and sociohistoric contexts in their seminal work on racial formations. In the case of Mexican immigrants and Mexican Americans, Telles and Ortiz (2008), building on the seminal work of Grebler, Moore, and Guzmán (1970) through follow-up surveys decades after the initial study, provide empirical evidence illustrating how certain segments of the Mexican-origin population of Los Angeles County and the city of San Antonio experienced limited social mobility as a consequence of occupying minority status in a society heavily stratified by perceived racial difference, among other factors. The authors also note that "in education, which best determines life chances in the United States, assimilation is interrupted by the second generation and stagnates thereafter" (Telles and Ortiz 2008, 265). Telles and Ortiz go on to say, "Mexican Americans, three or four generations removed from their immigrant ancestors, are less likely than the Mexican American second generation of similar characteristics to have completed high school or college" (265). In other words, the educational system is failing them. This further highlights the importance of structural factors beyond issues of race and language in a shot at achieving the American Dream.

Ultimately, the symbolic narrative fashioned through the American Dream, as such, though seemingly embracing the universalizing claims of citizenship and democracy, instead generates a sociological formation that maintains white supremacy by underplaying the sociohistoric contexts that have produced second-class citizens based on racial difference. This silencing blames the lack of success on the individual to the extent that social inequality is denied its structural roots. And as it applies to the present discussion, contemporary post-1965 immigration is decontextualized from the broader processes of transnational political economies and global inequality that catalyze mobility, and instead the migrant subject is viewed through the lens of legal absolutism and subsequently criminalized. This scripting casts new racialized migrants as both imprudent subjects and "forever foreign" (Lipsitz 2006)—in a sense the "American Dream" is not for them because they are not "real Americans." This understanding of the American Dream was even perpetuated by some scholars. Samuel P. Huntington (2004), as quoted by Telles and Ortiz (2008), notes, "There is no Americano Dream. There is only the American Dream created by an Anglo Protestant society. Mexican Americans will share in that dream and in that society only if they dream in English" (Telles and Ortiz 2008, 7). No matter to what degree new immigrants assimilate or "succeed," especially when it comes to issues of culture and language, they are consistently accused of being unwilling or unable to integrate into US society.

GLOBALIZING THE AMERICAN DREAM

However, there are yet other reasons to support moving the notion of the American Dream beyond the idea of upward social mobility and cultural assimilation. Globalization has led to the rise of "consumer culture" (capitalist-oriented consumption patterns) around the world and has especially been perpetuated through various forms of media and the Internet, which now are available at the click of a button in far-off, distant places. The American Dream is no exception. And while abject poverty and economic necessity remain important factors driving migration flows, unauthorized international migration is most prevalent between semi-periphery and core countries that share a political border in the world system. Therefore the impact of *relative deprivation*, or the feeling that arises when one compares what one has with what one feels he or she ought to have (Gurr 1970), must also be considered when examining the initiation and perpetuation of international migration flows. We must be aware of the role that increased globalization and the spread of consumerism play in exacerbating the conditions of relative deprivation (Aas 2013) and lead people to seek a "little more" for themselves and their families. Is it not reasonable for a person to search for the American Dream by working abroad and sending remittances home in an effort to not only meet basic economic needs but for the chance of having "something more" as well? We argue that for many potential migrants this in fact precedes the initial decision to migrate. This argument is supported by studies that have found that previous waves of unauthorized Mexican migrants did not necessarily migrate with the intention of permanently settling and establishing a new life abroad, but rather migrated in an effort to fund short-term projects back home such as the purchase of an automobile, the expansion of a house, or establishing a business. This underlying logic is further articulated in the "new economics of migration," a theory that holds that people enter the migrant stream in an effort to overcome failures in or the absence of certain markets, including capital markets, unemployment insurance, and crop insurance markets, among others (Lauby and Stark 1988; Taylor 1986; Stark and Taylor 1991; Massey et al. 1993). However, these reasons for engaging in repeat migration are now changing in an era of increased enforcement, which has led migrants to spend longer periods of time abroad and thus decrease the probability of returning to their countries of origin (Massey, Durand, and Malone 2003), a point to which we devote further attention below.

Beyond the American Dream

Upward social mobility and cultural integration into a host society is far from a seamless, linear process, as history shows. Rather, it is complex and contingent upon various factors, including the levels of financial and human capital immigrants bring with them, immigrants' racial and ethnic backgrounds and how these backgrounds map onto the host society's racial schema, as well as the host society's willingness to accept the newly arriving group (Alba and Nee 2003). In other words, achieving the American Dream—in the most essentialized sense of joining the economic mainstream via cultural assimilation—has just as much to do with the willingness of a host society to accept an immigrant group as it does with the immigrants themselves. For these reasons, we make a deliberate effort to move the discussion away from issues of cultural integration and upward social mobility and focus more on people's motives for migration and how these factors map the meanings of mobility and how those meanings are subsequently compared to notions of the American Dream.

While it is beyond the scope of this chapter to provide an exhaustive account of the theories that drive migration flows, they do merit some discussion considering that a central and often overlapping theme of these theories is the drive for improving people's life chances—a theme that is central to the notion of the American Dream. The American Dream itself, following in the epistemological direction of economic and sociological theories of migration, relies on the ideal of a "rational actor." However, the rational actor ideal ignores a number of other contextual circumstances that initiate, facilitate, and sustain migration flows, including relationships on the level of household, community, region, and nation (Massey et al. 1993). And migrants' "ways of speaking" about their own experiences and intentions indeed reveal how these relationships factor into their decisions to migrate, aspects of which we intend to interpret through discourse analyses of individual experience.

Neoclassical economists have often reduced migration intentions to an individual level cost-benefit decision, while sociologists have focused greater attention on the importance of a variety of markets and social institutions in the migration process. Sociologists have also described migration as a "coming of age" experience for young men or as a way for women to escape patriarchal gender norms at the family or community level. Macrolevel theorists have pointed to factors that "push" people out of their home countries, such as poverty or the absence of economic opportunities, as well as factors that "pull" them to new destinations, including the structurally embedded demand for immigrant labor, family reunification, or better life prospects. Over the past three decades these "push" and "pull" factors have been exacerbated by neoliberal reforms that have led to economic restructuring and ultimately displaced people around the world (Martínez et al. 2014).

Changes in immigration control efforts have actually transformed would-be seasonal migrants into a relatively permanent "underclass" of immigrants residing in the United States without legal status, which in itself limits people's abilities to interact and engage with the broader community. Prior studies have demonstrated the undeniable connection between intensified border enforcement efforts and the growth of the unauthorized population (Massey, Durand, and Malone 2003), which currently stands at 11.3 million people (Passel et al. 2014). Although economic factors and the search for the American Dream are cited as important reasons for migrants leaving their hometowns in our research, these factors become less salient among those who have spent considerable time living and working in the United States in an unauthorized manner. Longer spells in the United States have resulted in migrants developing strong ties to this country, such as starting a business, family, or household. As such, the border build-up over the past two decades has resulted in unauthorized migrants putting down roots and developing a strong "sense of place" here in the United States. It is possible that the emergence of an identity based not on nationality, citizenship, or race/ethnicity, but rather a "sense of place"—notably where one's home is located—becomes a vital factor in terms of explicating people's future crossing intentions upon repatriation, especially when compared to those who have never lived in the United States. In cases in which people have never lived or worked in the country, the search for the American Dream and economic considerations may remain relevant.

In this regard, we hypothesize that transnational migrants will powerfully invoke their own social personae in forming identities that foot shared and circulating "concepts of personhood and agency" within and across national boundaries (Dick 2010b, 106). This is to say, in narrating the meanings of their own migration, transnational migrants likely rely on the readability of cultural experiences of a social life en route—a dynamic semiotic display of time-space imaginings that rebuke the borders of the nation-state and reduce noncitizens to less than human others, and thus disorder the problematic and linear meanings embedded in the American Dream chronotope (Dick 2010b, 106). In what follows, we make a concerted effort to highlight migrants' "voice[s]" (Ladson-Billings and Tate 1995) in the conceptualization of the American Dream and how these notions shape future migration decisions. Based on these insights, as will be highlighted throughout the chapter, we have ultimately come to understand the American Dream from the view-point of our respondents—simply put, the American Dream is equated with striving for "something better" for one's self and family at home or abroad such that "something better" can simply mean having a sense of place with one's loved ones. Given that our understanding is sourced from the perspectives of migrants, in addition to the complexities outlined above, we therefore do not perceive the American Dream in terms of upward social mobility into middle-class status in the United States, nor the cultural integration or assimilation of Mexican immigrants into US society.

Data

Data used in this chapter come from Wave II of the Migrant Border Crossing Study (MBCS). The MBCS is a study consisting of open- and closed-ended responses as well as in-depth interviews aimed at better understanding recent Mexican deportees' unauthorized crossing and deportation experiences, encounters with US authorities, and time spent living and working in the United States. Because of increasing competition and overlap between human smuggling and drug smuggling corridors along the US-Mexico border, as well as the diversification of drug trafficking organizations' (for example, Los Zetas) illicit activities, such as kidnapping and extortion of migrants, violence experienced or witnessed during the migration experience was also a focus of the study (see Slack 2015).

All MBCS respondents were randomly selected outside of ports of entry and in migrant shelters in Tijuana and Mexicali, Baja California; Nogales, Sonora; Ciudad Juárez, Chihuahua; Nuevo Laredo, Tamaulipas; and Mexico City. In order to be eligible to participate in the study, migrants had to have attempted a border crossing sometime after September 11, 2001, been apprehended by any US authority, and deported a month or less prior to being interviewed. We established these criteria in order to allow for reasonable comparison across cases in a post-9/11 era of increased securitization. All respondents were eighteen years of age or older. In contrast to other surveys of Mexican migrants, which tend to be carried out in sending or receiving communities long after a person's most recent crossing attempt, all MBCS surveys were carried out immediately postdeportation, and therefore are much less susceptible to retrospective bias. Interviews were executed between 2009 and 2012; however, the overwhelming majority was completed in 2011. In all, 1,110 Mexican deportees were interviewed, with a 94 percent response rate. Wave II of the MBCS was a binational, multi-institution collaborative effort including twelve institutions and sixty researchers in the United States and Mexico (see Slack et al. [2013] and Slack et al. [2015] for a description of the MBCS II methodology).

Analytical Plan

For the purpose of this chapter, we rely on univariate descriptive statistics and bivariate associations, using Pearson's chi-square tests, to examine the role that coded open-ended responses consistent with the notion of the American Dream have on explicating people's immediate crossing intentions upon deportation. Specifically, we use univariate descriptive analyses to provide a demographic profile of MBCS respondents, which includes demographic characteristics, prior unauthorized migration experiences, social ties to the United States, lived experience in the country, and migrants' Mexican region of origin and the region of their desired destination in the United States. We also use univariate descriptive analyses to address the following research questions: "Why did you leave the place you were last living in Mexico?" and the main dependent variable of interest in the chapter: "Do you plan on crossing the border again within the next week, or not?" Further, we deploy bivariate analyses (Pearson's chi-squares) to examine the relationship between intending to cross again within the next week and having previously lived in the United States, as well as the association between *not* wanting to cross again postdeportation and prior US experience. Finally, we draw on migrant narratives elicited using our open-ended responses to help contextualize and humanize our quantitative findings. Specifically, in sections of interviews quoted, we engage in a deeper ethnographic discourse analysis to frame the data in the rich context of experience. We examine migrants' narrative constructions of their crossing experiences and how these constructions frame their attachments to the United States, that is, how they link their present social location to imagined communities and social groupings.

Results

Demographic Profile

Table 1 provides a demographic profile of MBCS II respondents. Generally speaking, consistent with other data sources of unauthorized border crossers, respondents tend to be male, near the age of thirty, with eight years of formal education, and from relatively impoverished backgrounds. On average, the typical migrant reported a mean monthly household income of around $360

Table 1. Profile of MBCS Respondents, Wave II

Variables	Percent/Mean	Std. Dev.	N
Demographic Characteristics			
Biological sex			1,104
Male	0.82	0.38	
Female	0.18	0.38	
Age	0.31	8.98	1,107
Indigenous Language Speaker	0.10	0.30	1,088
Years of formal education	8.04	3.01	1,071
Household income before last crossing	$358.89	$423.29	928
Sole Economic Provider for household	0.42	0.49	1,076
Employed Before most recent crossing	0.62	0.48	1,074
Migration Experience			
Lifetime Unauthorized Crossing Attempts	4.88	9.32	1,082
Lifetime Apprehensions	3.91	7.48	1,081
First-time crosser	0.16	0.37	1,110
Social Ties to US and US Experience			
Has lived in US	0.74	0.43	1,100
Years in US	9.00	7.20	800
Family currently living in US	0.83	0.38	1,087
At least one family member with US Citizenship	0.51	0.50	1,021
Has at least one US Citizen child	0.22	0.41	1,100
Current home in US	0.28	0.45	1,056
Region of Origin in Mexico			1,085
West-Central ("Traditional")	0.34	0.48	
South	0.32	0.46	
Central	0.21	0.41	
North	0.12	0.33	
Region of Desired Destination in US			1,092
West	0.53	0.49	
South/Mid-Atlantic	0.31	0.46	
Midwest	0.09	0.28	
Northeast	0.05	0.22	
Don't Know	0.01	0.10	

Source: Migrant Border Crossing Study, Wave II (unweighted data)

before his or her most recent border-crossing attempt, with 42 percent of the sample indicating they were the sole economic provider for the household. About 10 percent of respondents reported speaking an indigenous language in addition to Spanish.

Thirty-four percent of the sample originates from Mexico's west-central region, an area that has long been a source of the migrant stream to the United

States dating back to the Bracero program (1942–64) (Massey, Durand, and Malone 2003). On the other hand, nearly a third of respondents are from communities in southern Mexico, an area with a much more recent migration history. While some communities in southern Mexico have engaged in migration to the United States since the mid-twentieth century, most did not actively engage in the international migration process until after the 1994 North American Free Trade Agreement displaced rural *campesinos* to urban areas, northern Mexico, and abroad (Public Citizen 2014). Twelve percent were from the northern region of Mexico, which includes the six states that share a border with the United States, as well as Sinaloa and Baja California Sur.

Overall, the majority of respondents are experienced border crossers, with only 16 percent indicating their most recent crossing attempt had been their first. MBCS II respondents reported an average of 4.8 lifetime unauthorized crossing attempts, including the most recent crossing, yet the mean number of lifetime apprehensions by US authorities is only 3.9. This figure is consistent with previous research noting that the number of times people attempt to cross the border generally exceeds the number of times they are apprehended, suggesting migrants continue to try to cross the border until they succeed (Parks et al. 2009). Approximately one-third of MBCS respondents successfully arrived at their desired destination but were later apprehended by local law enforcement officials (Slack et al. 2013). The majority of people surveyed (53 percent) were attempting to get to the western United States, and an additional one-third (31 percent) indicated that a southern or mid-Atlantic state was their desired destination.

MBCS II respondents, like most recent deportees, have extensive social ties to the United States. Over 80 percent indicate they have family currently residing in the country, and over half state they have at least one US citizen family member. More important, around one in five indicate they have a US citizen child under the age of eighteen. Three-quarters have previously lived in the United States, with nearly one in three respondents noting that they consider their current home to be located here, not in Mexico. This, along with economic necessity and wanting a better life for their family members, plays important role in explicating people's future crossing intentions upon repatriation.

REASONS FOR FIRST LEAVING MEXICO

At the beginning of our interviews, we asked respondents to elaborate on the reasons that they had initially left their hometowns in Mexico. Table 2 illustrates a breakdown of these responses, which include multiple men-

Table 2. Reasons for Leaving Hometown Most Recently, All Respondents

Reasons (includes multiple mentions)	Percent
TO WORK IN THE US/ECONOMIC REASONS/LACK OF WORK	69
Family Reunification	13
In Search of the "American Dream"/ A Better Life	13
Looking for Adventure / to Get to Know the US	4
Left as a Child	3
Violence in Mexico	2
Personal or Family Reasons	2
Other	5

N = 1,014

Source: Migrant Border Crossing Study, Wave II (unweighted data)

tions. The overwhelming majority (nearly 70 percent) of respondents stated that they left their hometown for "economic reasons," which included low wages, underemployment, unemployment, or to search for work in the United States. Thirteen percent cited "family reunification" as a reason for leaving Mexico, and 13 percent explicitly mentioned leaving in search of the "American Dream" or a "better life." One could arguably perceive "economic betterment" (that is, "for better pay," "for better work") as being implicitly related to the American Dream, but we were more interested in the subgroup of respondents that explicitly mentioned leaving in search of the "American Dream" or a "better life" because it encompasses people's broader perceptions of the American Dream beyond economic factors.

Considering the extensive body of literature outlining the extant theories of migration, it is not surprising that the overwhelming majority of respondents mentioned one of these three factors ("economic reasons," "family reunification," or "the American Dream") as a reason for leaving home. Nevertheless, our main focus of this chapter is to examine people's decisions *postdeportation* in an era of increased border enforcement, and how those decisions are shaped by the continued search for the American Dream, which is tied not only to economic necessity but also the reality of having forged strong social ties in the United States over time.

IMMEDIATE CROSSING INTENTIONS POSTDEPORTATION
Table 3 illustrates descriptions and descriptive statistics for the dependent variables of interest in this chapter: "Are you planning on crossing the border

Table 3. Descriptions and Descriptive Statistics for Dependent Variables

Variable	Description	Percent	Std. Dev.
Plan on crossing again *next week*?			
Yes	R plans on crossing next week	25.7	0.43
No	R does not plan on crossing next week	60.6	0.48
Don't Know	R does not know if they'll cross again next week	13.7	0.34

N = 1097

Source: Migrant Border Crossing Study, Wave II (unweighted data)

again within the next week, or not?" Nearly 26 percent of respondents indicated they intended to cross the border again within the week following the survey, while 61 percent said they did not intend on crossing within that time frame. An additional 14 percent did not know if they would cross again within the next week or not. When asked more broadly at the end of the interview, "Is it possible that you will cross again in the future?" the share of "yes" and "don't know" responses increased to 56 percent and 19 percent, respectively. On the other hand, the percent of people who responded "no" decreased to 25 percent. However, because we did not include an open-ended follow-up question asking people to expand on this response, we focus our attention on people's crossing intentions within the week following the interview.

The parameter we established for this question (that is, a one-week window) and the moment in which it was asked (that is, immediately following deportation) likely underestimate the true rate at which people are planning on crossing in the relative short run. Nevertheless, these parameters also help ensure greater validity of open-ended responses for people who responded in the affirmative, as it is likely these people have decisively made up their minds about their next move while in a state of limbo at the border. For the sake of parsimony, we divide our analysis in this chapter into two parts, (1) an examination of reasons people plan on crossing again and (2) an examination of the factors mentioned for *not* wanting to cross again. The following section further explores respondents' open-ended responses and how they vary with having previously lived in the United States.

REASONS FOR WANTING TO CROSS AGAIN

The first column in table 4, which includes multiple mentions, illustrates the most frequent responses for the 277 respondents who expressed interest in

Table 4. Reasons for Wanting to Cross Again *Next Week, "Have Lived in US"* *vs "Never Lived in US"*

Reasons (includes multiple mentions)	% of All Respondents	% of "Have Lived in US"	% of "Never Lived in US"	Difference
Family in the US	52	60	21	(38)***
To Work in the US	24	21	35	(24)*
Economic Necessity	11	9	19	(10)*
Better Life in US	8	7	12	(5)
Poor Economic or Social Conditions in Mexico	8	6	14	(8)†
Has Established Life in US	5	6	-	-
Debt	4	3	9	(6)*
Other	6	5	10	(5)

N = 277

Note: †p < 0.10, *p < 0.05, **p < 0.01,***p < 0.001 indicates the difference is statistically significant

Source: Migrant Border Crossing Study, Wave II

crossing again. The majority of migrants (52 percent) cited having "family in the United States" as a reason for wanting to cross, followed by wanting "to work in the United States" (24 percent), "economic necessity" (11 percent), "in search of a better life" (8 percent), and "poor economic or social conditions in Mexico" (8 percent). Five percent of those surveyed indicated that they had "an established life in the United States" to which they were trying to return.

Many of these responses are consistent with the idea of the American Dream, most notably "in search of a better life," and to a lesser extent, "to work in the United States" and "poor economic or social conditions in Mexico." Nevertheless, people's immediate crossing intentions are shaped by the degree to which they have a direct and personal connection to the United States. In other words, the motives driving repeat migration are likely different for people who are relatively inexperienced border crossers or who have not lived in the United States when compared to those who have previously spent some time in the country.[1] Although it is likely that all unauthorized migrants initially left Mexico in search of a better life or new economic opportunities, the proximate factors driving people's immediate crossing intentions upon deportation likely vary according to whether or not they have previously lived in the United States. The following section examines bivariate relationships between lived experience in the United States and short-term crossing intentions immediately following deportation.

Factors driving immediate, short-term migration intentions after deportation while still near the US-Mexico border are shaped by the degree to which people feel a deeper placial attachment to the United States. We examine this relationship by comparing people's reasons for wanting to attempt a future crossing according to whether or not they have previously lived in the United States. The second and third columns in table 4 compare these differences. Statistically significant differences are noted.

Overall, having family in the United States appears to be an important reason for wanting to cross again among all migrants. But this reason stands out more among those who have previously lived in the United States. As noted in table 4, 60 percent of people who have previously lived in the United States cite "family in the United States" as a reason for wanting to cross again, compared to just 21 percent of those who have never lived in the country. Reasons for wanting to cross again consistent with the notion of the "American Dream" appear to be much more proximate among people who have never lived in the United States. For instance, 35 percent of people who have never lived in the United States cite wanting "to work in the United States" as a reason, compared to just 21 percent of those who have lived in the country. Similarly, 19 percent and 14 percent of those having never lived in the United States cite "economic necessity" or "poor economic or social conditions in Mexico," respectively, compared to 9 percent and 8 percent of people who have prior US experience. Although 12 percent of those who have not lived in the United States note they want to cross in search of a better life compared to just 7 percent of those who have lived in the country, this difference is not statistically significant. However, it demonstrates that the most important factors of family and investment in the United States are no longer a dream, but have become a day-to-day reality.[2]

BIVARIATE FINDINGS: NOT WANTING TO CROSS AGAIN AND
LIVED US EXPERIENCE

Because all MBCS respondents are recent deportees, it is clear that, at one time or another, they all had made the decision to attempt an unauthorized border crossing. However, only 56 percent indicate it is possible that they will cross again in the future, and just 26 percent state they will try again within

Table 5. Reasons for NOT Wanting to Cross Again *Next Week, "Have Lived in US"* *vs "Never Lived in US"*

Reasons (includes multiple mentions)	% of All Respondents	% of "Have Lived in US"	% of "Never Lived in US"	Difference
Net Risky Crossing	29	24	41	(17)***
Net Social Reasons	24	27	15	(12)**
Legal Implications	22	24	15	(8)*
Net Economic Factors	12	11	13	(2)
Net Proximate to Last Crossing	11	10	15	(5)†
Explore Legal Options	5	6	2	(4)*
Possibly Cross Again, but Not Next Week	5	5	5	(0)
Other	8	7	9	(2)

N = 657

Note: †p < 0.10, *p < 0.05, **p < 0.01, ***p < 0.001 indicates the difference is statistically significant

Source: Migrant Border Crossing Study, Wave II

the next week. And table 5 offers greater insight on some of the open-ended responses given as to why people *do not* plan on crossing again within the next week after being deported. Once again we differentiate between people who have previously lived in the United States and those who have not.

As noted in table 5, the most often cited reason for not wanting to cross again is having experienced a "risky crossing" during the most recent attempt. Mentions associated with a "risky crossing" include a difficult (15 percent) or dangerous (10 percent) crossing, extreme temperatures (4 percent), too much border enforcement (2 percent), and simply being scared (2 percent). Although 29 percent of all respondents cite a "risky crossing" as a reason for not wanting to cross, there are significant differences between people who have lived in the United States and those who have not—41 percent of people who have never lived in the United States, compared to only 24 percent of those who have spent time in the country. In a similar vein, factors "proximate to the last crossing" such as being too hurt, too tired, or needing to rest before crossing again, as well as having a "bad experience" during the last attempt or being mistreated while in US custody were reported more frequently by inexperienced migrants (15 percent) than more experienced migrants (10 percent).

Discussion: In Their Own Words

Walking toward the American Dream

People who have previously lived in the United States have forged strong personal connections to the United States, and therefore are less likely to be motivated to cross again for factors consistent with the trope of the American Dream. This is not to say that their *initial* reasons for leaving Mexico were not in search of the American Dream but rather that their most pressing reasons for wanting to cross again are largely social. Alejandro's experience evidences this.

Alejandro, a forty-year-old male originally from the southeastern Mexican state of Veracruz, has traveled back and forth between the United States and Mexico a considerable amount—five times in all—and has in fact spent twenty-two years of his life living and working in the United States. When last living in Veracruz he was earning about $250 per month. Inconsistent employment and meager pay led him to once again leave his hometown in search of alternative work opportunities in the United States. This time, however, he intended to stay permanently after crossing. He crossed the border in February 2004 by swimming across the Rio Grande outside of Reynosa, Tamaulipas, where he had had previous success. Although he made the border crossing attempt alone, he did rely on the services of a coyote to "avoid the dangers of crossing" the river. The coyote, who was recommended to him by friends from his hometown in Veracruz who had used his services long ago, only charged him $600 to guide him across the river and take him to his destination—a fee he paid using a portion of the money he had saved over several months.

After a relatively uneventful crossing attempt, Alejandro managed to avoid detection by US authorities and successfully made it to Tennessee, where he established a new life. He eventually got married, had three children, and found work painting houses.

In September 2011, Alejandro was stopped by local law enforcement during a routine traffic stop. He was subsequently turned over to Immigration and Customs Enforcement, processed, sent to a detention facility for ten days, and then deported to Nuevo Laredo, Tamaulipas, where members of our research team interviewed him. Despite being deported to one of the most dangerous cities along the US-Mexico border, an area controlled by the notorious Zetas drug trafficking organization known for preying on migrants in transit, the single most pressing thing on his mind was to return to the United

States to be with his family. When asked if he planned on crossing the border again within the next week, he simply replied "yes, I have my family in the United States" (interview September 21, 2011).

Here we see that Alejandro, a seasoned border crosser, initially left Mexico in search of better economic prospects. He managed to establish a new life in Tennessee, start a family, secure steady employment, and thus had no intentions of ever returning to Mexico. Nevertheless, a chance encounter with law enforcement officials altered his life circumstances, and now he was desperately trying to return to his wife and children in the United States. Although his initial reasons for leaving Mexico were economic, *social* connections forged with family now drive his desire to once again cross the border. Alejandro's decision to cross is tied to necessities generated by the contradictions of a country that at once prides itself as a nation of immigrants (who benefit from the American Dream) and simultaneously maintains a regime of deportability that exploits the labor of undocumented migrants. Further, as described at the beginning of this chapter, the American Dream narrative, as Hilary Parsons Dick describes, "relies on a chronotope of purity and fixity in which migrants are portrayed as an undifferentiated mass that moves unilinearly into the United States" (2011a, 229)—such a perspective conveniently elides the exploitative political economies in which migrants are positioned that catalyze their movements and through which they forge meaningful transnational ties. In the case of Alejandro, the meaning of his migration—his dream—is tied to a desire to be reunited with his family. His own imagined personhood is not that of an economic migrant and much less as an "illegal," but rather it is rooted in his role as a father and husband. These social ties are what drive Alejandro regardless of the dangers associated with crossing the border and the possible legal sanctions associated with doing so.

On the other hand, among those respondents who have never lived in the United States, we see that factors consistent with the notion of the American Dream continue to play an important role in their migration decision postdeportation. The following narrative further describes the motives and experiences of a relatively young, inexperienced migrant attempting to cross into the United States to pursue her dream of furthering her education.

We spoke to Lorena, an eighteen-year-old female from the west-central Mexican state of Nayarit who has never lived or worked in the United States. She left Nayarit on a bus two months ago with her mother, and the two made their way to Nogales, Sonora, where they planned on crossing the border and eventually settling in Los Angeles, California, where her mother's siblings were living and working.

Lorena, her mother, and a group of six others were guided to the outskirts of Nogales to a section of the border wall they were instructed to climb over. Although the coyote did not tell them they would be spending a considerable amount of time walking, the group spent four days in the desert, where they ran out of food after the first day and water on the last. The group was then guided to a remote area where a van picked them up to transport them to a "drop house" in Phoenix, Arizona. However, before reaching Phoenix they were pulled over by the US Border Patrol, processed, and deported to Nogales at 6:00 p.m. the evening prior to speaking with us. Lorena insisted that she and her mother would try to cross again within the next week. When asked why, Lorena stated:

> I have family there and I really want to see them. I also want to learn English for the degree I want to pursue. I'll learn it best in the United States, I really want to go to school in the United States, and the schools in Mexico can't teach me English.

Lorena has a tenth grade education and her dream is to pursue her studies in the United States. She went on to say, "I want to cross, I really do, I want to study and start my degree" (interviewed on July 11, 2011).

As noted, economic factors were cited most often as the reasons for why people initially left their hometowns in Mexico, and, as much research has shown, are perhaps the most significant "push/pull" factors driving the decision to migrate. However, among recent deportees, family separation prevails as the most important social factor that compels people to attempt another crossing in the short run. And although having family in the United States is an important reason for attempting a repeat crossing among all migrants, it is much more pressing for people who have previously lived, established a home, and developed a sense of "place" and attachment to social groupings in the country. On the other hand, as in the case of Lorena, responses consistent with the notion of the American Dream are much more pronounced among respondents who have no prior living experience in the United States.

Is the American Dream Becoming "la pesadilla Americana" (the American Nightmare)?

Although many unauthorized migrants plan on crossing the border immediately following deportation, more than twice as many in our sample indicate that they no longer plan on doing so in the short run. However, unlike those who plan on crossing again, parsing out the reasons for *not* wanting to cross again becomes much more challenging. Some cite difficulties associated with the journey itself, others indicate that living in the United States out of status takes its toll socially and psychologically, and yet others note that anti-immigrant sentiment in the United States has become overwhelming. For many, the search for the American Dream has turned into a nightmare. The following narrative provides a detailed account of the dangers and difficulties associated with undertaking a border-crossing attempt in an era of increased border militarization.

Jorge, twenty-five, departed Veracruz twenty days ago with a group of friends and began the journey to North Carolina. He says he left in search of a new experience, but mostly due to lack of employment back home. The group traveled from southeastern Mexico to Altar, Sonora, where they gathered supplies for the crossing and met a coyote who agreed to guide them across for a fee. The group set out for the border town of Sasabe, Sonora, where they would attempt their crossing. However, before arriving at Sasabe each group member was forced to pay a $150 toll to access an area controlled by a drug trafficking organization. Despite being told by the coyote they would only walk two-and-a-half days, the group spent four days crossing through the desert, surviving by drinking from small stagnant puddles. When asked if he would try crossing again now or anytime again in the future he replied, "no, you walk too much and if they catch you [US Border Patrol] they mistreat you. The border is a very dangerous place" (interviewed on September 30, 2011).

In Jorge's case, the realities of navigating an increasingly militarized border are too much to warrant another crossing attempt. However, unlike Jorge, it is likely that people who have lived in the United States for an extended period of time—and therefore have pressing social relationships to return to—have not attempted a crossing in quite some time, but rather were apprehended in the interior United States long after having crossed the border. Border enforcement efforts over the past two decades have made the crossing much more difficult, dangerous, and risky, such that the border today is a much different place than when people who have spent some time living in the United States last tried to cross.

Further, the legal implications of a potentially unsuccessful future crossing attempt, notably the possibility of being sent to an immigration detention facility or being charged with unauthorized reentry (which is a felony), also help explain why some do not wish to attempt another crossing. There appear to be notable differences between experienced and inexperienced migrants. Twenty-four percent of migrants who have lived in the United States cite legal implications, compared to just 15 percent of those who have not. People who have lived in the United States likely have received more information through various social networks of the adverse consequences of unsuccessful repeat crossing attempts. Moreover, it is possible that they are more likely to have had a formal deportation, as opposed to voluntary returns that carry relatively few legal consequences. The potential of being detained up to thirty-six months in a detention facility and charged with unauthorized reentry poses notable economic risks for many migrants. And just as social reasons play an important role in explicating who intends to cross in the short run, as in Alejandro's case, social reasons too help explain who does not plan on crossing again. Twenty-seven percent of people who previously lived in the United States cite wanting to visit family in Mexico or return to their community of origin as a reason for not crossing within the next week, compared to just 15 percent of people who have never lived in the United States. As previously discussed, increased border enforcement efforts have forced migrants who successfully make it to the United States to stay for longer periods of time than in the past. Many people living in the United States out of status have not been able to return to see their families in Mexico for quite some time and therefore take the opportunity to do so once deported.[3] The reality of not having seen family and friends in Mexico for some time—now exacerbated by increased border enforcement, which deters frequent back-and-forth crossings—highlights the continued attachments migrants have with their sending communities despite having also established a sense of place in the United States. Indeed, migrant personhood, in this regard, is linked to circulating notions of home and place that extend beyond the nation-state as the primary unit of identification, as their lives unfold in relation to transnational social groupings and real and imagined communities.

Unauthorized migrants take great risks to circumvent border enforcement efforts. Whether they are coming in search of new economic opportunities or to reconnect with family members already living and working in this country, they all come in search of something "more." Nevertheless, the social realities associated with residing in the United States clandestinely have a notable impact on people's hopes and desires to pursue the American Dream, such that that notion has come to mean something beyond the typically received narrative of upward mobility.

Although we are not conceptualizing the American Dream as being consistent with cultural integration, research has shown that migrants are in fact integrating socially and linguistically by the second and third generations (Chavez 2008; Telles and Ortiz 2008; Rumbaut and Massey 2013). Nevertheless, the Latino/a threat narrative—as identified by Leo Chavez (2008)—continues to frame Latino/a migrants as unwilling to integrate structurally and culturally into US society. In turn, this discourse, coupled with securitization and the "War on Terror," continues to drive anti-immigrant policies and increased border and immigration enforcement. Ironically, research has found that people's legal status affects the rates at which they integrate into US society and the opportunities afforded to them (Chavez 2008; Gonzales 2011). Meaning, the integration of migrants, documented and undocumented alike, has likely been disrupted by increased border and immigration enforcement over the past decade, including state-level initiatives such as Arizona's SB 1070, Alabama's HB 56, and Indiana's SB 590, as well as the federal Secure Communities Initiative. The constant threat of deportation has forced many families to navigate day-to-day activities with caution and, in many ways, impedes people's ability to structurally integrate into US society.

Despite Spener's (2009) important discussion of the "normalization of suffering" described in his seminal work on *coyotaje*, or human smuggling activities, the frustration and difficulties of navigating US society while being undocumented is something that frequently came up in our conversations with recent deportees. For example, Diego, a twenty-eight-year-old male from Veracruz, has lived off and on in Phoenix for the past ten years, having recently lived in Phoenix the past six years. He left Veracruz because all of his friends were getting married and life was different—he too wanted something different. However, when asked if he was going to cross again, he replied, "no, I don't like living there anymore. One goes from home to work, and back home. It's like living in prison" (interviewed on March 25, 2011). Marisol, a thirty-three-year-old female from Oaxaca, expressed a similar sentiment. She originally left Oaxaca because she needed to help her family financially and spent nearly five years living in Las Vegas, Nevada. When asked if she would cross again she replied, "no, I'm risking my life when I cross [the border], and it's too hard to find work. Every day I'm risking my life over there" (interviewed on March 3, 2011). Despite the financial need to help her family, the dangers of crossing the border, the difficulty in finding steady work, and the risks of navigating everyday life out of status all prove to be too challenging.

The insecurities associated with venturing outside of one's home while living and working in the United States were reiterated by several of our respondents. For instance, Miguel, a thirty-year-old *campesino* from Chiapas, had lived and worked in the United States on and off for eight years. Most recently, he had been living in the Phoenix area working as a landscaper to support not only his common law wife and two small children but his mother as well due to the unexpected death of his father. One night he left the relatively safe confines of his apartment and ventured out to use a public pay phone when he was stopped and questioned by local law enforcement officials. As a consequence of the Secure Communities Initiative, a federal program requiring people's immigration status be checked once in local law enforcement custody, Miguel was turned over to Immigration and Customs Enforcement and eventually deported to Mexico. When asked if he planned on crossing the border again, he replied "no, there is no work over there . . . the United States is a very racist country, and the police treat us badly" (interviewed on June 28, 2011). The economic recession had limited Miguel's ability to find work as a self-employed landscaper. Not only that, but he had also begun to experience the constant threat of being profiled by law enforcement officials. Miguel is planning on returning to Chiapas to explore the limited economic options there.

The economic recession has also impacted the short-term migration intentions of people who have established significant roots in the United States. Esteban, a fifty-three-year-old male from Mexico City, last left the country for Los Angeles, California, six years ago due to economic reasons. However, he has lived in the United States on and off for sixteen years. His wife and two US citizen children currently live in their family's home in California's San Fernando Valley. He said he likely would not try to cross again within the next week because "there isn't any work right now and they are deporting a lot of people." Nevertheless, he said it is possible that he will try again at some point in the future. This is not surprising considering his wife and children remain in the United States (interviewed on October 19, 2011). However, other people, like David, a forty-seven-year-old male from Puebla, appear to have given up on their hopes of ever realizing the American Dream. Despite having never previously lived or worked in the United States, he left Puebla two months before our research team interviewed him because of "miserable wages" where he was working as a chauffeur and, previously, as a police officer. However, when asked if he would try to cross the border again, either within the next week or at some point again in the future, he replied, "No, I'm going to fight in my country, I'm going to use my imagination and hope for some luck. There are some options here." He went on to say, "I'm really disappointed with (President) Obama and all of these anti-immigrant policies. They are fighting a war against people who aren't the terrorists." By fiscal year 2013, the Obama administration had formally deported over two million people (Gonzalez-Barrera and Krogstad 2014)—more than any other prior administration (Foley 2013). Despite this increase in formal deporta-tions, the 2012 Deferred Action for Childhood Arrivals (DACA) and the 2014 Deferred Action for Parents (DAP) executive orders have given some unau-thorized migrants and their families hope of protection from deportation. Yet approximately 5.8 million unauthorized immigrants in the United States are ineligible for deportation protection under these orders (Krogstad and Passel 2014). Furthermore, these executive orders continued to be publicly contested at the publication of this chapter.

Using one's imagination, as David suggests, is what all migrants do in assigning meaning to their migration and in turn constructing senses of personhood that foot their movements across time and space, movements that unfold in relation to the political economies in which their lives are positioned, in this case, a transnational political economy deeply reliant on border security and immigration enforcement that render migrant sub-jects disposable commodities. Further, as noted previously, joining the eco-nomic mainstream via cultural assimilation—that is, achieving the American Dream—is not a seamless process, but rather is hindered by the US racial formation, which equates citizenship with whiteness, such that persons of color are assumed to lack the qualities and characteristics needed to become full members of the nation-state. Keenly aware of these structural realities, migrant articulations of their crossing experiences and lived life in both Mex-ico and the United States constitute a type of position taking that displays a critical distance from the nation-state—and thus the uncritical narrative of the American Dream—while simultaneously claiming membership on the space of the US nation-state with developing a "sense of place," and that place is intimately connected to social groupings, family or otherwise.

Transnational mobility, economy, and social relationships are thus nego-tiated through mobility—voluntary and forced—and the idea of walking toward the American Dream, in this regard, is to resume and cultivate social ties under these circumstances. The American Dream, for migrants, is over-laid with human connections, not mere economic independence. And these meanings reveal a discursive breach in conventional understandings of both their reasons for migrating and the narrative of the American Dream. The former understanding usually positions migrants as mere laborers and the latter does the same more broadly for all subjects, although it tries to coat its ethic of work and duty with more noble platitudes like family values. How-ever, this moral framing falls apart when considering the lived conditions of deportability for transnational migrants—those who indeed contribute significantly to the US economy through their labor, but yet are denied family, intimacy, and are treated as disposable subjects. Their families, their lives, their connections don't matter—this indeed is a nightmare.

Conclusion

Our data show how people have left Mexico looking for something that approximates the American Dream as the search for opportunity, but after they have been deported, this no longer figures as the predominate reason to go back. Social and economic necessities drive people to *return* to the United States, not dreams. Deportation destroys dreams; it ruins people's families and everything for which they have worked so hard. Further, the security apparatus, the detention system, and the mistreatment migrants experience while in US custody also contribute to the nightmare for families living in the United States. Although the nature of Mexican migration to the United States has been transformed by globalization, it has also been reshaped by the "new border"—a border that now follows migrants into their receiving communities in the form of intensified immigration enforcement.

While it is true that the American Dream has always contained an exclusionary bias, it is time to reconsider what drives people to come to the United States and what keeps them here despite all its flaws. The search for the American Dream is not simply driven by a sense of relative deprivation or an abstract search for "something better," but rather the "Latino/a American Dream" is increasingly connected to keeping one's family together and fostering an emerging sense of "place" and "home" in the United States—for the people in our study, it is not as economically centered as is often assumed. The event-specific data and narrative constructions analyzed—those emerging from recent deportation—interrupt typified notions of migrant motivations for crossing the border. The chronotopic imaginings that migrants have of moving, working, and living in the United States are not reliant on the conventional concept of upward mobility, but on establishing real and lasting connections with places and people, particularly family, while thriving without the threat of economic insecurity or racially motivated exclusion. And while social and kin networks are interrupted by the deportation process and thus become more difficult to maintain, they are not destroyed. The "Latino/a American Dream" includes maintaining family despite barriers, and in so doing, forging a meaningful life, a dream that drives people to risk their lives time and again to be "here."

Notes

1. In a supplementary analysis, among people who have never lived in the United States, only 12 percent of respondents who initially mentioned leaving their hometowns in Mexico in search of the "American Dream" or "a better life" indicate they intend on crossing within the next week, compared to 21 percent of respondents who cite other reasons for leaving. Nevertheless, this difference is not statistically significant (p = 0.24), which is likely to due to a small number of observations. Only twenty-six individuals who have never lived in the United States *and* mentioned the "American Dream" as a reason for leaving their hometown intended on crossing the border within the next week compared to people who did not mention tropes consistent with the notion of the American Dream.

2. Interestingly, "debt" was mentioned more often among people who have never lived in the United States (9 percent) than those who had (3 percent). Migration is a costly endeavor. Many people take on loans from family members and friends to help finance their journey north. It is likely that people who have never lived in the United States have yet to pay off this initial debt, whereas people who have spent time living and working in the United States have been able pay down these loans.

3. This is not to say that they will not attempt another crossing down the road, they are just not planning on doing so within the next week.

References

Aas, Katja Franko. 2013. *Globalization and Crime.* 2nd ed. Thousand Oaks, CA: Sage.

Agha, Asif. 2007. *Language and Social Relations.* Cambridge: Cambridge University Press.

Alba, Richard, and Victor Nee. 2003. *Remaking the American Mainstream: Assimilation and Contemporary Immigration.* Cambridge, MA: Harvard University Press.

Bakhtin, Mikhail. [1935] 1981. "Discourse in the Novel." In *The Dialogic Imagination: Four Essays by M. M. Bakhtin,* edited by Michael Holquist, 269–424. Austin: University of Texas Press.

Chavez, Leo R. 2008. *The Latino Threat Narrative: Constructing Immigrants, Citizens, and the Nation.* Stanford, CA: Stanford University Press.

Delgado, Richard. 1989. "Storytelling for Oppositionists and Others: A Plea for a Narrative." *Michigan Law Review* 87: 2411–41.

Dick, Hilary Parsons. 2010a. "Imagined Lives and Modernist Chronotopes in Mexican Nonmigrant Discourse." *American Ethnologist* 37 (2): 275–90.

———. 2010b. "No Option but to Go: Poetic Rationalization and the Discursive Production of Mexican Migrant Identity." *Language and Communication* 30: 90–108.

———. 2011a. "Language and Migration to the United States." *Annual Review of Anthropology* 40: 227–40.

———. 2011b. "Making Immigrants Illegal in Small-Town USA." *Journal of Linguistic Anthropology* 21 (S1): E35–E55.

Dixson, Adrienne D., and Celia K. Rousseau. 2005. "And We Are Still Not Saved: Critical Race Theory in Education Ten Years Later." *Race Ethnicity and Education* 8 (1): 7–27.

Duranti, Alessandro. 1997. *Linguistic Anthropology*. Cambridge: Cambridge University Press.

Eisenlohr, Patrick. 2006. *Little India: Diaspora, Time, and Ethnolinguistic Belonging in Hindu Mauritius*. Berkeley: University of California Press.

Farr, Marcia. 2006. *Rancheros in Chicagoacán: Language and Identity in a Transnational Community*. Austin: University of Texas Press.

Foley, Elise. 2013. "Obama Deportation Toll Could Pass 2 Million at Current Rates." *Huffington Post*, January 31.

Fox, Cybelle, and Thomas A. Guglielmo. 2012. "Defining America's Racial Boundaries: Blacks, Mexicans, and European Immigrants, 1890–1945." *American Journal of Sociology* 118 (2): 327–79.

Gonzales, Roberto G. 2011. "Learning to Be Illegal: Undocumented Youth and Shifting Legal Contexts in the Transition to Adulthood." *American Sociological Review* 76 (4): 602–19.

Gonzalez-Barrera, Ana, and Jens Manuel Krogstad. 2014. "U.S. Deportations of Immigrants Reach Record High in 2013." Pew Research Center. Report. October 2. Available at: http://www.pewresearch .org/fact-tank/2014/10/02/u-s-deportations-of-immigrants-reach-record-high-in-2013/.

Grebler, Leo, Joan W. Moore, and Ralph Guzmán. 1970. *The Mexican American People: The Nation's Second Largest Minority*. New York: Free Press.

Guglielmo, Thomas A. 2004. *White on Arrival: Italians, Race, Color, and Power in Chicago, 1890–1945*. New York: Oxford University Press.

Gurr, Ted Robert. 1970. *Why Men Rebel*. Princeton, NJ: Princeton University Press.

Hanson, Sandra L., and John Kenneth White. 2011. *The American Dream in the 21st Century*. Philadelphia: Temple University Press.

Huntington, Samuel P. 2004. *Who Are We?: The Challenges to America's National Identity*. New York: Simon and Schuster.

Kasinitz, Philip. 2004. "Race, Assimilation, and 'Second Generation,' Past and Present." In *Not Just Black and White: Historical and Contemporary Perspectives on Immigration, Race, and Ethnicity in the United States*, edited by George Fredrickson and Nancy Foner, 278–300. New York: Russell Sage Foundation.

Krogstad, Jens Manuel, and Jeffrey S. Passel. 2014. "Those from Mexico Will

Benefit Most from Obama's Executive Action." Pew Research Center. Report. November 19. Available at: http://www.pewresearch.org/fact-tank/2014/11/20/those-from-mexico-will-benefit-most-from-obamas-executive-action/.

Ladson-Billings, G., and W. Tate. 1995. "Toward a Critical Race Theory of Education." *Teachers College Record* 97 (1): 47–68.

Lauby, Jennifer L., and Oded Stark. 1988. "Individual Migration as a Family Strategy: Young Women in the Philippines." *Population Studies* 42: 473–86.

Lipsitz, George. 2006. *The Possessive Investment in Whiteness: How White People Profit from Identity Politics.* Philadelphia: Temple University Press.

Lopez, Mark Hugo, and Ana Gonzalez-Barrera. 2013. "High Rate of Deportations Continue under Obama Despite Latino Disapproval." Pew Research Center. Report. September 19. Available at: http://www.pewresearch.org/fact-tank/2013/09/19/high-rate-of-deportations-continue-under-obama-despite-latino-disapproval/.

Martínez, Daniel E., Robin C. Reineke, Raquel Rubio-Goldsmith, and Bruce O. Parks. 2014. "Structural Violence and Migrant Deaths in Southern Arizona: Data from the Pima County Office of the Medical Examiner, 1990–2013." *Journal on Migration and Human Security* 2 (4): 257–86.

Massey, Douglas S., Joaquín Arango, Graeme Hugo, Ali Kouaouci, Adela Pellegrino, and J. Edward Taylor. 1993. "Theories of International Migration: A Review and Appraisal." *Population and Development Review* 19 (3): 431–66.

Massey, Douglas S., Jorge Durand, and Nolan J. Malone. 2003. *Beyond Smoke and Mirrors: Mexican Immigration in an Era of Economic Integration.* New York: Russell Sage Foundation.

Mendoza-Denton, Norma. 2008. *Homegirls: Language and Cultural Practice among Latina Youth Gangs.* Malden, MA: Blackwell.

Omi, Michael, and Howard Winant. 1994. *Racial Formation in the United States: From the 1960s to the 1990s.* 2nd ed. New York: Routledge.

Parks, Kristen, Gabriel Lozada, Miguel Mendoza, and Lourdes Garcia Santos. 2009. "Strategies for Success: Border Crossing in an Era of Heightened Security." In *Migration from the Mexican Mixteca: A Transnational Community in Oaxaca and California*, edited by Wayne A. Cornelius, David Fitzgerald, Jorge Hernández-Díaz, and Scott Borger. San Diego, CA: Center for Comparative Immigration Studies.

Passel, Jeffrey S., D'Vera Cohn, Jens Manuel Krogstad, and Ana Gonzalez-

Barrera. 2014. "As Growth Stalls, Unauthorized Immigrant Population Become More Settled." Pew Research Hispanic Trends Project. September 3.

Portes, Alejandro, and Rubén Rumbaut. 2001. *Legacies: The Story of the Immigrant Second Generation.* Berkeley: University of California Press.

Portes, Alejandro, and Min Zhou. 1993. "The New Second Generation: Segmented Assimilation and Its Variants." *Annals of the American Academy of Political Science* 530: 74–96.

Public Citizen's Global Trade Watch. 2014. "NAFTA's 20-Year Legacy and the Fate of the Trans-Pacific Partnership." Report. February. http://www .citizen.org/documents/NAFTA-at-20.pdf.

Rumbaut, Rubén G., and Douglas S. Massey. 2013. "Immigration and Language Diversity in the United States." *Daedalus* 142 (3): 141–54.

Slack, Jeremy. 2015. "Captive Bodies: Migrant Kidnapping and Deportation in Mexico." *Area.*

Slack, Jeremy, Daniel E. Martínez, Scott Whiteford, and Emily Peiffer. 2013. "In the Shadow of the Wall: Family Separation, Immigration Enforcement, and Security." Report. Center for Latin American Studies, University of Arizona. March 2013. Available at http://las.arizona.edu/sites/las .arizona.edu/files/UA_Immigration_Report2013print.pdf.

Slack, Jeremy, Daniel E. Martínez, Scott Whiteford, and Emily Peiffer. 2015. "In Harm's Way: Family Separation, Immigration Enforcement Programs and Security on the US-Mexico Border." *Journal on Migration and Human Security* 3(2): 109-128.

Spener, David. 2009. *Clandestine Crossings: Migrants and Coyotes on the Texas-Mexico Border.* Ithaca, NY: Cornell University Press.

Stark, Oded, and J. Edward Taylor. 1991. "Relative Deprivation and International Migration." *Demography* 26: 173–78.

Taylor, J. Edward. 1986. "Differential Migration, Networks, Information and Risk." In *Research in Human Capital and Development.* Vol. 4, *Migration, Human Capital, and Development,* edited by Oded Stark. Greenwich, CT: JAI Press.

Telles, Edward E., and Vilma Ortiz. 2008. *Generations of Exclusion: Mexican Americans, Assimilation, and Race.* New York: Russell Sage Foundation.

Waters, Mary C. 1999. *Black Identities: West Indian Immigrant Dreams and American Realities.* Cambridge, MA: Harvard University Press.

4

Hispanics and the American Dream

Lessons from the Experiences of Hispanics across
Nationalities Residing in Washington, DC

Enrique S. Pumar

Introduction

Recent interviews with diverse immigrant Hispanic[1] groups from around
the Washington, DC, metro region reveal a generalized longing for future
opportunities to attain more prosperity for themselves and their children.
In analyzing the experiences of immigrant Hispanic groups, one must
consider how individual social and human capital associated with levels of
national development impact immigrants' aspirations. Neither the emotional
and material costs of their journeys, the trepidations after their arrival, nor
the uncertain path to citizenship seem to diminish immigrants' optimism
about the opportunities the United States often provides. On the contrary,
the American Dream motivates immigrants to push for immigration reform
and a legal path toward citizenship.

While many cases could be cited in support of how Hispanic nationals
perceive the American Dream, the following three examples suffice. In one
interview, a Guatemalan emotionally described how he left his homeland
after his village was pillaged and many neighbors were either killed or kidnapped by the military during that country's civil war. Today, he has completed an associate degree and has found artistic expressions to promote his
culture and identity around Washington, DC. Along the way, he has gained
the social status he never enjoyed back home. In another case, a Bolivian
described the many hardships she encountered after moving to the region
and how she managed to build on those painful memories to become a notable civic community leader and a successful professional. Lastly, a Salvadoran
recounted how he arrived in Washington, DC, penniless and without social
support. Now he is a successful business owner and community leader, and

two of his children completed degrees in prestigious universities he could only have dreamed of attending back home.

To be sure, the historical record also suggests that the American Dream today is as much an assimilation ideology as it was when James Truslow Adams first introduced it in 1931 in his landmark book *The Epic of America.* As Adams himself put it lucently in a *New York Times* piece that came out just two years after his book was published, "The Dream is a vision of a better, deeper, richer life for every individual, regardless of the position in society which he or she may occupy by the accident of birth" (Adams 1933). The promise of the array of opportunities the United States usually offers to all Americans promotes conformity, discipline, and assertiveness.

Using data from in-depth interviews of Hispanic immigrants who currently reside around the Washington, DC, metro region, this chapter posits three points largely neglected by the literature associated with migration and the American Dream. First, the Dream is as much a "pulling" mechanism to attract migrants to our shores as it is an ideology to legitimize the relative success of migrants and their various rates of incorporation into American society. More importantly, the American Dream is not only consumed in the United States. The values embedded in the Dream, which were once exported abroad to sustain American interests, are internalized by migrants from all over the world, motivating them to come to the United States in order to materialize the Dream that only America seems to offer.

Second, among recent migrants, the American Dream manifests itself in different ways than it does for most Americans. In fact, there are at least two overriding visions of the Dream among migrants. The first relates to attaining legal citizenship rights and a peaceful lifestyle away from the perils, personal persecutions, and the arbitrary rule of praetorian regimes. It is only the second version of the Dream that attests to the pursuit of higher standards of living and a much brighter future, as it also does for other Americans.

Lastly, the different rates of success of recent migrants correlate with levels of national development, casting at least some doubt on the extent to which self-reliance alone guarantees success in America today.[2] In short, one of the ironies of social mobility among migrants is that their achievement depends on structural conditions they do not fully control, and these structural features are conditioned by ethnic nationalities. In other words, the effects of different levels of national development on migration explain a lot of the variation we find across immigrant communities with regard to attaining social mobility.

To illustrate these points, I triangulate statistical data from the 2010 census with the 2000 United Nations Human Development Report and qualitative findings from twenty-nine in-depth interviews I conducted with Hispanic immigrants throughout the Washington, DC, metro region beginning in 2013. The Hispanic population around the District constitutes a representative demographic microcosm of the landscape of Hispanic nationals residing throughout the United States. My focus on one case study discounts exogenous regional ecological effects from across the country.

Accounting for about 10 percent of the total population of Washington, DC, Hispanic residents constitute one of the largest immigrant groups among the foreign born in the city. Hispanics are also a very diverse group with practically all ethnic nationalities represented, although Salvadorans and Mexicans outnumber other fellow coethnics, and both groups account for more than half of all Hispanics residents. As in the rest of the nation, the number of Hispanics has also increased dramatically in recent years. In the Washington, DC, metro region alone, there were roughly 17,000 Hispanic residents in 1980, but the figure grew to nearly 63,000 by 2012. Washington, DC, metro area Hispanics are younger than average, tend to live in families, are well represented in all occupational brackets, and show a skewed distribution of educational attainment. They are overrepresented among those with less than a high school diploma and are underrepresented among those holding a bachelor's degree. Hispanics in the Washington, DC, metro region stand out above the national average in earnings and employment. They have lower unemployment rates and earned about $17,000 more in 2012 than Hispanic families elsewhere in the United States.

In this study, I disaggregate the data about social attainment among metro Hispanics by ethnic nationality rather than by standard social categories of race, gender, or social class for several reasons. First, in survey after survey, Hispanics identify themselves primarily with their country of origin. This ethnic identification is also prevalent among policy studies. Consequently, my study also contributes the structural aspects of inequality and social mobility often neglected in this literature. Second, some of the dimensions associated with standard stratification categories are further complicated by the unique labor market composition of Washington, DC. The District of Columbia is home to perhaps the largest group of Hispanic middle-class professionals in part because of the number of federal and international civil servants residing in the city. However, there is no empirical data that capture the achievements of Hispanics by class, making cross-class comparisons virtually impossible. The consideration of specific social categories other than nationality is further complicated by the presence of indigenous immigrant communities. Evidence discerns that social cleavages and attainment rates are conditioned by the legacy of social exclusions of this population, but again there is no empirical evidence to document this conclusion and compare indigenous with other groups across nationalities.

The Challenges and Prospects of the American Dream

Aspirations and motivations are other similarities between Hispanic migrants who reside in the Washington, DC, region and elsewhere in the nation. A recent national Gallup poll shows that a growing number of first-generation Hispanics ranked economic growth and health care among their chief concerns. By contrast, concerns with immigration policies erode even further among the second and third generations, according to the poll. For these two cohorts, other social issues related to the American Dream, like employment rates, the decline of the middle class, and the growing income gap between rich and poor gained more attention, according to Gallup (Saad 2012).

Despite multiple legal obstacles to attain full citizenship through immigration reform, the more than occasional hostile public reception, and mounting economic disadvantages, a poll released in 2012 by the Pew Hispanic Center also corroborates the above average support for the Dream among Hispanics across the nation. When asked about one of the values that anchors the American Dream—if most people can still get ahead in the United States through hard work—the overwhelming majority of Hispanics agreed regardless of whether they were native or foreign born, first or second generation, bilingual or not. In addition to the endorsement of the Dream, the support rate among Hispanics outpaced the fervor from other Americans by nearly 20 percent in this survey[3] (Taylor et al. 2012, fig. 2.2).

The paradoxical situation of espousing optimism about the future in the midst of austere economic conditions and multiple personal hardships serves as the background for this chapter. In particular, I will argue that the consumption of the American Dream even before Hispanics arrived on United States shores shapes an imaginary vision of what living in the United States is like. This is evident in the prevailing optimism about achieving the Dream across generations of Hispanic nationals, even among the first generation.

A more thought-provoking question relates to how Hispanics attain some key objectives associated with the American Dream. I propose to disaggregate pan-ethnic identities along ethnic nationalities. In other words, different Hispanic nationals follow different paths of incorporation and attain the American Dream with different rates of success according to the levels of development of the societies they come from (Pumar 2012). The promotional video, *Chasing the Dream: Different Paths, One Shared Future*, recently produced by the Service Employees International Union (SEIU), captures this idea succinctly. In this chapter, I first interpret how the Dream functions as a mechanism of assimilation. Then, against this background, I examine the rate of attainment of the American Dream among Hispanic DC residents.

The American Dream as an Assimilation Regime

To characterize the American Dream as an ideological mechanism of assimilation we do not have to look far beyond Adams's *New York Times* essay. With his usual flare and witty prose, Adams dismisses any doubts about America's future by insinuating that the general destitution brought about by the Depression was temporal, not structural, as some social critics of the time suggested. Adams notes that this was not the first time American pessimism had fluctuated with cycles of optimistic prospects about our human potential and despairs about our mutual limitations.

The implications of this characterization could not be more revealing for assimilation policies today. First, Adams's message is unambiguous: economic troubles could be overcome because they are temporal, not systemic. This presents a less fatalistic outlook of the future, giving hope to migrants that their hardship conditions and personal determination would reverse their desperate fate. In his essay he claims that the American Dream "develops our capacities to the full, unhampered by unjust restrictions of caste and customs" (Adams 1933). Therefore, it seems that Adams believes that American exceptionalism consists of providing equal opportunities to attain happiness and prosperity for all, but it is up to our individual efforts to fulfill this promise. When he criticizes the reckless behavior and opulent accoutrements that characterized the prosperous years before the Depression and equates the instant gratification of consumerism to fallacies about happiness and the delusion of the good life, he seems to be warning immigrants against indulging in excesses in order to compensate for the years of deprivation that motivated them to migrate in the first place. Falling back on Puritan norms, there are no ambiguities about what Adams associates with success in America.

Finally, the ambiguities associated with the propositions that compose the American Dream enable individual interpretations of success. This means that no two experiences are alike, and immigrants manage to define the values of the American Dream according to their own individual needs and purposes. For those seeking relative prosperity, the Dream assures them that

America offers an exceptional opportunity to attain that goal. This ideal also holds true for those escaping political persecution and repression, as well as for those simply wanting to break with traditions. Beneath every Dream there is ecology of freedom sustaining it. Aberrations with individual success, intentionally or not, gradually corrode shared ethnic values, collective identities, and mutual relations of trust and obligations that so often characterize patterns of socialization in ethnic enclaves.[4]

By implication, the optimistic faith about the future in their newly adopted homeland also presents immigrants with contrasting differences about the grim experiences they left behind. Interviews revealed the promise of a more thriving future was very vivid in the minds of Hispanics in Washington, DC. One of my interviewees, a Salvadoran who journeyed north to escape the intense fighting in his native village during the country's civil war, described in dramatic detail how he arrived illegally and labored hard in the fields of California before landing in Washington, DC. As I listened attentively to his story, I realized how he constructed his own meaning of the American Dream. While still struggling to make ends meet, he conveyed a proud sense of accomplishment for overcoming numerous personal obstacles, even as he exhibited abundant confidence in the future.

Consuming the Dream: How Immigrants Absorbed the Values of the American Dream.

Conventional wisdom assumes that immigrants learn the American Dream after they land on American shores.[5] However, evidence gathered from multiple interviews overwhelmingly points in a different direction. Numerous interviews suggest that the allures of the American vision resonate well beyond our borders. When it comes to migration, the American Dream is as much a mechanism of assimilation as it is one of the pulling factors that often attract immigrants to the United States. Values associated with the American Dream are often diffused intergenerationally through the closed transnational interpersonal ties that bind friends and relatives in immigrant communities. As Rogers (1995, 92–93) inferred from Doug McAdam's study of the Freedom Summer project (*Freedom Summer* 1988), having strong connections with other participants in the Freedom March was the strongest predictor of whether or not participants joined the civil rights demonstrations in 1964. Likewise, among migration flows, individuals with ties to other migrants are more likely to migrate themselves.

Perhaps another unexpected source of diffusion was the so-called soft power side of American diplomacy. Particularly during the Cold War, American diplomats doubled their efforts to promote American values abroad, along the lines of what we term today "cultural diplomacy." The promotion of cultural diplomacy took many forms, such as goodwill visits by prominent American industrialists, tours of politicos and public personalities, and United States Information Agency–sponsored educational exchange programs and artistic performances. While the means of cultural dissemination might have varied, the goal was to project a picturesque outlook of the American way of life abroad that was characterized by a welcoming notion of a melting pot with unmatched opportunities and the promise of a peaceful and prosperous future. Meanwhile, little if any mention was made of the social cleavages or the packets of poverty throughout the country. Even when the misfortune of specific segments of the population was exposed in these programs, despair was described as a rare condition or the outcome of deviant behavior among outliers.

As historian Emily S. Rosenberg documents in her book *Spreading the American Dream* (1982), the marketing of American Dream values throughout Latin America started a few years after the outbreak of World War II when Nelson Rockefeller grew concerned about the spread of Axis influence through the hemisphere, particularly in South America. After the president appointed Rockefeller to head the Office of Inter-American Affairs in the State Department in 1940, Rockefeller immediately used popular culture, communication, and educational programs to sell the American Dream and counterbalance Nazi influence. Once in place, these programs were implemented every time there was a perceived threat or perilous instability. During the 1960s, along with the Alliance for Progress, cultural diplomacy became the cornerstone of the peripheral containment policies to stop Soviet subversion throughout the hemisphere.

As such, the effect of selling the American Dream on the promotion of migration flows to the United States was unintended. While migration flows have been sustained over time by structural factors such as income differentials and transnational network ties, it is curious why Hispanics chose the treacherous journey north[6] to the United States rather than settling in other neighboring countries. Even after one accounts for strong economic outputs, geographical proximity, and shared regional cultures, the insinuation, intended or not, that the possibility of a more abundant future can become reality only in America is surely one of the main motivations that continues to attract Hispanic migrants to the United States. One of the lessons to be drawn from the encounter of Hispanics with the American Dream is that more than any other ethnic group, Hispanics first consumed the virtues of the Dream back in their countries of origin, even before they arrived in the United States.

The Meaning of the American Dream

For Hispanics, the Dream connotes two orders of values that I refer to as first- and second-order values, respectively. The former relates to basic rights of citizenship involving the quest for security, peace, tranquility, and the right to aspire to legal residency. For Hispanics, as for other migrants from the Global South, these values are part of the American Dream because the political instability and rancor back home do not always render these rights attainable. An assessment of how first-order values fare among Hispanics is mixed. Migrating to the United States offers an opportunity to live in peace and without fear of persecution. It also affords the desire to live in a society governed by a fair implementation of the law and a well-institutionalized polity. However, not all Hispanic nationals fare equally with respect to their chances to legalize their immigration status. Often, the prospects of citizenship depend not on the merits of each case but on the migrants' timing of arrival, nationality, or whether they are considered asylum seekers or economic migrants.

The longing for peace and security is intimately tied to the vision of a prosperous future. A recent survey of Mexicans residing in Mexico supports this point and sheds further light about the priorities and possible motivations for migrating north of the border. When asked about conditions in Mexico, the overwhelming majority of respondents did not approve of the direction the country was heading. Six out of ten Mexican nationals stated that their compatriots who left for the United States enjoy a better quality of life. When asked to rank the order of the major problems the country faces, Mexicans named crime first (81 percent), followed by economic problems (75 percent), illegal drugs (73 percent), and then corruption (68 percent) (Pew Global Attitudes Project 2009).

Recently, most of the country's attention to citizens' rights has centered on the fate of an estimated eleven million citizens who unlawfully entered the United States. Much has been said about the political impasse around comprehensive immigration reform legislation and the rising political capital of this undocumented population. The literature is also extensive regarding the various strategies of political mobilization and framing among immigrants trying to pressure Congress and the White House to pass some form of comprehensive immigration reform.

Now I will explore how first order values within the American Dream promote migration before turning to social mobility. In Latin America, the question of political rights is not correlated to one political persuasion since divisive ideologies and winner-take-all elections often result in gross human rights violations. For example, during the 1960s, Cuban refugees fled to the United States to escape the systematic and arbitrary intrusions into their private lives and the massive incarcerations of dissidents once their nation turned communist. This desire for freedom motivated other nationals to migrate as well. In the 1970s, repressive bureaucratic-authoritarian regimes headed by military officers dominated South American politics, resulting in numerous persecutions and the massive exodus of middle-class artists and intellectuals. Washington, DC, was one of the major US cities that benefited most from this immigration since this wave of immigrants was responsible for promoting civic engagement and the rich Hispanic cultural scene in the city.

In his penetrating book *Predatory States* (2005), Patrice McSherry exposes how a series of cross-border counterinsurgency programs, labeled Operation Condor, systematically crushed organized dissent against regimes in the Southern Cone. Later in the 1980s, civil wars exploded all over Central America causing one of the largest spikes in human migration to the United States since the 1920s. These Central American refugees were often victims of abductions and violence by both the military on the right and leftist insurgencies.

Finally, since the mid-1980s, an explosion of drug trafficking has destabilized the lives of millions throughout Latin America, principally in Colombia, Central America, and Mexico. According to reports by the United Nations Office of Drugs and Crime (UNODC), drug trafficking corrupts all spheres of civil life and produces countries with fragile institutional governmental infrastructures. In its latest annual report, the UNODC states that the most perilous societies in the world are located along the Central American drug trafficking corridor. Between 2000 and 2011 in Honduras alone, the homicide rate jumped from 51 to 92 per 100,000. Belize experienced an increase of 23 homicides per 100,000 in the last ten years since 2000 (UNODC 2013, 48).

Since the early 1960s, political instability, human rights abuse, and personal crime have contributed to a jump in the migration rates from Latin America to the United States. Hispanics come to the United States to live in peace and without fear of persecution, abductions, and crime. The opportunity to live in a society where basic human rights are respected and there are relatively low levels of crime is a part of every migrant's Dream.

The American Dream of Hispanics in Washington, DC

I analyze different rates of social attainment among Hispanics residing in the District of Columbia to show the lingering effects of levels of national development on assimilation among Hispanics. Accordingly, I focus my analysis on two key concepts of the migrant experience: (1) social capabilities and (2) the indexing of experiences. My argument is that social capabilities associated with conditions of the national development contextualize the experiences immigrants transfer with them when they embark on the journey to reside abroad. Experiences from their home nations shape the bias, prejudices, and values that form attitudes toward everyday life. These attitudes—in addition to the social and human capital and the modes of incorporation—influence the pace of segmented assimilation among immigrant populations today. Attitudes and values are reinforced across generational and friendship networks. Transnational village (Levitt 2001) mentalities also show that immigrants' stock of knowledge consists of inspiring values associated with the American Dream, as well as the social constraints and opportunities that levels of national development afford them.

The concept of capabilities has been operationalized by Amartya Sen in his book *Development as Freedom* (2000). According to Sen, the capabilities of any human being are "the substantive freedoms he or she enjoys to lead the kind of life he or she has reason to value" (87). The degrees of freedom a person enjoys are usually habituated by conditions of national development, the strategies of development, and the levels of development a society manages to achieve. These factors combined constitute the conditions of national development.

To show one illustration from Latin America since at least the past decade, Argentina and Barbados have achieved almost identical development indexes (0.797 and 0.793, respectively), according to the United Nations Development Programme. However, those familiar with the region would affirm that nationals from these two nations experience different conditions of development. Therefore by considering levels of the national development index alone, one would not have been able to predict the different patterns of assimilation between these two particular groups of ethnic nationals.

An examination of the effects of the social impact of national developments is further complicated when one takes into account social stratification. It is generally accepted that neoliberal development policies have disproportionally benefited those possessing enough transferable human and social capital to compete globally. For Sen the relationship between the conditions of development and personal capabilities are also conditioned by such factors as location, gender, social roles, and even epidemiological atmosphere over which individuals have very little control.

Finally, for some individuals two or more of these parametric variations are coupled resulting in further disadvantages (Sen 2000, 88). Sen describes development as the equivalent to freedom because the former could potentially condense the detrimental effects of capabilities' deprivations, another useful term from Sen's study. Conversely, capability deprivation describes how national poverty limits the freedom of individuals to achieve a relatively prosperous life and full potential. Among other reasons, this concept is useful for our purpose because it allows us to study the legacy of structural conditions of poverty on a particular group without even considering the controversial issue of the culture of poverty. Capability deprivation is associated not only with the capacity of individuals to be free but also with the range of experiences, family values, and social norms that immigrants acquire through their socialization in their home countries. In the context of today's economic migration, capability deprivation becomes a useful concept to use to understand how populations who migrate in search of a better life face constraints and opportunities, and to understand the difficulties they face overcoming these conditions.

One could argue that migration presents an attempt to free oneself from the effects of uneven national development. Following this interpretation, deprivation does not foster a culture of poverty, as some social scientists have argued, since the effects of deprivation can be overcome, hyphenated, or eroded over time. Instead, the effects of poverty materialize into temporal social habits and norms. The extent to which social habits and norms endure across first- and second-generation Hispanics in Washington, DC, is often predisposed by differential socialization, network ties, and the personal longing for national symbols and cultural rituals these immigrants leave behind. When immigrants congregate in ethnic enclaves and socialize with other conationals with comparable class positions and status, habits are reproduced and become internalized or indexed in ethnic identities. In some cases, marginalization and the relative social isolation many immigrants experience once they settle in new enclave destinations also reproduce the effects of deprivation.

Because capability deprivations manifest themselves differently across social classes from country to country, different ethnic nationals are predisposed, and in some cases also become willing, to assimilate not just according to their human and social capital but also by the "indexing" of personal experiences. As Cicourel (1973) explains:

> Indexical expressions force all members to retrieve by recall or invention particular ethnographic features from context-sensitive settings that will provide acceptable normative meanings to present activities and accounts of past activities. (Cicourel 1973, 85)

In sum, along with various manifestations of social and human capital, the experiences associated with conditions of national development should also be taken into account to determine the rate of incorporation of various immigrant nationals. To determine the different rate of incorporation within ethnic groups, it is useful to take into account how conditions of national development determine the levels of capabilities each of these group experiences. Once we take these factors into account, the effects of national development on immigrants' formative years become relevant to understanding how these groups interpret their own values and identities in receiving societies.

To illustrate these points, I shall select eight different Hispanic groups living in Washington, DC, and show their relative assimilation according to five standard measurements from the migration literature. I drew the ethnic nationalities from a quota sample according to the levels of national development as measured by the United Nations (UN) Development Programme's Human Development Indicators (HDIs). The HDI is a composite index of four basic variables that measure quality of life across nations. The measuring variables in the UN index are life expectancy at birth, mean years of schooling, expected years of schooling, and gross national income per capita. Each of these variables has an expressed value ranging from 0 to 1. Furthermore, to classify the countries in my pool, I took the 2000 HDI ranking and ranked selected sending societies according to the overall HDI values. Nations with 0.75 or higher were considered in the higher rank, those between 0.74 and 0.65 were the medium rank, and at 0.64 or below were the low rank.

Table 1 describes the HDI values, the national ranking, and the percentage of the Washington, DC, population of each of the ethnic nationals selected. For the assimilation variables in table 2, I chose educational attainment, measured by the percentage of college or higher degree graduates; the abil-

Table 1. Sample Hispanic demographic

Country Nationals	HDI	HD Country Ranking	Percent of DC Population
Mexicans	78	High	14
Cubans	78		3
Colombians	77		5
Dominicans	73	Medium	10
Salvadorans	71		37
Hondurans	64	Low	2
Nicaraguans	64		2
Guatemalans	61		2

Source: 2000 United Nations Human Development Indicators and 2010 Census.

ity to speak English very well; occupation, measured by the percentage of profession-related occupations; the percentage of home ownership; and the percentage of homeowners occupying homes valued at $200,000 or above. All the data is considered standard in the migration literature, and all, with the exception of home values, were taken from the 2010 United States Census Bureau's American Fact Finder. Home value information was also gathered from the census, but it was reported from a 2000 sample.

In the context of Washington, DC, where unemployment is relatively low but there is ample evidence of residential segregation, calculating the value of the home provides an important measure of the type of neighborhoods immigrants live in and to what extent they are able to afford higher and more comfortable living quarters.

While some critics may point to the lack of data about generations and their time of arrival, it is important to keep in mind that one of the purposes of this chapter is to call attention to the fact that some lagging effects of national development are not washed off easily—despite the fact that these effects could be altered by discrimination, ethnic competition, and solidarity among conationals.

The data presented in table 2 suggest a strong association between the capabilities derived from conditions of national development, as measured by HDI, and the degrees of segmented attainment of the American Dream among the eight Hispanic groups in the sample. Although there is considerable variation among the values in each case within the three levels of HDI,

Table 2. The American Dream attainment among Hispanic Washington, DC, residents

Ethnic Nationals	HDI	Education	Language	Occupation	Home Ownership	Home Value	Attainment Index
High							
Mexicans	78	55	48	28	23	55	42
Cubans	78	59	63	39	42	48	50
Colombians	77	86	59	45	29	59	56
Medium							
Dominicans	73		50	12	23	6	23
Salvadorans	71	34	27	3	23	12	20
Low							
Hondurans	64	9	27	2	13		13
Guatemalans	64	17	27	4	18	25	18
Nicaraguans	61	9	41	6	35		23

Note: All figures are expressed in percentages. Data was taken from the 2010 census. Missing values were not reported by the Census Bureau. Attainment index rates were rounded.

the trend indicates that Hispanic nationals who migrate from countries with relatively high levels of socioeconomic development tend to do better in the Washington, DC, region than those from middle- and low-development societies. Practically all the groups from high human development conditions scored substantially higher than the rest on every one of the five selected indicators. There are two exceptions to this generalization. Both Mexicans and Colombians, despite their high level of human capital, do not show a comparable degree of homeownership. Likewise, Nicaraguans show low levels of education and occupational status but unusually high levels of homeownership. This finding deserves further study than this chapter can afford. However, the unexpected levels of homeownership in these cases might be related to the transient nature of many professionals in and around Washington, DC. Perhaps many of the Mexican and Colombian nationals who participated in the census lived or expected to live in Washington, DC, for a brief period and did not own their living quarters.

Another interesting finding that supports the association between high capability and assimilation is that populations migrating from high-HDI societies seem to be more able to translate their relatively high human capital and their language acquisition abilities and education into higher occupational status than any group coming from medium- and low-HDI countries. Thus, Colombians, like Cubans for example, show one of the highest levels of human capital and occupation. Conversely, Nicaraguans and Dominicans show the fifth and fourth highest degree of English acquisition, respectively, but one of the lowest educational and occupational attainment levels. Salvadorans reported a considerable level of education attainment, but the second lowest numbers of professional occupations. Finally, when the HDI and attainment indexes are compared, the two flow in conjunction with each other. With the exception of Nicaraguans and Dominicans, the attainment index increases with national development levels. In fact, the differences between high and medium index levels more than double, and between high and low more than triple.

At the very least, these findings support the need to further explore the association between levels of national development and its impact on the segmented attainment of the American Dream. As Sen discusses in his book, the effects of development indicators should be examined in their totality, considering the social and psychological effects in addition to the material opportunities brought to individuals. Taking into consideration the effects of national capabilities might also explain why some immigrant groups—as seems to be the case with Salvadorans and to some extent with Dominicans in this sample—experienced relative downward mobility once they left their nations.

Another indication of the success endured by immigrants from higher HDI societies is reflected in the average value of the homes they occupy. Without exception, the percentage of homeowners among the group of immigrants coming from high-HDI societies who resided in homes valued at $200,000 or more in 2000 was double or more than other ethnic nationals. Like most cities, the Washington, DC, real estate market offers homes at a wide array of prices, and home values correlate with the quality of home units and the neighborhoods where they are located. Consequently, on average, Mexican, Cuban, and Colombian nationals enjoy more comfortable living quarters, and probably a more affluent lifestyle, than other Hispanics in the city.

Directions for Future Research

Future studies of how Hispanics conceive and struggle to attain the American Dream should consider how social cleavages and mechanisms of exclusion impact social cohesion among Hispanics. As the recent work of Edward Telles demonstrates, even ambiguous interpretations of skin color often problematize notions of racial identities among Hispanics. Telles pointedly observes: "Skin color is a continuous and clearly visible characteristic that may discriminate among people who identify in the same race category but who are actually of different color" (Telles 2014, 11).

Another important consideration for future research would be to explore how specific labor market segmentations impact the socioeconomic performance of Hispanics according to measurable indicators of the Dream. To undertake such a study, it would be necessary to follow a comparative analysis of different Hispanic groups across multiple cities. Such an approach would certainly challenge general findings that are historically rich but are only centered on a single metropolitan region as well as broader national studies that overlook distinct urban conditions.

Conclusion

The experience of Hispanic attainment demonstrates a few valuable lessons for students of migration and American studies. Perhaps one of the most significant points we ought to consider carefully is that the consumption of the American Dream usually takes place before immigrants arrive on our shores. Years of cultural diplomacy, promoting American values abroad to legitimize our national interest, also cultivate an aberration with achieving the Dream, increasing migration among some. An unintended consequence of this effort is that these values have become a pulling factor attracting immigrants to our country. Another significant lesson from this study is that migrants conceive the Dream slightly differently than other Americans. Hispanic immigrants value securing citizenship rights as much as economic prosperity and often perceive both as inseparable. This dual order is rooted in the particular historical context of Hispanic migration and the political economy of the Global South.

The study also suggests that it is a mistake to continue to assume that all ethnic groups fare similarly when they pursue the Dream. More often than not, the attainment of the American Dream depends on the legacy of structural factors such as levels of national development and how these structural conditions affect individual capabilities and stocks of knowledge. As the experience of Hispanics residing in Washington, DC, demonstrates, immigrants who come from countries with higher levels of national development also show higher success rates when it comes to attaining the American Dream.

To illustrate the advantages of closely examining variations in attainment rates among Hispanics according to national origins, an analysis of education suffices. In a report published in 2013, the Pew Research Center concludes, "overall, the District of Columbia has the highest college degree attainment rate among Hispanic adults, with 36.2% of those ages 25 or older holding a bachelor's degree" (Cuddington and Lopez 2013). However, as my research indicates, this assertion holds for some Hispanic groups but not others. Education rates among Colombian, Cuban, and Mexican residents of the District of Columbia are rather high, reaching 86, 59, and 55 percent respectively. But this is not the case for other Hispanics. Among Hondurans and Nicaraguans education level does not surpass single digits and for Guatemalans is 17 percent.

To be sure, the policy and academic implications of these findings should not be underestimated. From an analytical point of view, taking levels of national development into account requires us to reinterpret various conceptual manifestations of assimilation. While different conceptions of this term vary substantially, pretty much all assimilation theories assume that the success of immigrants in America rests on how individual efforts or the effects of generational legacies are conditioned by structural factors. This chapter calls for a reexamination of these assumptions.

Although somewhat less controversial, the chapter illustrates the need to move away from pan-ethnic denominations. Many pan-ethnic rubrics are socially constructed and highly politicized—witness the contentious implications of the terms *Hispanics* and *Latino/as*, to cite one example. Moreover, pan-ethnic concepts provide little meaning to understand relative achievements within ethnic groups. Even when we aggregate the data and compare one ethnic group with another, the rates of variations of specific ethnic nationals dissipate, causing significant misconceptions. Notice for instance the idea of Asian Americans as a "model minority" and the implied disregard for the fact that many Hispanic groups show greater chances of achieving the American Dream than some of their Asian counterparts.

At a more practical level, the findings of this chapter call for policy makers to dedicate more attention to two specific concerns. The first is the need to take into account, as demanding as it might be, the effects of unintended consequences in decision-making processes. This conclusion, once popularized by the late Albert O. Hirschman, is relevant to migration studies because it enriches the debate about the reasons why people transit across borders. It is obvious that initial efforts to export the ideals of the American Dream were never intended to stimulate migration. As it turns out, the consumption of American values abroad provides a feasible explanation as to why immigrants from all over the world still attempt to come to the United States more often than to other countries despite well-documented economic problems and immigration restrictions. At this junction it is worth remembering that about forty-five million immigrants currently call the United States home, more than four times the amount residing in any other nation. In short, when we ask why immigrants still attempt to reach America, our cultural diplomacy might take center stage in the investigation.

If we take into account the weight of national development levels on the immigrant experience, as I have argued, this conclusion implies we need to be more patient before we begin to witness the fruits of resettlement and social programs designed to assimilate new comers. This does not mean we need to abandon or hamper support for these efforts. On the contrary, these programs might only work when they are sustained over time.

Acknowledgments

The ideas discussed in this paper were first presented at invited lectures at the Smithsonian Institution and the Eastern Sociological Society. An early draft of the paper benefited from the able comments and suggestions of my two colleagues who edited this volume, Sandra Hanson and John K. White, and my former graduate student Ashley Kopack. The findings I present here are my responsibility alone.

Notes

1. Throughout this paper, I use the term *Hispanic* to include Latino/as. I prefer the former in light of recent survey findings that suggest that Hispanics identify more often with the term *Hispanic* to characterize their identity.

2. My argument adds to the discussion on social capital popularized by Robert D. Putnam (2000) that most groups promote social capital, but some forms of capital are more fruitful than others (on this point see the work of Mario Small [2004]). I posit, however, that one way to explain the differentiation among various forms of migrant social capital is to examine the impact of levels of national development.

3. More specifically, the same survey finds that 75 percent of Hispanics interviewed agreed that with hard work people can get ahead, while only 21 percent, as opposed to 40 percent of the general population, stated that hard work alone is no guarantee for success.

4. For an exemplary discussion among marginalized populations, see the work of Lomnitz (1998).

5. This fallacy is certainly assumed in a tutorial book where Lionel Sosa (1998) lays down a plan for Hispanics about how they can succeed in the United States.

6. More than 11,000 Central American immigrants were kidnapped in Mexico and many more died crossing the country on their way to the US-Mexico border in 2010 alone.

References

Adams, James Truslow. 1933. "America Faces 1933's Realities."
    New York Times. http://www.nytimes.com/learning/teachers/
    archival/19330101AmericanDream.pdf.

Belmonte, Laura. 2008. *Selling the American Way: U.S. Propaganda and the Cold War*. Philadelphia: University of Pennsylvania Press.

Cicourel, Aaron. 1973. *The Social Organization of Juvenile Delinquency*. New York: Wiley.

Cohn, D'Vera, Ana Gonzalez-Barrera, and Danielle Cuddington. 2013. "Remittances to Latin America Recover—but Not to Mexico." Pew Research Hispanic Trends Project. http://www.pewhispanic.org/2013/11/15/remittances-to-latin-america-recover-but-not-to-mexico/.

Commager, Henry Steele. 1950. *The American Mind: An Interpretation of American Thought and Character since the 1880's*. New Haven, CT: Yale University Press.

Cuddington, Danielle, and Mark Hugo Lopez. 2013. "D.C., Virginia, and Maryland Have the Highest Share of College-Educated Latinos." Pew Research Center. http://www.pewresearch.org/fact-tank/2013/08/29/d-c-virginia-and-maryland-have-the-highest-shares-of-college-educated-latinos.

Foucault, Michel. 1980. *Power/Knowledge: Selected Interviews and Other Writings, 1972–1977*. Edited by Colin Gordon. New York: Pantheon.

Huntington, Samuel. 2009. "The Hispanic Challenge." *Foreign Policy Magazine*. http://www.foreignpolicy.com/articles/2004/03/01/the_hispanic_challenge#sthash.sPeLSt9J.dpbs.

Kazin, Michael. 2011. *American Dreamers: How the Left Changed a Nation*. New York: Knopf.

Levitt, Peggy. 2001. *The Transnational Villagers*. Berkeley: University of California Press.

Lomnitz, Larissa Adler de. 1998. *Redes sociales, cultural y poder: Ensayos de antropología latinoamericana*. Mexico City: FLACSO.

McSherry, J. Patrice. 2005. *Predatory States*. Lanham, MD: Rowman and Littlefield.

Messner, Steve, and Richard Rosenfeld. 1994. *Crime and the American Dream*. Belmont, CA: Wadsworth.

Pew Global Attitudes Project. 2009. *Trouble by Crime, the Economy, and Corruption*. Washington, DC. Pew Research Center.

Portes, Alejandro. 1997. "Globalization from Below: The Rise of Transnational Communities." Princeton University, WPTC-98-01.

Pumar, Enrique S. 2012. "National Development, Capability, and the Segmented Assimilation of Hispanics in Washington, DC." In *Hispanic Migration and Urban Development: Studies from Washington DC*, edited by Enrique S. Pumar, 25–44. London: Emerald Press.

Putnam, Robert D. 2000. *Bowling Alone.* New York: Simon and Schuster.

Reich, Robert B. 2011. *Aftershock: The Next Economy and America's Future.* New York: Vintage Press.

Rogers, Everett M. 1995. *Diffusion of Innovations.* 4th ed. New York: Free Press.

Román, Ediberto. 2013. *Those Damned Immigrants: America's Hysteria over Undocumented Immigration.* New York: New York University Press.

Rosenberg, Emily. 1982. *Spreading the American Dream: American Economic and Cultural Expansion, 1890–1945.* New York: Hill and Wang.

Saad, Lydia. 2012. "Hispanic Voters Put Other Issues Before Immigration." http://www.gallup.com/poll/155327/Hispanic-Voters-Put-Issues-Immi gration.aspx.

Sen, Amartya. 2000. *Development as Freedom.* New York: Anchor Books.

Small, Mario Luis. 2004. *Villa Victoria: The Transformation of Social Capital in a Boston Barrio.* Chicago: University of Chicago Press.

Smith, Hedrick. 2012. *Who Stole the American Dream?* New York: Random House.

Sosa, Lionel. 1998. *El sueño americano: Como los latinos pueden triunfar en Estados Unidos.* New York: Plume/Penguin.

Taylor, Paul, Mark Hugo Lopez, Jessica Martínez, and Gabriel Velasco. 2012. *When Labels Don't Fit: Hispanics and Their Views of Identity.* Washington, DC: Pew Hispanic Center.

Telles, Edward. 2014. *Pigmentocracies: Ethnicity, Race, and Color in Latin America.* Chapel Hill: University of North Carolina Press.

United Nations Office of Drugs and Crime. 2013. "World Drug Report." Vienna, Austria.

Vargas, Jose Antonio. 2011. "My Life as an Undocumented Immigrant." *New York Times,* June 22.

The Color of the Dream

Latino/as, African Americans, and the American Dream

Steven A. Tuch

Introduction

The dramatic increase in Latino/a immigration to the United States over the past several decades has fundamentally changed the racial and ethnic terrain of twenty-first-century America. In 2014 Latino/as constituted 17.4 percent of the US population—up from 6.4 percent in 1980, 9.0 percent in 1990, and 12.5 percent in 2000. In the first decade of this century Latino/as supplanted Africans Americans, who in 2013 composed 13.2 percent of the population, as the nation's largest minority group (US Census Bureau 2012, 2014).[1] It is projected that by 2050 Latino/as will compose nearly a quarter of the US population (Lee and Bean 2012), a figure that is expected to reach 31 percent by 2060 (Krogstad and Lopez 2014). Moreover, by midcentury the United States is expected to become a "majority-minority" nation in which members of racial and ethnic minorities will together constitute more than half of the population (Frey 2010). The significance of this demographic shift for the future of race and ethnic relations, and thus for race and ethnicity scholarship, is profound: the black-white binary that has traditionally garnered the lion's share of scholarly attention no longer captures the full dynamic of race and ethnicity in America. In addition to the focus on majority-minority relations, minority-minority comparisons are gaining more importance in our increasingly multiracial and multiethnic society.

This chapter examines Latino/as' and African Americans' views of the American Dream. Specifically, I ask: First, how optimistic are Latino/as and African Americans about their progress toward achieving the American Dream? Second, what economic and noneconomic factors shape perceptions of the Dream, and do these factors differ by racial-ethnic group? Third, do Latino/as and blacks view themselves as in zero-sum competition with each other for economic and other resources? Finally, do Latino/as' perceptions of economic competition with blacks, and African Americans' perceptions of economic competition with Latino/as, lead members of either group to fear that their progress toward achieving the Dream is in jeopardy? In order to address these questions I examine nationally representative survey data from 2000 to 2012. Throughout, similarities with and differences between Latino/as and African Americans, on the one hand, and non-Hispanic[2] whites, on the other, are also examined.

Theoretical Background

I use group position theory (Blumer 1958), which depicts racial attitudes as a reflection of intergroup competition and conflict over material rewards, power, and status, for insights. According to this framework, prejudice is rooted in a collective "sense of group position," and group interests, in turn, are the driving force underlying contentious intergroup relations. These interests include proprietary claims to scarce resources by a dominant group, challenges to which may be viewed as a threat to the prevailing racial order. Dominant group attitudes toward other racial groups are therefore "positional": shaped by a sense of superiority over other groups and a need to defend the dominant group against threats to its interests. The subordinate group, on the other hand, is motivated by a sense of unfair and exclusionary treatment at the hands of the dominant group and by an interest in securing a greater share of advantages; the greater the sense of oppression felt by minority group members, the more likely they are to favor change in the racial status quo (Bobo 1999). Thus, according to group position theory, racial dynamics reflect not merely individual feelings and beliefs but also relations between groups, especially fears of losing privileges or resources to competing racial groups (Blumer 1958; Quillian 1995; Bobo and Hutchings 1996; Kinder and Sanders 1996; Bobo 1999).

Traditionally, group position theory has been applied to majority-minority, not minority-minority, intergroup relations. However, some attempts have been made to extend Blumer's framework to multiethnic settings (for example, Bobo and Hutchings 1996; Bobo 1999). In this context, Bobo and Hutchings's discussion of "racial alienation" is especially relevant:

> Among subordinate racial groups the level of alienation will vary based
> on group differences in the persistence, pervasiveness across domains of
> life (i.e., economics, politics, education, etc.), and degree of inequality of

life chances. This argument implies that members of more recent (and voluntarily incorporated) subordinate groups will feel less alienated than will members of long-term (and involuntarily incorporated) subordinate groups. (Bobo and Hutchings 1996, 956)

Thus if Latino/as have a less crystallized, and African Americans a deeper and more crystallized, sense of relative group position vis-à-vis the other, we would expect Latino/as' views of the Dream to be less impacted than blacks' views by perceptions of economic threat.

Comparing Latino/a and African American Socioeconomic Status

Since discussions of the American Dream so often focus on the attainment of economic goals, a brief comparison of Latino/as and blacks with whites on several key indicators of economic well-being is presented.

In 2010 62.9 percent of Hispanics twenty-five years of age and older living in the United States had a high school education, compared to 84.2 percent of blacks and 87.6 percent of whites, and 13.9 percent of Latino/as twenty-five years old and older had at least a BA degree, compared to 19.8 percent of blacks and 30.3 percent of whites. Also in 2010, the median income for Hispanic households in the United States was $38,039, compared to $32,584 for black households—far below the comparable figure for whites ($51,861; all in constant 2009 dollars). Unemployment rates for Latino/as were 10.8 percent; for blacks, 13.4 percent; and for whites, 7.5 percent. Poverty rates showed similar disparities—25.3 percent and 25.8 percent of Latino/as and blacks, respectively, were in poverty in 2010, while the corresponding figure for whites was less than half that, 12.3 percent (US Census Bureau 2012). Thus with the exception of educational attainment, Hispanics in 2010 fared better than African Americans on each of these key indicators of socioeconomic status, though both groups lagged far behind whites.[3]

Also of note is that blacks and Hispanics are more residentially segregated from whites than they are from each other (Logan and Stults 2011; Loewen 2011). In 2010 the average index of dissimilarity score between blacks and whites residing in metropolitan areas in the United States was 59.1, the Hispanic-white dissimilarity score was 48.5, and the dissimilarity score between blacks and Hispanics was 45.9.[4] Lower levels of residential segregation between Latino/as and blacks increase the likelihood of contact and, possibly, competition between them.

Data and Methods

DATA

In order to address the research questions posed above, I analyze data from the 2000 to 2012 General Social Surveys (GSS). The GSS is administered biannually by the National Opinion Research Center (NORC) at the University of Chicago. The surveys are based on full probability sampling designs and are representative of the noninstitutionalized adult (eighteen years of age and older) population of the United States. The mode of administration is face-to-face interviews with an average of 2005 respondents in each survey year between 2000 and 2012. Combining data from these seven most recent GSS surveys (2000, 2002, 2004, 2006, 2008, 2010, and 2012) yields sufficient numbers of African American (N = 2,663) and Latino/a (N = 1,984) as well as white (N = 13,559) respondents to sustain comparative analyses by race/ethnicity.[5] The 2000 survey was the first year in which the GSS included an explicit Hispanic identification question, reducing ambiguity in measuring Hispanic ethnicity. Beginning in 2006 the GSS introduced the option of Spanish language interviews, allowing a determination as to whether or not language of interview matters for Latino/as' views.

MEASURES

The specific GSS questions I use to measure respondents' assessments of their progress toward achieving the American Dream focus on opportunities for, and barriers to, the "good life." The first three questions ask specifically about financial issues: (1) "We are interested in how people are getting along financially these days. So far as you and your family are concerned, would you say that you are pretty well satisfied with your present financial situation, more or less satisfied, or not satisfied at all?" (2) "During the last few years has your financial situation been getting better, worse, or has it stayed the same?" (3) "Compared with American families in general would you say your family income is far below average, below average, average, above average, or far above average?" The next set of questions ask respondents to compare their standard of living with that of various reference groups: (4) "The way things are in America, people like me and my family have a good chance of improving our standard of living—do you agree or disagree?" (5) "Compared to your parents when they were the age you are now, do you think your own standard of living now is much better, somewhat better, about the same, somewhat worse, or much worse than theirs was?" (6) "When your children are at the age you are now do you think their standard of living will be much better, somewhat better, about the same, somewhat worse, or much worse than yours is now?" The last question assesses respondents' views of the prerequisites for success: (7) "Some people say that people get ahead by their own hard work; others say that lucky breaks or help from other people are more important. Which do you think is most important?"

Findings

Figures 1 through 7 display responses to the GSS questions separately by racial group. As figure 1 shows, about a third (32.4 percent) of whites, but only 18.5 percent of African Americans and 17.2 percent of Latino/as, are "pretty well satisfied" with their present financial situation. Figure 2 indicates that approximately equal percentages of whites (35.9 percent), blacks (33.0 percent), and Latino/as (36.5 percent) describe their financial situations as having improved over the last few years. However, as shown in figure 3, about two-and-a-half times as many whites (25.2 percent) as blacks (10.8 percent)

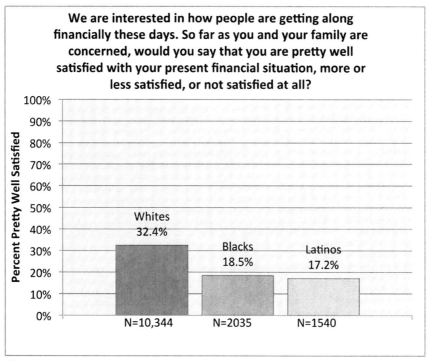

Figure 1

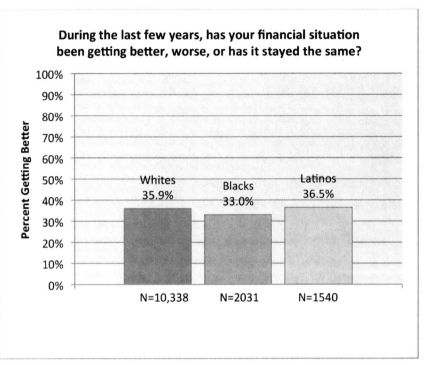

Figure 2

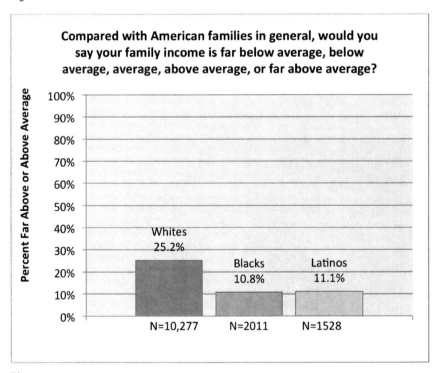

Figure 3

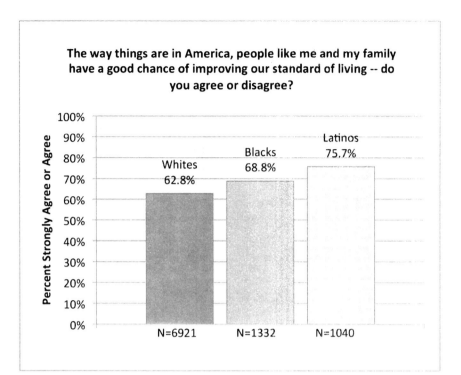

Figure 4

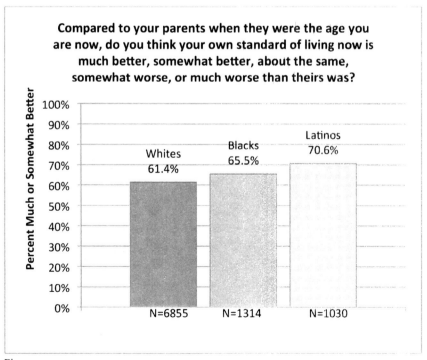

Figure 5

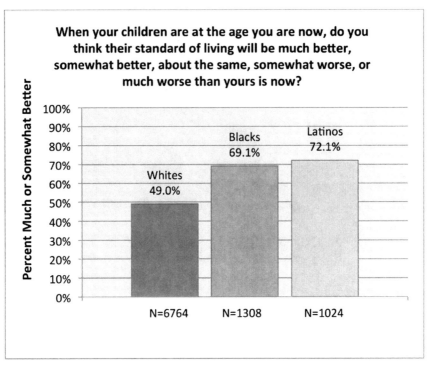

Figure 6

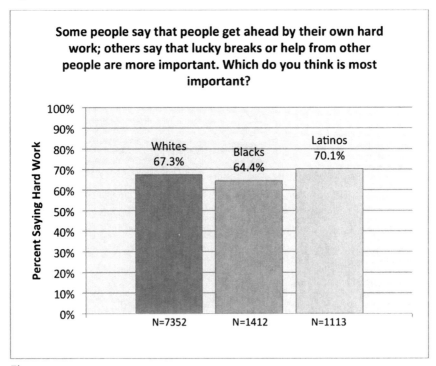

Figure 7

126

and Latino/as (11.1 percent) consider themselves to have above average family income.

The next question asks about respondents' prospects for improving their standard of living. Majorities of each group—though more Latino/as (75.7 percent) and African Americans (68.8 percent) than whites (62.8 percent)—agree that the chances are good (figure 4).

The next two questions ask for generational comparisons. Figure 5 displays respondents' assessments of their own standard of living as compared to that of their parents, and figure 6 shows an analogous comparison between respondents and their children. While majorities of all three groups assess their own standard of living as better than that of their parents (figure 5), Latino/as (70.6 percent) compare themselves more favorably to their parents than either whites (61.4 percent) or blacks (65.5 percent) do to theirs. Similarly, as figure 6 shows, Latino/as (72.1 percent) are also more likely than African Americans (69.1 percent), and much more likely than whites (49.0 percent), to predict that their children's standard of living will be much better or better than their own.

Finally, only minor differences are found in the percentages of each group who endorse hard work as the most important way to get ahead, with seven in ten Latino/as (70.1 percent) and nearly as many whites (67.3 percent) and African Americans (64.4 percent) in agreement (figure 7).

What conclusions do these figures support about how Latino/as, blacks, and whites view their progress toward achieving the American Dream? Three patterns stand out. First, consistent with the socioeconomic inequality data summarized earlier showing that Latino/as and blacks still lag far behind whites on most key indicators of economic status, members of both minority groups assess their financial situations less positively than whites assess theirs. As indicated in figures 1 and 3, whites are more satisfied than either Latino/as or blacks with the state of their finances, though only about a third of each group reports progress in financial health over the last few years (figure 2). Second, despite their economic disadvantages compared to whites, both Latino/as and blacks are more strongly committed than whites to the pursuit of the Dream. Both retrospectively and prospectively, as figures 4 through 6 show, blacks and Latino/as are steadfast in their belief that the Dream is attainable. Third, and consistent with the predictions of group position theory, Latino/as are more optimistic than African Americans about their prospects for attaining the Dream (figures 4 through 6), though the groups differ little about the role of hard work in doing so (figure 7).

Multivariate Analysis

Having described how Latino/a, African American, and white respondents assess their progress toward achieving the American Dream, I turn next to an examination of the factors that shape these beliefs. The question I address is whether the *process* by which beliefs about the Dream are formulated is invariant across racial-ethnic groups or if, instead, the process differs in important ways by group membership. By "process" I mean similarities or differences in whether and how the explanatory variables shape views of the Dream. In other words, is there a single American Dream that is shared by Latino/as and African Americans alike, or does the Dream mean different things to different groups? In this part of the analysis I focus on Latino/as and African Americans only.

Table 1 presents the results of fitting OLS regression models to the GSS data separately for Latino/as and blacks. The dependent variable in this analysis is a summated, unit-weighted index of six of the seven GSS survey items discussed above: satisfaction with one's present financial situation, assessment of recent changes in financial condition, comparison of one's family income with that of other families, beliefs about the prospects for improving one's standard of living in the future, a comparison of one's own living standard with that of respondent's parents at the same age, and an assessment of whether the interviewees expect their children's standard of living to exceed their own.[6] All variables are coded such that higher scores reflect more positive assessments of progress toward realizing the Dream. Cronbach's alpha reliability coefficient for the six-item index is 0.616 for Hispanics and 0.604 for African Americans, indicating that the items form a reliable measure.

The selection of explanatory variables for the models was guided by findings from the literature reviewed above as well as by the predictions of group position theory. Given the grounding of the American Dream, at least partially, in prospects for attaining economic success (Hanson and White 2011), economic factors are expected to be especially cogent predictors of beliefs about the Dream (but see Stout and Le 2012). Accordingly, I included in the models *household income* and other bases of economic inequality—*gender, educational attainment,*[7] *age,* and *work status*—as well as a measure of *subjective social class.*[8] In light of evidence that political liberals and conservatives have differing views regarding the value of neighborhood racial and ethnic diversity (Pew Research Center 2014), I also incorporated a measure of *self-reported political ideology* ranging on a continuum from extremely liberal to extremely conservative. If competition over scarce resources such as jobs, housing, and education is a factor in Latino/a-black relations, cities—especially large cities and their surrounding suburbs—are the most likely locales where such competition is experienced. Hence, whether *residence* is in a large- or medium-sized city (50,000 or more inhabitants) as compared to a small city or rural area (fewer than 50,000 inhabitants) is included in the models. The *region* of the country in which respondent resides and *marital status* are included as demographic controls. Moreover, I added two additional predictor variables for Latino/as: whether the respondent chose English or Spanish as the *interview language,* an option introduced by the GSS beginning in the 2006 survey year, and *generational status*—whether the respondent was foreign born or is second generation or later. The rationale for including choice of interview language is based on the possibility that Latino/as who prefer to be interviewed in Spanish may be less well integrated into American society, and thus less optimistic about their pursuit of the Dream, than those who choose English. Regarding generation, most immigrants, especially the majority who emigrate in search of better economic opportunities than are available in their home countries, typically start with few resources and expect to sacrifice (Washington Post 2014), while native-born Latino/as may be more likely to compare their status to that of other Americans, especially non-Hispanic whites (see, for example, Alvarez 1973). Thus, compared to later generation coethnics, immigrants may be even more likely to adhere to tenets of the Dream.[9] Finally, in separate models, I include proxy measures of *competition-threat.* For Latino/as I use a question that is often employed in racial attitude research to tap "racial resentment"—the notion that antiblack affect is rooted in a belief that African Americans violate such traditional values as self-reliance and hard work (Tuch and Hughes 2011; Hughes 1997).[10] For blacks I use a question about whether the number of immigrants to the United States should be increased, decreased, or kept at current levels.[11]

After eliminating cases with missing data on any of the variables in the model, 1,914 cases remain for analysis—841 Latino/as and 1,073 African Americans.[12]

Turning first to the statistically significant coefficients for Latino/as in table 1, older respondents, not surprisingly, are less positive than their younger coethnics about prospects for attaining the Dream. Equally unsurprising, and consistent with the findings of previous studies, those with higher household incomes are significantly more likely than those with lower incomes to positively evaluate their progress toward achieving the Dream. As expected, the higher the self-reported social class, the more hopeful Latino/a respondents are about the Dream, Latino/a city dwellers are significantly less hopeful than

Table 1. Regression of American Dream Beliefs on Predictor Variables, Latino/as and African Americans, 2000–2012 General Social Surveys

	Latino/as		African Americans	
	b	*beta*	*b*	*beta*
Female	-0.410	-0.063	-0.328	0.048
	(0.211) #		(0.192)	
Education	-0.010	-0.012	0.030	0.024
	(0.034)		(0.038)	
Age	-.039	-0.162**	-0.004±	-0.019
	(0.008)		(0.006)	
Income	0.122**	0.187**	0.100**	0.174
	(0.023)		(0.020)	
Work status	0.138	0.005	1.003	0.149**
	(0.237) +/-		(.213) +/-	
Subjective class	1.333**	0.245**	1.392	0.291**
	(0.179)		(0.136)	
Political views	-0.004	-0.002	-0.166	-0.073**
	(0.072) +/-		(0.064) +/-	
City	-0.721	-0.064*	-0.251	-0.030
	(0.353)		(0.250)	
Nonsouth	-0.162	-0.024	-0.209	-0.031
	(0.213)		(0.203)	
Foreign born	0.509	0.078*	----	----
	(0.240)		----	
Spanish language interview	0.845	0.116**	----	----
	(0.305)		----	----
Married	0.485	0.071*	0.223	0.030
	(0.215)		(0.224)	
Year	-0.121	-0.144**	-0.057	-0.071*
	(0.027)		(0.023)	
N	867		1073	
R-Square (adjusted)	0.174		0.182	

standard errors (in parentheses)
± *coefficients differ significantly*
*p 0.05; **p 0.01

their nonmetropolitan counterparts about their pursuit of the Dream, and the foreign-born are more positive than the native-born. Contrary to expectations, those in 2006 or later who opted for a Spanish language interview are *more* positive about their progress than those who chose to be interviewed in English. Married respondents are more hopeful about their pursuit of the Dream than the nonmarried. Finally, the significant negative effect of year indicates that respondents in later surveys were less positive than those in earlier years. No significant effects of gender, education, work status, political views, or region of residence exist among Latino/as.

The analogous regression coefficients for African Americans in table 1 indicate that income significantly shapes views of the Dream, with higher income blacks, as expected, more positive about their prospects for attaining the Dream than their lower income racial peers. Similarly, being employed and identifying with the middle class both elevate African Americans' sense of progress toward achieving the Dream. More politically conservative blacks, on the other hand, are less optimistic than the politically liberal, as are respondents who were interviewed later in the timeline. No significant effects of gender, education, age, region of residence, city versus noncity locale, or marital status exist among African Americans.

As indicated earlier, an important question is whether the factors that shape views of the Dream differ significantly by racial-ethnic group membership. In order to address this question I fit interaction terms between race-ethnicity and each of the explanatory variables that appear in both the Latino/a and African American models in table 1—in other words, every variable except foreign- versus native-born status and language of interview, both of which were asked only of Latino/a respondents. A significant interaction term indicates that the variable impacts views of the Dream differently for Latino/as and blacks. As indicated in table 1, only two significant interaction effects exist: the effects of work status in increasing optimism and of political views in decreasing it are significantly stronger for blacks than for Latino/as. The impacts of the other nine common predictors do not differ significantly by race-ethnicity. These findings support the conclusion that the *process* by which beliefs in the Dream are nurtured—the factors that shape those beliefs—is largely the same for Latino/as and blacks.

The last step in the OLS analysis is to increment the models in table 1 with the competition-threat terms discussed earlier. Focusing first on Latino/as, when the racial resentment variable is entered into the model its coefficient is -0.283 and significant: being resentful of African Americans decreases Latino/as' sense of making progress toward achieving the Dream (coefficients not shown in the table). The only changes to the coefficients for Latino/as in table 1 when racial resentment is controlled are that the effects of city size and interview language become nonsignificant. Among blacks, similarly, when immigration attitudes are entered into the model, the coefficient is -0.317 and significant: African Americans who believe that immigration should be reduced are less positive about the American Dream. Two changes to the coefficients for blacks in table 1 occur when immigration attitudes are controlled: city size becomes significant and year of interview loses significance. Overall, these results support the importance of perceptions of intergroup competition and threat in shaping views about the Dream for both Latino/as and African Americans but do not change the conclusion that the process by which views of the Dream are created is similar for both groups.[13]

Some implications of these findings are discussed next.

Summary, Conclusions, and Directions for Future Research

The analyses reported here support the conclusion that Latino/as and African Americans are more optimistic than non-Hispanic whites about the American Dream, despite both groups' inferior economic statuses compared to whites. Whether the focus is on their own current financial health, retrospective assessments of the financial status of their family of origin, or future expectations for their children, Latino/as and blacks are more optimistic about, and more committed to pursuing, the Dream than whites.

Consistent with the predictions of group position theory, however, the Dream is affected by feelings of group competition and threat. As noted, when proxy measures of competition and threat are entered into the multivariate models, their effects are significant for Latino/as and blacks alike. This finding is largely consistent with the zero-sum view of intergroup competition over resources expected on the basis of the group position framework generally, and with Bobo and Hutchings's (1996) discussion of racial alienation in a multiracial, multiethnic context specifically. Historically, blacks' subordinate status in society leads to heightened feelings of threat at the hands of other minority group members. For their part, Latino/as display a similar tendency, with increased perceptions of competition and threat resulting in less positive views of the Dream.

Perceptions of threat and competition tell only part of the story, however. Not only do Latino/as continue to pursue the Dream, they also remain vigilant in their belief that the pursuit will eventually be rewarded. In this respect

Latino/as are more optimistic than blacks. Moreover, compared to African Americans (and whites), Latino/as are more likely to believe that education is the single most important key to success, despite—or perhaps because of—the fact that they lag substantially behind African Americans (and whites) in educational attainment.

Finally, and notably, the hypothesis linking foreign-born Latino/as to greater confidence in the Dream than their native-born coethnics was also supported. However, it is possible that the foreign-born/native-born dichotomy used here masks important generational variation in beliefs about the Dream. The key comparison may be between the foreign born, on the one hand, and successively later generations of coethnics—second, third, fourth generation and beyond—on the other, a distinction that is lost by combining second and later generations into a single category.

Future research on racial-ethnic differences in the American Dream might clarify and extend the findings reported here by focusing on several factors. First, as mentioned earlier, disaggregating Latino/as by country of origin rather than implicitly assuming that they are monolithic is likely to reveal interesting intragroup differences; second, and also as noted, potential generational differences among Latino/as should be analyzed in finer detail than is done here; finally, attention should be paid to whether the intersection of race and ethnicity within the Latino/a community might shape views of the Dream. Do Latino/as who self-identify as white or black differ in their beliefs from those who self-identify as neither? Does the increase in mixed race and ethnic identities complicate matters further? Amid growing evidence that such designations matter (Frank, Akresh, and Lu 2010; Lee and Bean 2004), future studies should devote more attention to these issues.

Do Latino/as and African Americans share a common view of what constitutes the American Dream, how best to achieve it, and what factors, economic and noneconomic alike, shape it? The preponderance of evidence presented here indicates that they do. The *process* that shapes beliefs in the Dream is largely invariant across racial-ethnic lines—that is to say, with a few exceptions, the factors that matter most for Latino/as also matter for blacks, and the factors that matter most for blacks also matter for Latino/as. In short, despite their very different histories and experiences in America, there appears to be not two American Dreams—one for Latino/as and a different one for African Americans—but rather a common, shared Dream. In the America of the twenty-first century, where equality remains far more aspiration than reality, the Dream persists.

Acknowledgments

This research was supported in part by a Columbian College of Arts and Sciences Facilitating Fund grant from the George Washington University. That support, and the research assistance of Everly Jazi, are both gratefully acknowledged.

Notes

1. Those who identified as both African American and another race composed 15.2 percent of the US population in 2013 (US Census Bureau 2014).

2. The terms "Hispanic" and "Latino/a" are used interchangeably in this chapter.

3. Importantly, these comparisons do not disaggregate Latino/as by country of origin or generation and thus risk obscuring important intragroup differences. This issue is discussed further in the conclusion.

4. The index of dissimilarity measures the proportion of one group or the other that would have to change neighborhoods in order to achieve integration. The index ranges from a low of 0 (total integration) to a high of 100 (total segregation).

5. Sample sizes are prior to deleting cases with missing data on other study variables. The GSS incorporated a panel design beginning in 2006. The analyses here use only the cross-sectional data. For a full discussion of sampling methodology see Smith et al. (2012).

6. The remaining item—whether hard work rather than luck or help from others is the pathway to success—had too few cases remaining for analysis after eliminating missing data on all predictor variables.

7. According to a 2013 survey conducted by the *Washington Post* in conjunction with the Miller Center at the University of Virginia, 64 percent of Hispanics believe "very much" that receiving a college education is an important part of achieving the American Dream; the figures for whites and blacks—50 and 48 percent, respectively—lagged substantially behind. Moreover, 41 percent of Hispanics, compared to 27 percent of whites and 34 percent of blacks, consider education to be the *single* most important factor for getting ahead. Thus Latino/as' faith in education as a gateway to the American Dream is stronger than that of both blacks and whites (Washington Post 2014).

8. The question wording is, "If you were asked to use one of four names for your social class, which would you say you belong in: the lower class, the working class, the middle class, or the upper class?"

9. Although 35.5 percent of Latino/as living in the United States in 2012 were foreign born, including 49.8 percent of Latino/a adults (Krogstad and Lopez 2014), recent data show that after four decades of growth in the number of foreign-born Latino/as their share is now in decline (US Census Bureau 2012). Since 2000, the primary source of Hispanic population growth in the United States has been native births. Thus if the hypothesis that native-born Latino/as become increasingly disenchanted with their prospects for achieving the American Dream, the upshot in terms of the sheer numbers affected will be substantial.

10. The question wording is, "Irish, Italians, Jews, and many other minorities overcame prejudice and worked their way up. Blacks should do the same without special favors." Response options range from "disagree strongly" to "agree strongly" on a 5-point continuum.

11. The question wording is, "Do you think the number of immigrants to America nowadays should be increased a lot, increased a little, remain the same as it is, reduced a little, or reduced a lot?"

12. With one exception, the loss of cases due to missing values is not attributable to any one predictor but rather is spread across several. The exception is household income. Accordingly, I used mean substitution, separately for Latino/as and blacks, to recapture cases with missing income data. As a rough barometer of the consequences of missing data I examined a series of models in which I deleted subsets of predictors with varying amounts of missing data and compared the results with the full model. In no case did the reduced models differ substantially from the results reported in table 1.

13. Entering the competition-threat variables into the model caused a substantial loss of cases due to missing data: the Ns dropped to 424 for Latino/as and to 394 for African Americans. Hence, some caution is in order in interpreting this last step in the multivariate analysis.

References

Alvarez, Rodolfo. 1973. "The Psycho-Historical and Socioeconomic Development of the Chicano Community in the United States." *Social Science Quarterly* 53: 920–42.

Blumer, Herbert. 1958. "Race Prejudice as a Sense of Group Prejudice." *Pacific Sociological Review* 1: 3–7.

Bobo, Lawrence. 1999. "Prejudice as Group Position." *Journal of Social Issues* 55: 445–72.

Bobo, Lawrence, and Vincent Hutchings. 1996. "Perceptions of Racial Group Competition: Extending Blumer's Theory of Group Position to a Multiracial Social Context." *American Sociological Review* 61: 951–72.

Frank, Reanne, Ilana Redstone Akresh, and Bo Lu. 2010. "Latino Immigrants and the U.S. Racial Order: How and Where Do They Fit In?" *American Sociological Review* 75: 378–401.

Frey, William H. 2010. "Race and Ethnicity." In *State of Metropolitan America*, 50–64. Washington, DC: Brookings Institution.

Hanson, Sandra L., and John K. White. 2011. *The American Dream in the 21st Century*. Philadelphia: Temple University Press.

Hughes, Michael. 1997. "Symbolic Racism, Old-Fashioned Racism, and Whites' Opposition to Affirmative Action." In *Racial Attitudes in the 1990s: Continuity and Change*, edited by Steven A. Tuch and Jack K. Martin, 45–75. Westport, CT: Praeger.

Kinder, David, and Lynn Sanders. 1996. *Divided by Color: Racial Politics and Demographic Ideals*. Chicago: University of Chicago Press.

Krogstad, Jens Manuel, and Mark Hugo Lopez. 2014. "Hispanic Nativity Shift: U.S. Births Drive Population Growth as Immigration Stalls." Washington, DC: Pew Research Center's Hispanic Trends Project.

Lee, Jennifer, and Frank D. Bean. 2004. "America's Changing Color Lines: Immigration, Race/Ethnicity, and Multiracial Identification." *Annual Review of Sociology* 30: 221–42.

———. 2012. "A Postracial Society or a Diversity Paradox? Race Immigration, and Multiraciality in the Twenty-First Century." *DuBois Review: Social Science Research on Race* 9: 419–37.

Loewen, James. 2011. "Dreaming in Black and White." In *The American*

Dream in the 21st Century, edited by Sandra L. Hanson and John K. White, 59–76. Philadelphia: Temple University Press.

Logan, John R., and Brian J. Stults. 2011. "The Persistence of Segregation in the Metropolis: New Findings from the 2010 Census." http://www.s4 .brown.edu/us2010.

Pew Research Center for People and the Press. 2012. Washington, DC.

———. 2014. Washington, DC.

Quillian, Lincoln. 1995. "Prejudice as a Response to Perceived Group Threat." *American Sociological Review* 60: 586–611.

Smith, Tom W., Peter V. Marsden, Michael Hout, and Jibum Kim. 2012. *General Social Surveys, 1972–2012*. Chicago: NORC.

Stout, Christopher T., and Danvy Le. 2012. "Living the Dream: Barack Obama and Blacks' Changing Perceptions of the American Dream." *Social Science Quarterly* 93: 1338–59.

Tuch, Steven A., and Michael Hughes. 2011. "Whites' Racial Policy Attitudes in the 21st Century: The Continuing Significance of Racial Resentment." *Annals of the American Academy of Political and Social Science* 634: 134–52.

US Bureau of the Census. 2012.

———. 2014.

Washington Post. 2014. "Hispanics Often Lead the Way in Their Faith in the American Dream." February 2.

From the Margins to the Center

The US Catholic Bishops, Latino/as, and the American Dream
in the Twentieth Century

MARIA MAZZENGA AND TODD SCRIBNER

The US Catholic Bishops and Latino/a Immigrants in the Twentieth Century

In introducing their 1986 pastoral letter, *Economic Justice for All*, the US Catholic Bishops set out principles for addressing the economy in the context of the Catholic social doctrine tradition and in an increasingly global world. The document, intended to serve as a guide for Catholics on matters economic, stressed consideration of the moral dimensions of economic activity, particularly how such activities affected "the poor and vulnerable." Among the most vulnerable were immigrants, including millions of Latino/a Catholics living and working in the United States.

The Bishops' letter also referenced the American Dream in support of their religiously based arguments for economic justice:

> As *Americans*, we are grateful for the gift of freedom and [we are] committed to the dream of "liberty and justice for all." This nation, blessed with extraordinary resources, has provided an unprecedented standard of living for millions of people. We are proud of the strength, productivity, and creativity of our economy, but we also remember those who have been left behind in our progress. (US Catholic Conference 1987, no. 9)

The Bishops here suggest a "'New American Experiment'—to implement economic rights, to broaden the sharing of economic power, and to make economic decisions more accountable to the common good." This experiment would not simply include those within the physical boundaries of the United States; the Bishops recognized that while many of the faithful were tied to the US economy, others moved in and outside of its borders regularly. Since "part of the American dream has been to make this world a better place for people to live in; at this moment of history that dream must include everyone on this globe" (US Catholic Conference, 1987, no. 89).

For members of the US Catholic hierarchy, there is both an American and Catholic character to the American Dream. The relationship between the two has been evolving since the early twentieth century, when the Bishops first established formal programs to minister to Latino/a migrants. First, the Bishops believed that immigrants from around the world would come to the United States and pursue an *American* dream, wherein they would settle, adapt to a specific set of cultural and political practices, acquire middle-class status using individual and group talents, and live prosperous lives. Second, the Bishops' programs on behalf of immigrants melded this vision of the American Dream with *Catholic* elements. The Catholic version of the Dream was middle class, English speaking—though maintaining specific ethnic group characteristics that meshed with American democratic and civic ideals—and expressive of Catholic communal life and doctrinal teaching. Hence, the Bishops' version of the Dream—particularly in the first half of the twentieth century—was assimilationist in the sense that the immigrants were ideally expected to embrace English and middle-class values, and divergent from mainstream American Protestantism in that Catholic immigrant programs emphasized Catholic social teaching and often put them at odds with American Protestants.

This essay draws from the archival record of the Bishops' Conference of the United States to trace evolving attitudes and practices of the formal hierarchy of the Catholic Church toward Latino/a Catholic immigrants (usually referred to as Hispanic Catholics by the US Bishops' Conference; we use Hispanic and Latino/a interchangeably in this essay).[1] Throughout the twentieth century the Catholic bishops of the United States engaged the Latino/as through Americanization programs, pastoral support, and advocacy efforts aimed at improving the social and political standing of Latino/as who were living in the United States.

This chapter will examine the extent to which these efforts made the American Dream more accessible to Latino/as and, in doing so, sought to enable them to move from the margins of American life to its center. It is our contention that the Bishops' engagement on behalf of Latino/as, while well intended and consistently applied during the period under discussion, often met with practical obstacles and opposition from the wider community that worked to undermine the Bishops' efforts in this arena. Given the historic interest of the Bishops in Latino/a immigrants, their efforts provide an interesting perspective into the institutional Catholic church's engagement with this migrant population; further research needs to be done to explore the ways in which the wider church has contributed to these same objectives.

We begin by looking at the way in which the Catholic Bishops of the United States engaged in Americanization efforts that focused on Latino/a communities and how these programs helped these populations to function in an American milieu. Next, we examine their work with respect to Mexicans crossing the Southwest border and, second, alongside Latino/as living in Florida. This opens the door to a more expansive discussion to some of the pressing problems confronting Latino/as living in the United States and obstacles hindering their achieving the American Dream. In particular we examine the Bishops' critique of the Bracero program and the growing importance of Hispanic ministry. We finish the chapter with a discussion related to the contours of comprehensive immigration reform and the way in which it continues to shape various dynamics related to Latino/as and the American Dream.

The Bishops' Conference, Latino/a Immigrants, and Early Views of Americanization

The Bishops' Conference first organized to address the needs of Catholic soldiers during World War I. Their organization evolved in 1919 into the National Catholic Welfare Council with the aim of serving and leading American Catholics generally, and eventually into the National Catholic Welfare Conference (NCWC) three years later. Just after the Second Vatican Council in the early 1960s, the group was reorganized and renamed the National Conference of Catholic Bishops (NCCB) and its Secretariat, the United States Catholic Conference (USCC). In 2001, the NCCB and USCC were merged to form the current structure, the United States Conference of Catholic Bishops (USCCB) (Slawson 1992).

This complex organizational history notwithstanding, the US Bishops have maintained a steady and deep interest in immigration-related matters since the founding of the Conference. Most immigrants to the United States across the twentieth century were Catholic and working class, and the church established a specific interest in working-class-related matters with the issuance of the encyclical *Rerum Novarum* in 1891 by Pope Leo XIII. This document asserted that the working classes deserved consideration and respect in economies reshaped by industrialization. Not only was the message of *Rerum Novarum* recapitulated throughout the twentieth century by subsequent popes, but a host of American

Catholic intellectuals, beginning with Monsignor John A. Ryan, also drew from the encyclical to develop a body of thought related specifically to economic matters in the United States. Such writings further informed the US Bishops' practices toward Latino/a Catholic immigrants.

The US Bishops ran what they called "Americanization" programs in the early twentieth century and by midcentury turned toward global migration and refugee-related issues on the one hand, and economic issues and immigration legislation in the United States on the other. Ensuring economic justice within a Catholic and American matrix was a key concern of the US Bishops throughout most of the twentieth century. These programs ultimately sought to integrate immigrant Catholics into the US economic, cultural, and political system, but on Catholic terms. This meant that these immigrants would be able to function as citizens of the United States and also participate in Catholic religious and social institutions.

The NCWC sought to address matters of immigration from the establishment of the organization in 1919. Initially Americanization programs, which included English and citizenship classes, were run through its Social Action Department, headed by John A. Ryan from its origins in 1919 until 1945. But such programs were seen as insufficient in scope early on. Catholic immigration to the United States had begun in earnest in the nineteenth century, with large numbers of Irish and Germans entering the country from the early nineteenth century, and eastern and southern European Catholics arriving by the late nineteenth and early twentieth century. Hispanic Catholics had already been in the United States by this time, of course, as original inhabitants of the Southwest and western United States. With the development of the Southwest at the end of the nineteenth century, more Mexicans crossed the relatively open border between the United States and Mexico to work in mining, railroad construction, and agriculture. Puerto Ricans and Cubans began migrating to the United States at this time as well. By 1910, there were over sixteen million Catholics in the United States, by 1920, nearly twenty million in a total US population of just over 106 million. As Timothy Matovina notes, Hispanic immigration to the United States accelerated as the European immigration declined, so processes of incorporation were not necessarily following a European Catholic model (Matovina 2012; Mazzenga and Scribner 2009).

The impetus for engaging Catholic immigration beyond Americanization programs for immigrants who had already settled in US communities was a fear that Protestants were attempting to convert Catholic immigrants at points of entry. From the perspective of the Protestant groups attempting to convert the Latino/as, these Catholic immigrants were viewed as a challenge to the Protestant version of America. Hence, the Catholic programs may have embraced some assimilationist elements, such as English speaking as an ideal, but they nonetheless affirmed what Gary Gerstle calls a transformationist version of incorporation into America in that they resisted the marginalization of the Latino/as' Catholicism as the immigrants adapted to American life. This transformationist version of incorporation meshed Catholic ideals with Protestant versions of America for a Latino/a Catholic Americanism (Gerstle 2013, 307).

In 1920, reports of Protestant proselytizing led to the establishment of the NCWC Bureau of Immigration, headed for the next forty-five years by Bruce Mohler, an American who had served as the Red Cross commissioner in Poland during World War I. The bureau was headquartered in Washington, DC, and opened offices in New York City and at Ellis Island in 1921, eventually expanding to several other cities as well (Mazzenga and Scribner 2009).

The Bishops and Mexican Immigration to the Southwestern United States

Initially, the bureau put most of its energies into assisting European Catholics. However, particularly after restrictive immigration laws curtailed Catholic migration from southern and eastern Europe and migration from Mexico skyrocketed, staff began to recognize the need to assist immigrants to the southwestern United States.[2] In 1920 there were 725,332 Mexican immigrants in the United States. By 1928 there were over two million, largely settled in the four border states and Colorado. In 1921, a full report on the conditions of Mexican immigrants in El Paso, Texas, generated interest in using NCWC resources to assist them. The executive secretary of the NCWC's National Council of Catholic Men (NCCM), Michael Slattery, who had spent much time in El Paso, reported to Father John J. Burke in 1921 that sources had relayed to him that "El Paso has one of the most serious immigration situations the Church has to confront in the country." Protestant organizations like the YWCA and YMCA were "spending profusely" on Mexican immigrants. Sacred Heart parish alone had "about 18,000 Mexicans," but there was no social area for these people to gather, so they used the spaces sponsored by Protestants. Slattery believed that El Paso "was one of the wildest towns in the Southwest, and while the Mexican trade during the past 18 years has somewhat developed the town, at the same time, the feeling against the Mexican has never been eradicated; in fact, a Texan hates a Mexican worse than he hates a Negro." El Paso, he estimated, was 50 percent Mexican. He then asked if $10,000 could be set aside for welfare work among that population. When Burke pressed Slattery for details on how the money would be spent, Slattery responded that the "average Mexican peon is used to living in a shack or a box-car, and it has been my experience while I was living in Mexico that once you were able to lift him out of the shack and put him into a house of adobe brick he began immediately to change for the better" (Slattery 1921, June 28; National Catholic Welfare Conference 1928, Bressette).

Slattery believed that elevating the economic circumstances of the Mexicans would raise their sense of themselves as Catholics and as Americans. This fits into a view conditioned by the American Dream, one that held that one could change one's life circumstance through proper integration into the American context. In other words, the Mexican was not fixed in identity and by nature prone to poverty; instead, Mexicans could come to the United States and work themselves out of poverty with a little help from the Catholic Church, thereby becoming American Catholics. Note that Slattery saw the Protestant version of doing the same thing as not having the same effect— indeed this was a Catholic American vision for the Mexican.

After further consideration, the NCWC decided to move ahead on establishing a formal Catholic presence to assist migrants along the Mexico-US border. Father John J. Burke, the general secretary of the NCWC at the time, was keenly interested in the Mexican Catholic population in the Southwest and believed they would be an important "asset to the Church" in the future. Caroline Boone, a social worker from New York, was selected to establish an office along the border.[3] Boone's plan for ministering to these migrants was to set up staff at each of the main stations through which the migrants passed through; there were twelve in all, and these included at least one staff member on both sides of the border. The work at the stations consisted of record taking of the names of the immigrants passing through, which would form the basis for follow up by local church leaders later on. This "religious assistance" and information was a form of integration, wherein the immigrants would be adapted to the "social and governmental machinery of their city or locality for the benefit of the alien who needs help" (Boone 1922). Americanization entailed the following, according to Boone: "Cooperating for the benefit of the immigrant with existing agencies in the border towns and states, and of stimulating interest among other agencies or groups for the undertaking by them of friendly visiting among aliens, making Church and pastor connections for them, providing English and citizenship classes, etc." (ibid.). Boone also planned to establish contacts with Mexican consuls and government officials on both sides of the border toward "mutual understanding and the securing of their cooperation" (ibid.). Ultimately, the goal was to keep Mexicans within US Catholic institutions, provide a range of services to them within those institutions, and eventually incorporate the immigrants into those institutions.

The US Bishops and Latino/a Immigrants in Florida

The NCWC was not only interested in the Latino/a Catholics of the Southwest, they also sought to work with the Cuban immigrants of Key West and Tampa, Florida. In 1922, of a total population of about 19,000, there were about 8,000 Cubans, both immigrant and later generation, in Key West. The Cuban American population there was generally not observant of Catholicism, and were generally working poor, with jobs centered primarily in the cigar factories. According to a Father A. L. Maureau's report on the Cuban population of Key West to the NCWC that year, the Cubans would become "pagans, socialists, bolshevists—unless the Church remedies the evil in time." Maureau himself had been working with the population for three years by that time and had learned Spanish to interact with the largely Spanish-speaking population. His plan was to establish free Catholic schooling toward attracting the Catholics in the public schools and to provide clothing for the needy (Maureau 1922). By early 1923, the NCWC had complied with Maureau's request for resources, sending Joseph I. Breen as a representative of the Bureau of Immigration. As with Boone, Breen would represent the NCWC and serve under the direction of the bureau's head, Bruce Mohler. The aim would be to "give a permanent foundation" to work with the Key West Cuban Americans (Burke 1923).

Breen would also serve the Catholics in Tampa and Ybor City. According to Father Joseph Farrell, a Tampa priest, in 1923 there were "nearly 45,000 people of the Latin races, Italian, Spaniards, and Cubans and they are rapidly increasing in numbers. Only a few hundred of them practice their religion" (Farrell 1923). Breen reported that according to the 1920 census 30,000 of the 45,000 Latino/as were "of either Cuban or Spanish extraction," and a number of them attended Tampa's Catholic Church and boys' and girls' high schools, though a large proportion of the Latino/a population ignored the city's Catholic institutions. In Breen's view, Tampa's Catholic problem was due to an impoverished population unable or unwilling to maintain traditional religious practices, lack of Catholic institutional infrastructure and trained staff, and a lack of general funding to assist needy Catholics (Breen 1923).

Consequently, Protestant proselytization efforts were undertaken with some success among the Catholic immigrants. Breen saw the solution as related to improved Americanization efforts:

> It seems to me that the real problem here is one of Americanization and "follow up" which ought to be carried on by the local Catholics. . . . Most of these people know nothing whatever of America or its people they are strange to our customs and our ways and ignorant to an appalling extent of our laws and our government. Many of them know no English at all, they are poor and ignorant and seem to me to be almost ideal cannon fodder for the false and pessimistic teachings of socialism, bolshevism, and other such isms which threaten the future of this nation. (Breen 1923)

Breen believed that the Latino/a Catholics of Tampa presented the church with a "very excellent opportunity for genuine service to both Church and State in the molding of a fine citizenship, devoted and loyal to America and her institutions and to the upbuilding of a strong, militant Catholicity." He recommended creating a day nursery for children, a boys club, and a girls club; holding sewing and cooking classes; luring more religious sisters to teach in the schools; and completing a partially built church in Ybor City. A new school should be built, and a community center, as part "of a general Americanization plan," where an evening night school would enroll adults in classes on English, American history, civics, and naturalization laws. If such a program were not enacted, wrote Breen, "another generation will see in this place 100,000 people without even a trace of their Catholic faith and probably, without any religion of any kind" (Breen 1923). For Breen, this lack of faith meant that the Latino/as would not in fact be properly integrated into the American social and cultural system. Indeed, Catholicism was the matrix of integration into the American system, and Latino/a Catholics could not real-ize the American dream if they did not realize it in the context of Catholicism.

The Bureau of Immigration and Latino/a Catholics in the United States

By 1924, against the protests of the NCWC Bureau of Immigration, legislation dramatically limiting the numbers of immigrants from southern and east-ern Europe became US law. Timothy Matovina points out that as "European immigration declined and the process of their incorporation into American life quickened over the course of the twentieth century, nascent Hispanic immigration accelerated." Mexicans were exempted from the exclusions of the legislation of the 1920s, work in the Southwest was plentiful, and political unrest in Mexico in the wake of president Plutarco Elías Calles's enforcement of the anticlerical articles of that nation's constitution generated a rise in emigration from Mexico to the north. By the 1930s, the Great Depression—combined with nativism in the United States—would lead to a forced repatriation of Mexican immigrants and the illegal deportation of many Mexican American citizens to Mexico (Matovina 2012, 28).

In 1926, Boone had left her post in El Paso and was replaced by Cleofás Calleros, an emigrant from Chihuahua, Mexico, to El Paso. Calleros worked for the NCWC Bureau of Immigration as the Mexican border representative for the next forty-two years, handling over a million migration cases. Calleros himself can be viewed as an example of achievement of the Latino/a Catholic American Dream. Arriving in the United States in 1902, he attended Catholic schools and graduated from Sacred Heart School as valedictorian of his class. He went on to acquire an accounting degree in college. Serving in World War I, Calleros earned a Purple Heart for injuries acquired during the Meuse-Argonne offensive. Upon his return to the United States, he served as chief line clerk for the Santa Fe Railroad and held memberships in dozens of charitable, civic, and veterans' organizations. A historian, he also authored several books on the Southwest and taught citizenship classes to Mexican immigrants for more than fifty years. Underscoring his Catholic Americanism, Calleros once said that "of two things I have always been very proud," are "my altar boy regalia and my army uniform" (Sánchez-Walker 1999, 28–29).

Calleros watched with concern the treatment of Mexicans in the 1920s and 1930s on both sides of the border. He was constantly involved in interpretation and clarification of the law where Mexican immigrants were involved. Historian Marjorie Sánchez-Walker contends that while Calleros was not quite an activist in the modern sense, he did "work to establish a Mexican American society of equal standing with those of the Anglo community. . . . This is not to say that Anglo society was open to Mexican integration, but Calleros embraced the concept of proving Mexicans equal in similar activities" (Sánchez-Walker 1999, 30).

Although Calleros was explicitly instructed to follow a hierarchical chain of command in all of his activities—gaining approval from the NCWC Bureau of Immigration director Bruce Mohler if he sought to initiate any new pursuits—he would occasionally conduct controversial activities without permission if he saw them in ethical terms. For example, he protested without the consent of the NCWC when authorities in El Paso sought to reclassify Mexican Americans as "colored" on documents related to vital statistics. He tried to maintain the status of Mexicans as "white," calling for a citywide protest, "I will spend my last cent to fight such a proposal" (Sánchez-Walker 1999, 30) Hence, Calleros saw Mexican Americanness in terms of being white and not being classified as "colored" due to the social, legal, and economic status such a classification would confer. At this time, the Catholic church itself was segregated into black and white, so it made some sense that he would work outside institutional religious structures to maintain Mexican American whiteness. Fulfillment of the Latino/a American dream, in Calleros's view, required classification as white.

By 1933, Sánchez-Walker notes, the Immigration Bureau of the NCWC at El Paso "had earned the 'complete confidence of [US government] officials' to handle needy cases that fell outside the scope of the Immigration and Naturalization Service (INS). Improved relations between the NCWC and INS signified a sharp contrast to the attitude prevailing towards the Bureau in its first ten years of service. However, by this time immigration policy in the U.S. had become more exclusionary. Mexican policy had shifted in only a decade from relatively open to one of exclusion and deportation. Once deported, readmission to the U.S. was almost impossible. Hence, by 1933, most people seeking assistance from the NCWC sought to secure alien residence or validate their citizenship status, toward preventing deportation" (Sánchez-Walker 1999, 67, 72).

The Bishops' Conference and the Bracero Program

The Bracero program, officially called the Farm Labor Transportation Program, ran from 1942 to 1964 and brought about five million contract workers into the United States during those years. Undocumented workers also crossed the border into the United States at this time, and even after the program ended, such undocumented migration continued (Matovina 2012, 28). Although the Mexican government was skeptical of the so-called Bracero program from the start, given the abuses of Mexican workers in the United States throughout the early twentieth century, they signed the agreement starting the program in August 1942, allowing Mexican workers temporary contract employment. The agreement was intended to have Mexican workers supplement rather than replace domestic workers, and stipulated that guest workers be provided transportation, a minimum wage of 30 cents an hour, and housing and medical treatment. The Farm Security Administration of the US Department of Agriculture was charged with overseeing the program, but its efforts were inadequate. Housing and sanitation were subpar, food was of low quality, and there was a lack of community and recreational facilities. Hence, it is no surprise that the Mexican government suspended recruitment for the program, and the United States renegotiated the agreement so that the Mexican workers would receive wages, housing, and medical care matching that of other US agricultural workers. The program reached a peak between 1955 and 1959 when about a half a million guest workers labored in thirty-eight states. By the 1960s, the need for workers diminished, and the program ended for all practical purposes in 1963 (Jones 1945; O'Brien 2005, 140–41).

As Monsignor George G. Higgins, director of the Social Action Department of the Bishops' Conference, recognized, the Bracero program not only set up a temporary nonnational workforce that was easily abused by growers, but it essentially was "a form of indentured servitude that is contrary to American principles" (Higgins 1973, 1977; O'Brien 2005, 141). Braceros were segregated both economically and physically from the rest of the population and were viewed as racially inferior. Additionally, their status as "temporary" excluded them from fully accessing middle-class status, the educational system, and citizenship—hence, the program barred Latino/as from the American Dream.

Although officially eliminated in 1964, the Bracero program was phased out over the next three years and, in 1968, the flow of braceros dwindled to zero. Its elimination coincided with passage of the Immigration and Nationality Act of 1965, and the implementation of a cap on Western Hemisphere migration (120,000 annually)—the first of its kind—that limited the number of immigrants from Latin America into the United States every year. In 1976, Congress further limited Western Hemisphere immigration by incorporating a 20,000 per country cap and eliminating the rights of minors to sponsor the immigration of parents (Massey 1995, 639).

The tightening of regulations with respect to admissions into the United States from Mexico and Central America did not stop migrants from trying to enter the United States, but merely proscribed them from legally doing so. As sociologist Douglas Massey puts it, "When avenues for legal entry were suddenly curtailed after 1965, the migratory flows did not disappear but simply continued without authorization or documentation" (Massey and Pren 2012, 4). This contributed to an increase in the population of unauthorized migrants from Latin America living in the United States, which jumped from negligible in 1965 to nearly ten million in 2008. Illegal immigration from this geographical region thus accounted for about 80 percent of the total unauthorized immigration to the United States during that period (Massey and Pren 2012, 2).

Paired with the increase in illegal immigration, legal immigration from Latin America also grew substantially. The Pew Research Center estimates the number of Hispanics who lived in the United States in the year 2012 at fifty-four million, a sixfold increase from thirty years earlier (Brown 2014). Key to understanding this surge is the 1965 law to exempt close family members from the per-country cap. Although there was a cap on Western Hemisphere migration, spouses, minor children, and parents of American citizens were exempt from the numerical ceiling. These exemptions laid the groundwork for "chain migration," a trend that intensified as legal immigration from Latin America continued and incentives for US citizenship became pronounced (Massey and Pren 2012; Tichenor 2002).[4]

The Catholic Church and Hispanic Ministry

The growth of both legal and illegal immigration from Latin America posed a significant challenge to the hierarchy of the United States, particularly given the large proportion of newly arriving Hispanics who were Catholic. The bishops' response to this population mirrored commitments they had made to European immigrants earlier in the century. Reflecting on these similarities, the bishops wrote in their pastoral letter *The Hispanic Presence* (1983) that the earlier European-focused outreach "must inspire in the Church's approach to recent Hispanic immigrants and migrants a similar authority, compassion, and decisiveness" (US Conference of Catholic Bishops 2012b, no. 4). Much like these earlier waves of migrants, which brought with them large numbers of low-skilled, non-English-speaking Catholics, the American hierarchy recognized an obligation to help "gain for Hispanics participation in the benefits of society . . . to secure their empowerment in our democracy and the political participation that is their right and duty" (US Conference of Catholic Bishops 2012b, 15).

Through Catholic churches, schools, and related institutions, the hierarchy provided resources to the Hispanic community that would help them to grow and thrive in an American context. These efforts aimed at providing for the needs of newly arrived Hispanics, so as to ensure that their religious, spiritual, and material needs were met, and to remove obstacles that would prevent this from happening. Although such efforts became pronounced in the 1970s and 1980s, the foundations for this kind of outreach were established decades earlier.

In 1945, Archbishop Robert Lucey of San Antonio coordinated the first national effort in Hispanic ministry with the founding of the Bishops' Committee for the Spanish Speaking. His work in this field led to the establishment of diocesan Catholic councils across the United States that aimed at enhancing ministry efforts among Hispanics. The Hispanic office founded by Archbishop Lucey was moved to Washington, DC, in 1968, and was established as the "Division for the Spanish Speaking" in the Social Action Department at the NCCB/USCC. Seven years later it was elevated to the status of a Secretariat for the Spanish Speaking (Matovina 2012).

It was through this secretariat that a series of "Encuentros" were planned and executed in 1972, 1977, and 1985. They focused on the continued evangelization of Hispanics and sought to construct an infrastructure in the church and society that would empower their community. At their first meeting, church leadership made the commitment to develop a pastoral plan of action aimed at developing structures within the church and establish pastoral institutes across the United States, hire bilingual staff on the national and local level, and push for more Hispanic bishops and related forms of Hispanic leadership (Division for the Spanish Speaking 1972). Efforts to develop such a plan continued throughout the Encuentro process, with the findings from the third Encuentro functioning as a framework for the development of the pastoral plan. The capstone of this process was the production of the *National Pastoral Plan for Hispanic Ministry* that responded "to the reality and needs of the Hispanic people in their efforts to achieve integration and participation in the life of our Church and in the building of the Kingdom of God" (US Catholic Conference 1987, 2).

Efforts by the hierarchy to establish an infrastructure in the church that would respond to the needs of the Hispanic community have borne fruit, but they have not always been successful in achieving the overarching objectives that initiated these efforts in the first place. On the positive side, prior to the first Encuentro only three Hispanic bishops oversaw dioceses in the United States, but by the time of the third Encuentro the number of Hispanic bishops had increased to seventeen. At the time of this essay twenty Hispanic bishops had been appointed to lead dioceses in the United States.[5] By 2001, over 75 percent of the dioceses had established an office for Hispanic ministry and over four thousand parishes provided pastoral services to Hispanics in Spanish (US Conference of Catholic Bishops 2003, 7). In 2008, the United

States Conference of Catholic Bishops reorganized the Conference, at which point they established the Committee on Cultural Diversity in the Church and set as one of the priorities of the United States Conference of Catholic Bishops the "recognition of cultural diversity with a special emphasis on Hispanic ministry in the Spirit of Encuentro 2000" (US Conference of Catholic Bishops 2010, 9). While one might argue that officially establishing such a priority only in 2008 was done decades too late, in reality the bishops' work on behalf of Hispanic Catholics has been ongoing for some time.

While the bishops have made important strides toward responding to the needs of Hispanics living in the United States, recent research published by the Pew Forum has raised reason for some concern. This research has pointed to the important role that Hispanics play in the life of the contemporary American church, but it simultaneously highlights the difficulty of maintaining a strong Catholic identity among this population. As reported in their *U.S. Religious Landscape Survey,* since 1972 the Catholic share of the total population has remained steady at about 25 percent. While this proportional consistency suggests a stable picture of the American church, it hides demographic changes that will have a long-lasting effect on American Catholic identity and practice. Their findings point to some trends related to the formation of young Catholics; many appear to have abandoned the faith in favor of another religious tradition or have become largely indifferent to religion altogether. While 31 percent of Americans were raised Catholic, only 24 percent currently define themselves as such. Taken as a portion of the entire population, Pew reports that approximately 10 percent of the American population was raised Catholic but has since left the Church (Pew Research Center 2008, 6–8).

What has helped to keep the Catholic share of the population constant since the early 1970s is the influx of Hispanic Catholics, primarily from Mexico and Latin America. Mexican migrants, who make up a plurality of immigrants coming to the United States (34 percent), are overwhelmingly Catholic (72 percent) in their affiliation. Of immigrants coming from other countries, slightly more than half identify with the Catholic faith (51 percent) (Pew Research Center 2008, 51). While nearly half of adult Catholics under the age of forty are Latino/a, they account for only 17 percent of Catholics aged sixty or older (Pew Research Center 2008, 8). Overall, Hispanics continue to make up an increasingly larger proportion of the Catholic Church in the United States, with one-third of all Catholics being Hispanic (Pew Research Center 2014, 10). Nevertheless, the proportion of Hispanics who are Catholic has fallen in recent years; as recently as 2010 the Pew Forum estimated that approximately 67 percent of Hispanics were Catholic, a number that has dropped to 55 percent by 2014. Almost one-quarter of Hispanic adults are *former* Catholics (Pew Research Center 2014, 5–11). Most of these ex-Catholic Hispanics have either converted to Evangelical Protestantism or have entered the ranks of the religious nones.

Pinpointing why the church has failed to keep Hispanics within the fold is difficult, but it is clearly important for the bishops and the wider church to wrestle with this problem further. Fifty-seven percent of Hispanics who were raised Catholic but are now unaffiliated cite a loss of belief in church teaching as being the primary reason for their departure, while nearly half of Hispanics raised Catholic but who converted to Protestantism reported that they found a church that helps its members more as the reason for leaving (Pew Research Center 2014, 14). Secularization, the failure to provide more effective catechetical training, and not adequately meeting the psychological, social, or material needs of Hispanics—these are all possible explanations for the decline in the Hispanic Catholic population in recent years. Given the significance of this population for the Catholic Church in the United States, failing to adjust accordingly in the future could have a substantially negative effect on its future makeup and size.

How effectively the bishops, not to mention the myriad church organizations, lay leaders, and related Catholic associations, respond to this matter of the retention of Hispanics remains an open question. What is apparent, however, is the important role that Hispanics have in the demographic makeup of the church. Part of this has to do with the comparatively high reproduction rates within Latino/a communities, but it also has to do with the influx of migrants into the United States from countries that have relatively high Catholic populations. This clearly points to the central role that immigration has for the church, a role that is made more complex when the politics of immigration comes into play.

Hispanics, Immigration, and the American Bishops

For Hispanics legally present in the country, the work of the bishops has often focused on the economic, political, and cultural disparities affecting this community and the need to provide resources to assist in increasing its members' upward mobility. This is evident through the range of social services that Catholic charities, hospitals, and other organizations provide to Hispanic communities, not to mention the extensive advocacy efforts they have undertaken on poverty- and employment-related issues. Themes expressed in a statement made by the eight Hispanic bishops of the United States in 1977 typified this commitment. Here they dedicated the church to the betterment of Hispanics everywhere and "denounced the many injustices which continue to afflict our people: institutional and personal racism both from within and from without the church; discrimination in language, culture and education; political under-representation; poor housing and few job opportunities" (Spanish Speaking Bishops of the United States 1977).

Viewed through the prism of the American Dream, the bishops' efforts to improve the material conditions of Latino/a communities and enhance their political and social standing in the United States aimed at helping Latino/as move from the margins of American life to its center. Archbishop Joseph Bernardin of Chicago made this obligation explicit when, during the convocation of the Second Encuentro, he stated that the church must, as a matter of strict justice, "help people in their struggle to overcome everything which condemns them to a marginal existence," including political powerlessness, economic injustice, and inadequate educational opportunities (Bernardin 1978, 50).

The obstacles preventing the move from the margins to the mainstream are particularly acute for Hispanics and other migrants living in the United States illegally. As historian Mae Ngai argues in her book *Impossible Subjects*, while the illegal alien is physically present here she "remains at the outermost point of exclusion from national membership" (Ngai 2004, 6). By virtue of their doubly marginalized existence in the United States, unauthorized Hispanic migrants are particularly vulnerable to exploitation, abuse, and harassment. Given the bishops' emphasis on empowering disempowered communities, it is not surprising that they focused extensively on this population as its presence became more visible and the "threat" that it posed to American life and culture became more widely discussed.

Unauthorized migration became a contentious topic by the early 1970s and elicited a predictable response from some members of Congress who spearheaded efforts to confront and control it. Consideration of space prohibits us from going into detail here on either the legislative and political debates that occurred following the upsurge of illegal immigration or the bishops' involvement in these debates. Both topics have been addressed elsewhere (Scribner 2013; Tichenor 2002). A brief overview of both aspects will have to suffice. In particular, we will highlight some of the primary themes that have informed the bishops' efforts in this arena from the mid-1970s to the present, with an eye to how they affected Hispanics. Given the high proportion of unauthorized migrants who came from Mexico and Central

America—unauthorized migration from Mexico alone counts for approximately 52 percent of all unauthorized migrants—the bishops' legislative efforts would necessarily have an outsized effect on these populations (Pew Research Center 2014, 16).

Between 1971, when representative Peter Rodino (D-NJ) initiated hearings aimed at addressing the problem of illegal immigration, through 1986, when the Immigration Reform and Control Act became law, Congress repeatedly attempted and failed to enact meaningful legislation related to the immigration issue. Most of these efforts focused on the implementation of employer sanctions so as to eliminate the magnet that promoted unauthorized migration to the United States (Hohl 1973, 323). The failure to pass legislation during this period contributed to Congress's decision to establish the Select Commission on Immigration and Refugee Policy (SCIRP) in 1978. In its final report to Congress, SCIRP recommended closing "the back door to undocumented/illegal migration, [while] opening the front door a little more to accommodate legal migration in the interests of this country," and clarifying the objectives and the processes through which US immigration policies could be adjudicated more fairly (Select Commission 1981, 5). To do so, the committee report promoted increased funding for the border patrol, the establishment of employer sanctions that would make it illegal for employers to hire undocumented workers, the provision of additional visas that would help to clear preexisting backlogs, and the implementation of an amnesty for migrants who were currently in the country illegally.

The recommendations made by SCIRP in their final report provided the general framework for the Immigration Reform and Control Act (IRCA), which was signed into law by Ronald Reagan in the fall of 1986. While legalizing millions of unauthorized migrants living in the United States and authorizing enforcement measures to limit future illegal immigration, it provided for only a temporary pause in the debate that raged over immigration. It was expected that a generous legalization program would "clean the slate" by significantly reducing the number of people living in irregular status, and enforcement measures would prevent it from happening in the future. Such was not the case. By the early 1990s concerns about illegal immigration resurfaced and calls to reinforce border security and build a wall to protect America from a foreign invasion of "illegals" became widely voiced. The federal government responded to these demands by substantially increasing resources for enforcement over the next two decades. By 2012, spending by the federal government's two primary immigration enforcement agencies— US Customs and Border Protection and the US Immigration and Customs

Enforcement—surpassed $17.9 billion, which is "nearly fifteen times the spending level of the US Immigration and Naturalization Service when IRCA was enacted" (Meissner et al. 2013, 2). Despite the increase in enforcement measures, the number of unauthorized immigrants grew from a few million in the early 1990s to over eleven million by 2012.

Following the uptick in illegal immigration beginning in the 1990s, many of the same issues came to the forefront that had occurred prior to the passage of IRCA, with the question of what to do with the millions of people living in the country illegally being central to discussions surrounding this issue. From the mid-1970s onward, the bishops consistently supported a legalization process for unauthorized migrants and became increasingly critical of "enforcement only" or "enforcement first" approaches that had become the standard approach to dealing with unauthorized migration (Higgins 1975; US Conference of Catholic Bishops 2003, nos. 78–80). As early as 1975, Bishop James Rausch, then general secretary of the Bishops' Conference, for example, argued that enacting an employer sanctions strategy prior to an amnesty would lead to the dislocation of hard-working immigrants who were members of long-standing communities and who had families who were dependent on them for their basic economic sustenance. Such a consequence would be "inhumane" and "immoral" (Rausch 1975).

The bishops' support for a legalization program and a path to citizenship rested on their concern that those living in an unauthorized status were subject to abuse and exploitation. It was also closely tied to the conviction that failing to do so would lead to the dislocation of millions of migrants who had lived in the United States—in some cases for decades—and promote the separation of families (Rausch 1975; US Conference of Catholic Bishops 2003, nos. 68–71). While never couching their calls for an amnesty or, in later years, for a legalization with a path to citizenship in the language of the American Dream, one can understand the logic of such a connection through that lens. Legalization would bring unauthorized populations from the sidelines to the mainstream and would remove the risk of deportation, thus providing these populations with an opportunity to make it in America. Absent such a process, unauthorized migrants are effectively restricted to a marginal status in American life. Given the bishops' emphasis on the family as a building block of society, keeping families together and emphasizing reunification in the immigration process will provide the institutional structures for individual immigrants to succeed. Finally, implementing a temporary worker program, provided that it included protections against abuse and exploitation, would enable migrants to come to the United States, work, and have access to opportunities and freedoms not available to them if they stayed in their home country (US Catholic Conference 1987, no. 6; US Conference of Catholic Bishops 2003, nos. 72–6). It would also allow them to more effectively provide for their families, both here and in their country of origin.

This last issue, the expansion and use of employment-based immigration—and particularly of a temporary variety—is an issue with which church leadership has struggled. The bishops had been long troubled by abuses that occurred in programs that brought temporary workers into the United States for seasonal or short-term employment, and repeatedly warned against creating new ones or expanding already existing programs (Hoye 1982). Too often these types of programs benefited the powerful at the expense of the poor, and the farm owner rather than the migrant farm worker. In this vein, Father Silvano Maria Tomasi noted during testimony at the US Catholic Bishops' Committee for the Bicentennial that the upside to a temporary worker program for those in positions of power "is the total control of the worker: no or very limited access to social benefits, no unemployment assistance, an easy dismissal in case of economic crisis," and that because of the power differential at play here, "most illegal immigrants ... suffer all the negative consequences of fear, insecurity, marginality and exploitation" (Tomasi 1975).[6]

Speaking before Congress in 1975, Archbishop Robert Sanchez of Santa Fe made an explicit comparison between efforts to institute a new temporary worker program to the Bracero program, claiming that "arguments against the latter program, which persuaded Congress to put an end to the program in 1964 apply with even greater force to the recruitment proposal" outlined in proposed legislation (Sanchez 1976a). Similar concerns continued into the 1980s as the debate over temporary worker programs received heightened attention. Nevertheless, the bishops eventually warmed to the idea of implementing a program that would provide an increase in work-related visas so long as proper protections were put into place (US Conference of Catholic Bishops 2003, no. 73). With the proper protections in place, these types of visas could help to respond to the needs of the domestic marketplace while simultaneously providing opportunities to migrants who want to come here and work.

Not surprisingly, critics of the bishops' immigration position provide a very different perspective on the benefits of a legalization process, or with the suggestion that employment-based visas be increased to provide more opportunities for foreign-born laborers to come to the United States. One of the central reasons for their skepticism centers on the conviction that these types of programs would disadvantage native workers and eliminate opportunities that would otherwise be available to them without the added competition of foreign-born labor. Certainly, while such proposals would benefit Latino/a, Asian, and other migrants who are in the United States illegally—a legalization process would after all provide an opportunity to live and work in the United States without fear of reprisal—these same legislative proposals hurt native-born workers and particularly those who occupied low-skilled employment. Legalization would create competition with native-born workers, thus making it more difficult for them to be competitive in the market place and thus disadvantaging them in their pursuit of the American dream (Camarota and Zeigler 2013).

Additional criticisms have focused on the way in which the bishops' proposals would undermine the rule of law and lay the groundwork, not for a solution to the problem but for an expansion of unauthorized migration in the future: Why bother dealing with the hassle of the legal process if one knows that he or she can enter illegally and still be awarded with legal status sometime down the road? (Addington 2013; Cotton 2013). Rewarding behavior of this sort by providing an amnesty threatens to erode the rule of law in other areas of American life. If the federal government is going to overlook and even reward illegal behavior, what area of law can Americans expect will be respected? Society depends on an array of positive laws that help to create uniformity, predictability, and a healthy social order. Disregarding positive laws that aim at building up a healthy social order, including immigration laws, runs the risk of introducing a "socially destructive anarchy" (Holloway 2013). In the long run, undermining the social order only serves to damage the economic, social, and cultural bonds that provide America with the unique character that makes possible the American Dream, for native or foreign born.

A more cynical line of criticism that extends beyond a purely economic or philosophical sort has targeted the bishops directly. Such a line of attack argues that at its core the bishops' primary motivation for supporting a legalization process for undocumented, and particularly Hispanic, migrants is not due to social justice, but self-interest. As one critic, a Catholic himself, put it, "immigration reform as it now stands is a baldly political business, and that's as true of the bishops as it is of the politicians: votes for the latter; devotees for the former" (Miner 2013). In short, given that the Catholic Church has in recent decades failed to properly fold young, native-born Catholics into the faith and has, as a consequence, lost many of them to other religions or to none at all, there is need for a new constituency. The influx of Hispanics provides such an audience; by advocating on behalf of the millions of Catholic-heavy and undocumented Hispanic migrants, the church could ensure that their pews, not to mention their coffers, would remain filled for some time to come.

While this criticism makes some intuitive sense, it is based on a narrow historical horizon that fails to appreciate the length of time that the bishops have engaged Hispanics living in the United States. Since the establishment of the NCWC and the founding of the Bureau of Immigration in the early 1920s, the bishops provided support not only to Europeans who arrived in the various port cities along the East Coast, but also to Hispanics as they crossed the border from Mexico into the United States and other Latino/a communities living in parts of Florida. The bishops' efforts in this regard focused on the idea of a distinct form of Catholic Americanization, which included an embrace of American middle-class values centered on achievement of the American Dream: attaining middle-class status, acquiring citizenship, achieving English language proficiency, and practicing an officially approved Catholicism. Within a few short decades the bishops initiated efforts in the arena of Hispanic ministry, with the hope of providing for the material and, in particular, spiritual needs of these communities. With the emergence of illegal immigration as a problem in the 1970s, advocacy efforts in support of amnesty and, later, the more robust notion of comprehensive reform became central to the institutional church's activities. All of these efforts took place long before any demographic crisis in the church emerged, thus making it difficult to blame the demographic crisis as the reason—a wholly self-interested reason—for the bishops' engagement with Latino/a migrants in recent years.

Conclusion

The Catholic bishops engaged Latino/a communities in different ways during the twentieth century in an attempt to empower these communities in the public square, and simultaneously nurture their commitment to the church. Efforts by the hierarchy aimed at helping Latino/as "make it" in America and better access the American dream. These efforts have not been an unadulterated success; a variety of obstacles that originated both inside and outside the church have hindered the bishops' ability to fully realize their broader objectives of empowering Latino/as living in the United States.

Prior to World War II Catholics were often on the margin of American life looking in on a largely Anglo-Saxon culture. At the time, the Protestant majority was both suspicious of Catholics, whose tradition they often saw at odds with the American political tradition, and hostile to migrants originating from areas other than northern Europe. Caught in the middle of this tension, American Catholics were often torn between their desire to maintain a distinctive identity and their desire to prove that they were as American as any Protestant. Consequently, Americanization efforts aimed at empowering Latino/a communities in America were at times heavy-handed in their approach, pressuring Latino/as to abandon their cultural and ethnic identity and instead assimilate in such a way as to embody an Anglo-Saxon model of being an American. This emphasis on assimilation carried with it the danger of undercutting Latino/a culture and failed to promote a more even-handed effort to integrate these populations into American life. Taken to the extreme, Americanization efforts promised access to the American Dream on the condition that Latino/as abandon their ethnic cultural identity, and in doing so become more fully American.

In addition to their socially and politically oriented Americanization efforts, by midcentury the bishops' pastoral outreach became more pronounced. These efforts have not always realized the overarching objective that initiated them in the first place: ensuring that Latino/as remain comfortably established in the Catholic community. Recently published research has shown that the success of these efforts has been decidedly mixed. On the one hand, church leadership has significantly developed and expanded the infrastructure charged with responding to the spiritual and religious needs of Latino/as. Nevertheless, the number of Latino/as who identify as Catholics has decreased rather substantially in recent years, with as many as one-quarter of adult Latino/as living in the United States identifying as former Catholics. It is not entirely clear why Latino/as are leaving the church, but it is likely due to a mix of factors, including secularization, a breakdown within the church's catechetical initiatives, and perhaps even a failure by the church to respond to some of the more basic material and psychological needs of these communities.

Finally, attempts by the bishops to push forward their legislative agenda have met with resistance from sources outside the Church, which is nothing new, and from within it. Catholic intellectuals, political leaders, and even the average, church-attending layperson have in recent decades shown a willingness to publicly object to the bishops' support for comprehensive immigration reform, the DREAM Act, and related legislation. The widespread resistance offered by influential lay Catholics points to the tenuous authority that, in practice, the bishops hold over the American Catholic Church. Vocal opposition by lay Catholics to the bishops' legislative priorities would be difficult to fathom in the earlier part of the twentieth century, but it is now an increasingly commonplace phenomenon. Part of this is attributable to a growing confidence within the lay community following Vatican II, but much has to do with more generalized changes occurring in American religious life during this same period.

By midcentury the Catholic community as a whole began to move from the margins of American life to its mainstream; the integration of Catholics into the wider culture occurred rapidly. With this shift, long-standing religious tensions that had once functioned as the primary point of division between Catholics and their non-Catholic religious contemporaries began to wane, a transition indicative of a much broader trend. In the post–World War II world, the denominational structure that had functioned as the primary marker of religious identity and belonging became "less significant as a basis for social and cultural tensions and divisions" (Wuthnow 1990, 94). In its place, political affiliation became a more important factor that determined who cooperated with whom and on what issues. The religion scholar Robert Wuthnow highlighted the importance of this shift when he noted that "the division between religious liberals and conservatives is one that cuts across denominational lines, rather than pitting one set of denominations against another" (Wuthnow 1990, 221). Political action was driven less by religious bonds created by a shared denominational identity and instead became increasingly correlated with those who are politically like-minded but of a potentially religiously different commitments.

The tendency for political ideology to trump religious identity, paired with the increase in political polarization in American life, has often left the bishops torn between competing segments of the church. The loss of consensus within the church that could provide a general framework for understanding and engaging political issues—from pro-life to social-justice-oriented causes—creates problems for the bishops when they try to garner grassroots support, as such efforts simultaneously fan the flames of opposition in other segments of the church. On issues like immigration that break along partisan lines, this fragmentation is crucial for understanding the loss of authority within religious institutions. Given the divisions that exist between Catholics on contentious political issues, it is easy to understand why the laity might resist pronouncements of bishops that offend that layperson's political sensibilities. It is more difficult to figure out how religious identity can again play a role in defining a coherent philosophical framework that reflects the church's moral tradition and simultaneously overcomes political differences between Catholics that in recent decades has become entrenched.

Notes

The ideas expressed in this essay do not necessarily reflect the perspective of the Catholic bishops of the United States or of the United States Conference of Catholic Bishops, but are the views of the authors.

1. The US Catholic Bishops have traditionally used the term "Hispanic" rather than "Latino/a." In their 2002 document "Encuentro and Mission" the former term was adopted by the bishops as a way to help "define a people with a common identity, vision, and mission." For the purpose of this essay these terms will be used interchangeably (US Conference of Catholic Bishops 2012a).

2. As the Bureau of Immigration staff formulated immigration policy in 1920, they noted "Mexican immigration should not be dealt with by the bureau at this time until preliminary studies of the problem by the Social Action Department were completed" ("Immediate Steps to Be Taken" 1920, 2).

3. Boone, who had extensive experience working in immigration, estimated between June 1920 and June 1921, "a little over 30,000 cases were legitimately admitted to the United States over the Mexican border, amounting to 600 a week divided among twelve stations" along the border, including Eagle Pass and Laredo (Boone 1922).

4. The Immigration Reform and Control Act of 1986 made millions of unauthorized immigrants eligible for citizenship. Soon thereafter Congress began to place restrictions on eligibility benefits for social services, generally restricting such benefits to citizens. Simultaneously, Congress reduced protections for noncitizens (e.g., curtailing judicial protections for noncitizens), thus incentivizing them to become citizens. This enabled them to sponsor immediate family members back home outside the cap, thus increasing immigration to the United States.

5. For the most comprehensive analysis of the role of Latino/as in the American Catholic Church, see Matovina (2012).

6. Tomasi was then the director of the Center for Migration Studies in New York and since has risen to the position of Permanent Observer of the Holy See to the United Nations in Geneva.

References

Addington, David. 2013. "Encouraging Lawful Immigration and Discouraging Unlawful Immigration." *Heritage Foundation Backgrounder* 2786 (March 27).

Appleby, K. 2013. "Moving Forward: Next Steps toward Immigration Reform." In *On Strangers No Longer: Perspectives on the Historic U.S-Mexican Catholic Bishops' Pastoral Letter on Migration*, edited by Todd Scribner and J. Kevin Appleby. New York: Paulist Press.

Bernardin, J. 1978. "Convocation." *Proceedings of the II Encuentro Nacional Hispano de Pastoral*. Washington, DC: United States Catholic Conference.

Blaire, S. 2011. "USCCB Labor Day Statement: Human Costs and Moral Challenges of a Broken Economy." *Origins* 41 (September 8).

Boone, C. 1922. December 17. Tentative outline of plan for N.C.W.C. program on the Mexican border. National Catholic Welfare Conference, Office of the General Secretary Records, Box 39, Folder 26. American Catholic History Research Center and University Archives, Catholic University, Washington, DC.

Breen, J. I. 1923. January 17. [Letter to Bruce Mohler] National Catholic Welfare Conference, Office of the General Secretary Records, Box 39, Folder 26. American Catholic History Research Center and University Archives, Catholic University, Washington, DC.

Brown, A. 2014. "The U.S. Hispanic Population Has Increased Sixfold since 1970." Pew Research Center (February 14).

Burke, J. J. 1923. January 3. [Letter to Father A. L. Maureau], National Catholic Welfare Conference, Office of the General Secretary Records, Box 39, Folder 26, American Catholic History Research Center and University Archives, Catholic University, Washington, DC.

Camarota, Steven, and Karen Zeigler. 2013. *Immigrant Gains and Native Job Losses in the Market, 2000–2013*. Washington, DC: Center for Immigration Studies (July).

Campese, G. 2007. "Beyond Ethnic and National Imagination: Toward a Catholic Theology of U.S. Immigration." In *Religion and Social Justice for Immigrants*, edited by Pierrette Hondagneu-Sotelo, 175–90. New Brunswick, NJ: Rutgers University Press.

———. 2012. "The Irruption of Migrants: Theology of Migration in the 21st Century." *Theological Studies* 73 (6).

Cotton, Tom. 2013. "It's the House Bill or Nothing on Immigration." *Wall Street Journal*, July 10.

Deck, A. 2008. "A Response to MT Dávila." *Catholic Theological Society of America Proceedings* 63 (9).

Division for the Spanish Speaking. 1972. *Conclusions for the First Encuentro*. Washington, DC: United States Catholic Conference.

Farrell, J. 1923. February 12. [Letter to Bishop Patrick Barry] National Catholic Welfare Conference, Office of the General Secretary, Box 39, Folder 26. American Catholic History Research Center and University Archives, Catholic University, Washington, DC.

Gerstle, Gary. 2013. "Acquiescence or Transformation: Divergent Paths of Political Incorporation in America." In *Outsiders No More? Models of Immigrant Political Incorporation*, edited by Jennifer Hochschid, Jacqueline Chattopadhyay, Claudine Gay, and Michael Jones-Correa, 306–20. New York: Oxford University Press.

Groody, D. 2009. "Theology in an Age of Migration." *National Catholic Reporter*. September 14. http://ncronline.org/news/global/theology-age-migration.

Higgins, G. 1973. July 9. And August 1, 1977. "Why Revive the Old Bracero Program?" *The Yardstick* (syndicated column).

———. 1975. "Testimony Regarding Illegal Immigrants." *Origins* 4 (1).

Hohl, D. 1973. "The Illegal Alien and the Western Hemisphere Immigration Dilemma." *International Migration Review* 7 (3).

———. 1982. "The Status of Undocumented Aliens." *Origins* 12 (15).

———. 1986a. Letter to Congress, October 15. United States Catholic Conference Files. Washington, DC: United States Conference of Catholic Bishops.

———. 1986b. Letter to the House of Representatives, September 25. United States Catholic Conference Files. Washington, DC: United States Conference of Catholic Bishops.

Holloway, Carson. 2013. "Illegal Immigration and the Rule of Law." *Public Discourse*. The Witherspoon Institute. December 1. Retrieved from http://www.thepublicdiscourse.com/2010/12/2109/.

"Immediate Steps to Be Taken." 1920. December 18. National Catholic Welfare Conference, Office of the General Secretary Records, Box 39, Folder 25. American Catholic History Research Center and University Archives, Catholic University, Washington, DC.

Jones, R. C. 1945. "Mexican War Workers in the United States: The Mexico-United States Manpower Recruiting Program and its Operation." Washington, DC: Division of Labor and Social Information. National Catholic Welfare Conference, Office of the General Secretary Records, Box 31, Folder 7. American Catholic History Research Center and University Archives, Catholic University, Washington, DC.

Kelly, T. 1977. "U.S. Catholic Conference Reacts to Carter Immigration Plan." *Origins* 7 (10).

———. 1982. "Testimony before the Republican and Democratic Party Platform Committees." *Origins* 10 (5).

Lemay, M. 1989. "Assessing the Impact of IRCA's Employer Sanctions Provisions." In *In Defense of the Alien*, vol. 12, edited by Lydio Tomasi, 146–70. New York: Center for Migration Studies.

Massey, D. 1995. "The New Immigration and Ethnicity in the United States." *Population and Development Review* 21 (3).

———. 2005. "Backfire at the Border: Why Enforcement without Legalization Cannot Stop Illegal Immigration." *Trade Policy Analysis* 29 (June 13). Washington DC: Cato Institute.

Massey, D., and J. Philips. 1999. "The New Labor Market: Immigrants and Wages after IRCA." *Demography* 36 (2): 233–46.

Massey, D., and K. Pren. 2012. "Unintended Consequences of US Immigration Policy: Explaining the Post-1965 Surge from Latin America." *Population and Development Review* 38 (1).

Matovina, T. M. 2012. *Latino Catholicism: Transformation in America's Largest Church.* Princeton, NJ: Princeton University Press.

Maureau, A. L. 1922. October 26. Condition of Cuban Catholicity in Key West, Florida.

Mazzenga, M., and Todd Scribner. 2009. The U.S. Conference of Catholic Bishops and Immigration. American Catholic History Classroom. Retrieved from http://cuomeka.wrlc.org/exhibits/show/immigration/background/immigration-intro.

Meissner, D., D. Kerwin, M. Chishti, and Clare Bergeron. 2013. *Immigration Enforcement in the United States: The Rise of a Formidable Machinery.* Washington, DC: Migration Policy Institute.

Miner, Brad. 2013. "Why the Catholic Bishops Are Wrong on Immigration." *Catholic Thing.* July 29. Retrieved from http://www.thecatholicthing.org/columns/2013/why-the-catholic-bishops-are-wrong-on-immigration.

National Catholic Welfare Conference. Office of the General Secretary. Box 39, Folder 26. American Catholic History Research Center and University Archives, Catholic University, Washington, DC.

National Catholic Welfare Conference. 1928. Mexicans in the United States; a report and brief survey. Washington, DC. Bressette, L., National Catholic Welfare Conference, Social Action Department Records, Box 31, Folder 7. American Catholic History Research Center and University Archives, Catholic University, Washington, DC.

National Conference of Catholic Bishops. 1986. *Economic Justice for All: Pastoral Letter on Catholic Social Teaching and the U.S. Economy.* Washington, DC: US Catholic Conference.

Ngai, M. M. 2004. *Impossible Subjects: Illegal Aliens and the Making of Modern America.* Princeton, NJ: Princeton University Press.

O'Brien, J. J. 2005. *George G. Higgins and the Quest for Worker Justice: The Evolution of Catholic Social Thought in America.* Lanham, MD: Rowman and Littlefield.

Passel, Jeffrey, D'Vera Cohn, and Ana Gonzalez-Barrera. 2013. *Population Decline of Unauthorized Immigrants Stalls, May Have Reversed.* Washington, DC: Pew Research Center. September 23.

Paul VI. 1975. *Evangelii Nuntiandi.* December 8.

Pew Research Center. 2008. *U.S. Religious Landscape Survey.* February.

———. 2014. *The Shifting Religious Identity of Latinos in the United States.* Washington, DC. May 7.

Rausch, J. 1975. "Illegal Alien Bill Criticized." *Origins* 5 (11).

Sanchez, R. 1976a. "Testimony before the Senate Judiciary Committee's Sub-committee on Immigration and Naturalization." *Origins* 5 (43).

———. 1976b. "USCC Testimony on Proposed Legislation to Reform U.S. Immigration Laws." *Origins* 5 (43).

Sánchez-Walker, M. 1999. "Migration Quicksand: Immigration Law and Immigration Advocates at the El Paso–Ciudad Juárez Border Crossing, 1933–1941." Unpublished PhD diss., Washington State University, Pullman.

Scribner, T. 2013. "Immigration as a 'Sign of the Times': From the Nineteenth Century to the Present." In *"On Strangers No Longer": Perspectives on the Historic U.S.-Mexican Catholic Bishops' Pastoral Letter on Migration*, edited by Todd Scribner and J. Kevin Appleby. New York: Paulist Press.

Select Commission on Immigration and Refugee Policy. 1981. *U.S. Immigration Policy and the National Interest.* Washington, DC: US Government Printing Office.

Slattery, M. J. 1921. June 28. [Letter to John J. Burke]. Burke, J. J. to Slattery, June 30, 1921 [Letter to Michael Slattery]. Slattery, M. J. (July 8) [Letter to John Burke]; Barron, Mr. July 27, 1921 [Letter to Michael Slattery]. National Catholic Welfare Conference Records, Office of the General Secretary, Box 39, Folder 25. American Catholic History Research Center and University Archives, Catholic University, Washington, DC.

Slawson, D. J. 1992. *The Foundation and First Decade of the National Catholic Welfare Council.* Washington, DC: Catholic University of America Press.

Spanish Speaking Bishops of the United States. 1977. "A Message from the U.S. Spanish-Speaking Bishops." *Origins* 7 (11).

Statement on the hiring of Caroline Boone to staff the NCWC immigration program in El Paso. 1922. November. National Catholic Welfare Conference, Office of the General Secretary Records, Box 39, Folder 26. American Catholic History Research Center and University Archives, Catholic University, Washington, DC.

Tichenor, D. J. 2002. *Dividing Lines: The Politics of Immigration Control in America.* Princeton, NJ: Princeton University Press.

Tomasi, S. M. 1975. "The Church and the Problem of Immigration." *Origins* 4 (37).

———. 1985. "Resolution on Immigration Reform." *Origins* 15 (25).

United States Catholic Conference. 1972. *Conclusions of the First Encuentro.* Washington, DC: United States Catholic Conference.

———. 1987. *National Pastoral Plan for Hispanic Ministry*. Washington, DC: United States Catholic Conference.

United States Conference of Catholic Bishops. 2003. *Strangers No Longer: Together on the Journey of Hope*. Washington, DC: United States Conference of Catholic Bishops.

———. 2010. *Embracing the Multicultural Face of God*. Washington, DC: United States Conference of Catholic Bishops.

———. 2012a. "Encuentro and Mission: A Renewed Pastoral Framework for Hispanic Ministry," reprinted in *A New Beginning*. Washington, DC: United States Conference of Catholic Bishops.

———. 2012b. *The Hispanic Presence: Challenge and Commitment*, reprinted in *A New Beginning*. Washington, DC: United States Conference of Catholic Bishops.

Wuthnow, Robert. 1990. *The Restructuring of American Religion*. Princeton, NJ: Princeton University Press.

Changing for the Dream?

Latino/a Religious Change and Socioeconomic Success

Jessica Hamar Martínez and Phillip Connor

Historically, a majority of Latino/as in the United States have identified as Catholic. However, recent evidence shows a shift away from the Catholic Church among Latino/as (Pew Research Center 2014a). The share of Latino/as who are Catholic has declined in recent years, and the shares who are either Protestant or religiously unaffiliated are growing. While the change in religious affiliation is occurring among both foreign-born and native-born Latino/as, the native born are less likely to identify as Catholics than the foreign born.

Previous research suggests that for many ethnic groups with immigrant origins, practicing religion in the United States is part of the process of "becoming American" (Herberg 1960; Hirschman 2004; Kurien 1998). And because the predominant religious identity in the United States is Protestantism, an identity that plays a significant role in the country's history and culture, becoming Protestant can signify incorporation into mainstream American society. Some suggest that for Latino/as in particular, becoming Protestant also has been associated with upward economic mobility (Greeley 1988, 1997), though it is not clear whether Protestant affiliation leads to upward mobility, or vice versa. Others have hypothesized that Protestantism, and particularly Protestant traditions that promote the Prosperity Gospel—or the idea that those who have enough faith in God will be granted health and wealth—provides a theological perspective that helps followers reach toward the American Dream, providing them with tools to succeed in modern America (Lin 2010).

However, other research indicates that perhaps the way toward the American Dream—defined broadly as upward social mobility—is not necessarily to follow the Protestant path, but instead to leave religion behind altogether. In a study of Latino/as in Richmond, Virginia, Cavalcanti and Schleef (2005) found that the religiously unaffiliated experienced higher occupational attainment compared with Catholics and Protestants. Results for educational attainment were more mixed: Both the religiously unaffiliated and mainline Protestants had higher levels of educational attainment than Catholics, while evangelical Protestants had the lowest levels of educational attainment. While this study is based on a fairly small sample of Latino/as in one city within the United States, it suggests a need to further explore the possible relationship between religious nonaffiliation and socioeconomic status attainment.

In recent years, Latino/as as a group have experienced some socioeconomic gains; for example, Latino/as make up a growing share of eighteen- to twenty-four-year-olds enrolled in college (Fry and Lopez 2012). Nonetheless, Latino/as have higher rates of poverty than non-Latino/a white Americans (Lopez and Cohn 2011), and Latino/as were hit hardest by the recent recession in terms of wealth (Kochhar, Fry, and Taylor 2011). For a population that has historically been predominantly Catholic, but among whom we see increasing numbers of Protestants as well as those with no religious affiliation, to what degree—if any—is religion associated with socioeconomic status?

In this chapter, we use data from a 2013 survey of a nationally representative sample of Latino/as, conducted by the Pew Research Center, to examine how Latino/as of different religious groups experience the American Dream, loosely defined in terms of socioeconomic status. First, we briefly summarize previous literature on religious affiliation and religious change among Latino/as. Then we describe the data that we will use for our analysis and present estimates for religious affiliation and religious switching. In subsequent sections, we describe literature on the relationship between religion (namely, religious affiliation and participation) and socioeconomic status. We present results examining how religious affiliation, religious switching, and religious involvement are associated with income, employment status, and educational attainment.

Research on Religious Change among Latino/as

Literature on the religious affiliation of Latino/as is in agreement that Latino/as are predominantly Catholic (Greeley 1988; Hunt 1998, 1999; Perl, Greely, and Gray 2006). Some of this literature suggests, though, that the Catholic share among Latino/as has been shrinking (Greeley 1988, 1997; Hunt 1999). However, whether or not and to what degree the religious profile of Latino/as has changed has not been well established, largely due to a lack of good quality trend data (Hunt 1999; Perl, Greely, and Gray 2006).

Nonetheless, previous research has suggested that the religious profile of Latino/as has shifted in certain ways in recent decades. More than two decades ago, Andrew Greeley was among the first to notice that the Catholic Church was losing Latino/as from its pews. Using data from the General Social Survey (GSS), Greeley (1988) found that as much as 8 percent of the Latino/a Catholic population was leaving the church in the 1970s and 1980s. Greeley updated his analysis in 1997, extending it to the mid-1990s, and found further decline. In 1999, Hunt also extended Greeley's analysis of the GSS into the 1990s and also found a decline in the proportion of Latino/as who were Catholic.

A recent report from the Pew Research Center (2014a), drawing on three recent sources of trend data, suggests the share of Latino/as who are Catholic has declined by anywhere from eight to thirteen percentage points in less than a decade. This religious change among Latino/as is likely attributable to a variety of factors. Among Latino/a immigrants, for example, the religious profile is likely affected by religious change in Latin America more broadly, as Protestantism grows in several Latin American countries (Martin 1990; Stoll 1990; Pew Research Center 2014b). Additionally, it is possible that Latino/a Protestants are more likely to migrate than Latino/a Catholics (Connor 2012), increasing the share of Latino/a Protestants in the United States.

At the same time, the Latino/a population is relatively young compared with other major racial or ethnic groups in the United States, and more of this population's growth in the last decade can be attributed to births than immigration (Krogstad and Lopez 2014); young Latino/as (particularly those age eighteen to twenty-nine) are more likely to be religiously unaffiliated than older Latino/as (Pew Research Center 2014a). As those under eighteen come of age, they likely contribute to a growing share of religiously unaffiliated Latino/as overall.

Religious switching also contributes to the changing religious profile. Among all adult Latino/as in a recent Pew Research Center report (2014a), about a third reported having a different religious affiliation than the religion in which they were raised. While a majority of Latino/as in that survey still reported Catholic affiliation, far more said they were raised Catholic than say they are Catholic today.

If the proportion of Catholics is on the decline, to what religion are Latino/as moving? Greeley's (1988, 1997) analysis suggests those who were leaving the Catholic Church were headed to Protestant congregations. Hunt (1999) found evidence that both Protestant, though mainly mainline traditions, and unaffiliated shares had grown over the 1970s, 1980s, and early 1990s. While Greeley found evidence that Latino/a Protestants on average had higher levels of education, income, and occupational status than Latino/a Catholics, Hunt's analysis suggests this was only true for mainline Protestants. Neither analysis, however, looked specifically at these socioeconomic measures among those who had *switched* from Catholicism to Protestantism, or to no religion.

Further, a 2006 Pew Research Center survey of Latino/as also found evidence of some movement away from Catholicism and toward evangelical Protestantism, as well as no religion. In that survey, about four in ten (43 percent) evangelical Protestant Latino/as indicated they were converts from Catholicism, and among Latino/as unaffiliated with any religion nearly as many (39 percent) said the same (Pew Hispanic Center and Pew Forum on Religion and Public Life 2007). Similar to the analyses from Greeley (1988, 1997) and Hunt (1999), this survey showed higher levels of educational attainment and income among Protestants—both evangelical and mainline—when compared with Catholics.

In this chapter, we explore the question of whether or not religious affiliation (or disaffiliation) plays a role for Latino/as in achieving the American Dream. More specifically, we examine whether changing one's religious affiliation is associated with varying levels of socioeconomic attainment. First, though, we describe the current religious affiliation among Latino/as, and the degree to which religious change is occurring among Latino/as.

Data

Data for this chapter come from a recent Pew Research Center survey (2013) of a nationally representative sample of 5,103 Latino/a adults.[1] The survey was conducted between May 24 and July 28, 2013, via cell and landline telephone, in both English and Spanish.[2]

Throughout this chapter, we analyze differences among three main groups, categorized by religious affiliation: Catholics, Protestants, and the religiously unaffiliated. Catholics are those respondents who tell us they are Catholic in response to a question about religious affiliation. Protestants are those who tell us they are either Protestant or Christian in response to the religious affiliation question. And the unaffiliated are those who respond that they are atheist, agnostic, or nothing in particular.[3]

Additionally, we examine three religious change groups: respondents who have not changed religion since childhood, those who have become Protestant from a non-Protestant religion, and those who have become religiously unaffiliated after having been raised in a religion.[4] We code these categories using a measure of current religious affiliation, in combination with a measure of childhood religion. Those who were raised in a Protestant faith and are currently affiliated with a different Protestant faith are not considered religious switchers for the purposes of this analysis.

Religious Affiliation and Religious Switching among Latino/as

A majority of Latino/as ages twenty-five and older—57 percent—identify as Catholic. Just over one-fifth (22 percent) identify as Protestant, and 16 percent identify with no religion. The "Current religion" column in table 1 shows this religious affiliation breakdown.

The "Childhood religion" column of table 1 shows the breakdown of religions that Latino/as were raised in, and shows that a much larger majority were raised Catholic than are currently Catholic. Just over three-quarters of Latino/as ages twenty-five and older were raised Catholic (79 percent), compared with 57 percent who are currently Catholic. Nearly a quarter (24 percent) were raised Catholic and are no longer Catholic, while 2 percent are now Catholic but were raised in some other religion, for a Catholic net loss of twenty-two percentage points.

Corresponding net gains are somewhat evenly distributed between Protestantism and no religious affiliation. Thirteen percent of Latino/a adults were raised Protestant. While 4 percent have since left Protestantism, 14 percent are now Protestant who were raised in some other faith (or no faith), for a net gain of nine percentage points. Only 6 percent of Latino/as were raised with no religious affiliation. But while 3 percent have since become affiliated, 14 percent are now unaffiliated who were raised with some affiliation, for a net gain of ten percentage points.

First-generation Latino/as (those born outside the United States, including those born in Puerto Rico) are somewhat more likely than second- and third-generation Latino/as to have been raised Catholic; 82 percent of first-generation Latino/as were raised Catholic, compared with 76 percent of the second generation and 69 percent of the third or higher generations. While the first generation is also more likely to be Catholic today than the second or third generations, among all three groups there are net declines in the Catholic share of the population.

In each generation group, there are corresponding net gains among both Protestant affiliation and no affiliation, though the gains among the unaffiliated share appear to be the largest for the second generation. The three groups were about equally likely to be raised unaffiliated, but second- and

Table 1. Turnover among Latino/a Catholics, Protestants, and religiously unaffiliated from childhood to today

	Childhood religion %	Entering group	Leaving group	Current religion %	Net change
All Latino/as (age 25+)					
Catholic	79	+2	-24	57	-22
Protestant	13	+14	-4	22	+9
Unaffiliated	6	+14	-3	16	+10
First generation					
Catholic	82	+2	-23	62	-20
Protestant	11	+12	-3	20	+9
Unaffiliated	5	+12	-3	14	+9
Second generation					
Catholic	76	+1	-29	49	-27
Protestant	14	+15	-5	24	+10
Unaffiliated	5	+20	-2	23	+18
Third-plus generation					
Catholic	69	+1	-26	45	-25
Protestant	18	+17	-6	29	+11
Unaffiliated	8	+17	-4	21	+13

Source: Pew Research Center survey of Hispanic adults 2013. Based on respondents ages twenty-five years and older. Other religions not shown.

third-generation Latino/as are more likely than first-generation Latino/as to currently be unaffiliated.

In addition to differences by immigrant generation, it is also often important to account for other sources of diversity among Latino/as, such as country of origin and/or heritage. When it comes to religious switching, however, this survey shows few differences among major subgroups of Latino/as in the United States. Overall, about a third of Latino/a adults have changed religions since their childhood, and this includes roughly a third of Puerto Ricans, Cubans, Salvadorans, and Dominicans, and three in ten Mexicans (see Pew Research Center 2014a).

Demographics by Religious Group and Religious Switchers

Latino/a Catholics and Protestants (ages twenty-five and older) are very similar in terms of their gender composition (see table 2); each group is roughly evenly split between men and women. These two groups are also very similar in terms of their age distribution. Roughly four in ten of each group is under the age of forty, reflecting the fact that the Latino/a population is relatively young as a whole (Motel and Patten 2013).

Comparatively, a larger share of the religiously unaffiliated are male (58 percent) than are female (42 percent), and a majority of this group—six in ten—is under the age of thirty. In these two ways, the Latino/a unaffiliated population resembles the unaffiliated in the US general public overall (Pew Forum on Religion and Public Life 2012). Latino/a Catholics are somewhat more heavily foreign born than Latino/a Protestants or the unaffiliated—72 percent of Catholics, compared with 60 percent of Protestants and 56 percent of the unaffiliated.

Among Latino/as who have become Protestant (see table 3) after being raised in another tradition, the demographic characteristics are very similar to Latino/a Protestants overall. Likewise, the demographic characteristics of those who have become unaffiliated after being raised in a religion closely mirror the demographic characteristics of the unaffiliated overall: more male than female, and relatively young compared to other groups. Among those who have not changed their religion, the demographic breakdown is very similar overall to Latino/a Catholics—the majority religious group among Latino/as.

Religion and Socioeconomic Success of Latino/as in the United States

Although more recent research on religion and economics is scant (Wuthnow 1994), the relationship between religion and economic mobility has a long history in the social sciences.

Marx saw religion as an oppressive element of society, limiting the upward mobility of individuals through the religious dominance of society's superstructure (Marx 1978 [1844]). By contrast, Weber (2003 [1904]) argued in his study of Protestantism and the rise of capitalism that religion can sometimes have prosperous benefits on economic mobility.

More specifically in the United States, however, several sociological classics writing during the postwar period suggested the presence of a religious

Table 2. Demographic characteristics of Latino/a Catholics, Protestants, and religiously unaffiliated

	Catholic	Protestant	Unaffiliated
	%	%	%
Men	48	47	58
Women	52	53	42
	100	100	100
Age			
25–39	38	38	60
40–64	48	52	34
65+	14	9	6
	100	100	100
Census Region			
Northeast	15	15	17
North Central	8	5	6
South	36	40	40
West	41	40	37
	100	100	100
Foreign born	72	60	56
Native born	28	40	44
2nd generation	15	19	24
3rd generation	13	21	20
Don't know gen.	*	*	0
	100	100	100
N	1,949	1,288	744

Source: Pew Research Center survey of Hispanic adults 2013. Based on respondents ages twenty-five years and older.

stratification system in the United States (Lenski 1961; Niebuhr 1929; Warner 1963). More recent studies also point to the continuance of religious stratification in American society (Davidson 2008; Keister 2011; Massengill 2008; Smith and Faris 2005) with white mainline Protestants often located in the highest economic strata of society.

Table 3. Demographic characteristics of religious change groups

	No Religious Change	Change to Protestant	Change to Unaffiliated
	%	%	%
Men	48	46	58
Women	52	54	42
	100	100	100
Age			
25–39	39	33	63
40–64	48	57	31
65+	13	11	5
	100	100	100
Census Region			
Northeast	15	12	18
North Central	7	6	6
South	36	42	38
West	41	41	38
	100	100	100
Foreign born	69	60	56
Native born	31	40	44
2nd generation	16	20	26
3rd generation	14	20	18
Don't know gen.	*	*	0
	100	100	100
N	2,543	804	594

Source: Pew Research Center survey of Hispanic adults 2013. Based on respondents ages twenty-five years and older.

However, some religious minorities have made progress toward the American Dream, moving up the socioeconomic ladder. For example, Jews and Hindus have become part of America's upper class (Keister 2011; Pew Forum 2012). Jews may have originally experienced economic discrimination, but through education (Keister 2011) and entrepreneurialism (Portes and Manning 1986) are one of the wealthiest religious groups in the United States (Keister 2011). Mostly due to selective immigration of higher classes, Hindus also have high incomes (Pew Forum 2012). And as another example, many Catholics have been upwardly mobile from one generation to the next.[5]

This potential for upward mobility among religious minorities is consistent with immigrant studies demonstrating few economic disadvantages for immigrant religious minorities in the United States (Connor 2011; Connor and Koenig 2013).[6] As Foner and Alba have argued (2008), religion is not a bright boundary in the United States. The legal separation of church and state in addition to America's lengthy and relatively positive experience with religious diversity brought on by immigration (Eck 2001; Wuthnow 2005) has actually led religion to be more of a bridge rather than a barrier for upward mobility (Connor and Koenig 2013; Hirschman 2004; Mooney 2009).

However, some socioeconomic outcomes may operate differently from others when it comes to mobility and religious affiliation (Warner 2007). While previous studies indicate that occupation and employment seem to be rather innocuous from differences by religion, this is not the case for educational attainment. For example, Bankston and Zhou (1995) find that more religiously involved Vietnamese Catholic youth have greater educational success. Similarly, several studies of Latino/a youth find a positive relationship between educational attainment and involvement in religious groups (Liou, Antrop-Gonzalez, and Cooper 2009; Sikkink and Hernandez 2003). A variety of social mechanisms in religious organizations are posited to explain this positive effect, including more expansive social networks for additional educational opportunities, access to social capital in congregations that aid youth in their educational pursuits, and avoidance of certain behaviors (drinking alcohol, taking drugs) that lead to a more studious work ethic.

Previous studies indicate that Latino/as belonging to a non-Catholic religious group like evangelical Protestantism can offer measurable differences in their economic trajectory. For example, Smilde (2007) finds that Latin Americans in Central and South America who have converted to Protestant groups are able to increase their economic standing vis-à-vis Catholics. The causal arrow for this difference is difficult to determine, but Smilde speculates that both an independence from the obligations of family as well as a more disciplined lifestyle advocated by evangelical Protestants (namely, less drug and alcohol abuse) allows for greater freedom from extended-family responsibilities and instead offers greater individual focus for participants in Latin America's growing capitalist economies. On the other hand, Latino/as moving from a religious affiliation (mainly from Catholicism) to no religious affiliation could also be upwardly mobile. For instance, a study based in Richmond, Virginia (Cavalcanti and Schleef 2005), finds that Latino/as who no longer have a religious affiliation score more highly on several measures of integration.

Given the theoretical and empirical literature, we would expect few explicit differences in employment status or income between Latino/as by religious group in the United States, especially when other factors such as education, age, race, and gender are taken into account. These relatively few differences in concrete, economic measures between Latino/as of different religious groups would include those who have switched from one religion to another. However, there are reasons to expect educational differences between Latino/a religious groups and Latino/as who have switched religions.

To test this hypothesis, we rely once more on the Pew Research Center's 2013 survey of Hispanic adults. The analysis limits cases to those aged twenty-five years and older, combining men and women together (separate analysis by sex was conducted but did not provide different patterns). Findings are presented as cross-tabulations.[7] However, to ensure known spurious variables are not behind the relationships, multivariate regression was used to control for sex, age, geographic region of residence, primary language used in the home, race, weekly church attendance, education (for employment and income outcomes), and immigrant generation (when applicable). Statistically significant findings net of these controls are described in the text. Findings that may appear to be large differences across groups in the tables, but are not highlighted in the text, are not statistically significant when controlling for the aforementioned sociodemographic characteristics.

As anticipated, the religious affiliation of Latino/as doesn't seem to be strongly associated with their direct economic success (see table 4). About half of each of the major Latino/a religious groups is employed full time. (This is not a true employment rate as it includes people not in the labor force.) Similarly, about a quarter of US Latino/as among all religious groups have an annual family income of $50,000 or higher.

However, education levels do differ across religious groups. While slightly more than a third of US Latino/as have at least some years of postsecondary education, the share is much higher among religiously unaffiliated Latino/as. In fact, more than half of Latino/as with no religious affiliation have some postsecondary education.

A similar pattern of few differences in employment and income occurs when Latino/as are grouped into religious switching categories (see table 5). As earlier, about half of all Latino/as—whether they made no religious

Table 4. US Latino/a socioeconomic status and religion

% of U.S. Latino/as in each religious group who are...

	Employed Full Time	Annual Family Income 50k or Higher	Some Postsecond-ary Education
All Latino/as	51	24	37
Catholic	51	22	31
Protestant	50	26	37
Unaffiliated	56	25	54

Source: Pew Research Center survey of Hispanic adults 2013. Based on respondents ages twenty-five years and older.

Table 5. US Latino/a socioeconomic status and religious change

% of U.S. Latino/as in each religious change group who are....

	Employed Full time	Annual Family Income 50k or Higher	Some Post-secondary Education
All Latino/as	51	24	37
No religious change	50	23	32
To a Protestant religious group	50	26	37
To no religious affiliation	57	24	58

Source: Pew Research Center survey of Hispanic adults 2013. Based on respondents ages twenty-five years and older.

change, changed to a different religious group, or changed to no religious affiliation—are employed full time. And about a quarter of Latino/as across all religious-switching categories have an annual family income of $50,000 or higher.

By contrast, findings for education by religious-switching groups are much different. About one-third of Latino/as not changing religions or changing to Protestantism from a different religious group since adolescence have some postsecondary education. Meanwhile, well over half of Latino/as who have switched to no religious affiliation have some higher education. And when religiously unaffiliated Latino/as are compared between those who have changed *to* and those who were raised *with* no religious affiliation, the educational premium is higher for Latino/as who were not raised in a nonbe-lieving household (switchers).

As supported by previous studies and theory, few religious differences seem to exist among Latino/as for general economic indicators like employ-ment and income. However, religiously unaffiliated Latino/as, and more spe-cifically those who have changed to no religious affiliation, are more likely to have some postsecondary education. But is this pattern consistent across all immigrant generations? In other words, is the association between religious switching to no eligious affiliation stronger as each generation of Latino/as have become of age?

Not surprising, second-generation Latino/as (at least one foreign-born parent) are much more likely to have some higher education beyond a high school diploma than first-generation (foreign born) Latino/as (see table 6). However, as consistent with literature of stalled upward mobility of Latino/as in the United States (Telles and Ortiz 2008), about the same rate of Latino/as of subsequent generations (third-generation plus) have some postsecondary education.

However, the increase in educational attainment from first- to second-generation Latino/as is even more dramatic when examining differences by major religious groups. Although the share of Latino/as with some post-secondary education is about the same for both first-generation Latino/a religious groups, first-generation Latino/as with no religious affiliation are slightly more likely to have education beyond high school. This trend con-tinues into the second generation where an even greater difference in educa-tional attainment occurs for second-generation unaffiliated Latino/as com-pared with Catholic or Protestant Latino/as. (This premium in education for the religiously unaffiliated is maintained for subsequent generations as well.)

Similar to education findings for all Latino/as, the pattern of higher education for the religiously unaffiliated is most endemic of Latino/as who have switched to no religious affiliation. Looking only at second-generation Latino/as, 71 percent of religiously unaffiliated have some postsecondary edu-cation while 80 percent of second-generation Latino/as who have *switched* to no religious affiliation have the same level of education. Although the differ-ence is not large, it is still substantial.

As mentioned earlier, previous research suggests that religious involve-ment (rather than affiliation alone) is associated with educational attainment (Liou, Antrop-Gonzalez, and Cooper 2009; Sikkink and Hernandez 2003). Obviously, those with no religious affiliation rarely attend church or other religious services. But is it possible that Latino/as belonging to a religious

Table 6. US Latino/a education and religion by immigrant generation

% of US Latino/as in each religious group with some postsecondary education, by generation

	First Generation	Second Generation	Third-Plus Generation
All Latino/as	26	61	57
Catholic	23	60	46
Protestant	26	53	56
Unaffiliated	39	71	75

Source: Pew Research Center survey of Hispanic adults 2013. Based on respondents ages twenty-five years and older.

Table 7. US Latino/a education and religious change by immigrant generation

% of US Latino/as in each religious change group with some postsecondary education, by generation

	First Generation (Foreign born)	Second Generation	Third-Plus Generation
All Latino/as	26	61	57
No religious change	23	56	50
To a Protestant religious group	27	53	53
To no religious affiliation	40	80	84

Source: Pew Research Center survey of Hispanic adults 2013. Based on respondents ages twenty-five years and older.

group or switching to a different religious group and who also attend religious services are more likely to have higher education than Latino/as with no religious affiliation? Again looking at differences across immigrant generations, any positive relationship between religious attendance and education is seen in the second and third-plus generations (see table 8). Among second-generation Latino/as, more than ten percentage points (53 percent versus 41 percent) separate Protestant attendees and Protestant nonattendees. As hypothesized, religious attendance does seem to have a positive relationship with education for Latino/a Protestants in the United States. By contrast, attendance does not seem to be associated with education for Latino/a Catholics in the United States.

Table 8. US Latino/a education, religious group, and religious attendance by immigrant generation

% of US Latino/as in each religious group with some postsecondary education, by generation

	First Generation (Foreign born)	Second Generation	Third-Plus Generation
All Latino/as	26	61	57
Catholic attendees	21	60	49
Catholic nonattendees	25	60	44
Protestant attendees	25	60	56
Protestant nonattendees	29	44	57
Unaffiliated nonattendees	40	71	72

Source: Pew Research Center survey of Hispanic adults 2013. Based on respondents ages twenty-five years and older.

But is the apparent educational premium associated with religious attendance any greater than Latino/as with no religious affiliation and thus, largely no religious involvement? For both the second and third-plus generations, a greater share of Latino/as with no religious affiliation have some postsecondary education than Latino/as belonging to a religious group and attending religious services weekly or more often. For example, 71 percent of second-generation Latino/as with no religious affiliation have higher education while 60 percent of Protestant attendees and 60 percent of Catholic attendees have the same level of education.

The same pattern of a higher likelihood of higher education for religiously observant Latino/as continues when groups across generations are compared by their switching to and from different religious groups. However, Latino/as who have switched to no religious affiliation are still significantly more likely to have some postsecondary education compared to religious switchers with regular religious attendance.

Conclusion

The religious affiliation of Latino/as in the United States is shifting (Pew Research Center 2014a). Once almost entirely Catholic, an increasing share of Latino/as have become Protestant or have no religious affiliation. Although the precise mechanisms behind the growth of non-Catholics in the US

Latino/a population cannot be determined with the data used in this chapter, it is most likely a combination of a growing population of Protestants in Latin America migrating to the United States combined with a growing movement from Catholicism to other religious affiliations among immigrants and their children (Pew Research Center 2014a). There is also the possibility of religious selectivity of Protestants above Catholics among Latin Americans entering the United States (Connor 2012).

Since religion has long been considered a bridge in the United States for immigrant integration, perhaps playing a role in facilitating the American Dream for those who come seeking it, this shift in the religious landscape of Latino/as in the United States is important. Many scholars point to the benefits of active religious involvement and socioeconomic success, especially among immigrants (Hirschman 2004). Our analysis of a nationally representative survey of Latino/as in the United States finds that religious affiliation or switching of religious affiliations is not associated with higher or lower employment rates or income. However, the religion of Latino/as is associated with educational outcomes. More specifically, Latino/as who are Protestant and those who have no religious affiliation are more likely to have some postsecondary education, particularly for second-generation Latino/as. And while religiously active Protestants are more likely to have higher education than Protestants who are not religiously active in their congregations, the highest likelihood of having higher education occurs among Latino/as who have no religious affiliation. Particularly true for the second generation, Latino/as who were raised in a religion but currently claim no religious affiliation have the highest likelihood of all groups to have some postsecondary education.

So does involvement in Protestant congregations or having no religious affiliation lead to a more educated Latino/a population and thus, a closer approximation of the American Dream? Without panel data, the answer cannot be definitively assessed. It is possible that becoming Protestant or religiously unaffiliated could lead to higher education. At the same time, it is also possible for Latino/as with higher education to shed Catholic identity and become Protestant or religiously unaffiliated. Although the exact direction of the relationship cannot be determined with the data used in this chapter, we do know that more Latino/as who have switched to a Protestant religious group or have become religiously unaffiliated say they did so before becoming an adult than after adulthood. This small fact leans the directional arrow toward education as a consequence of religious change, but further research on the exact causal mechanisms between the relationship of religion, education, and socioeconomic success of Latino/as in the United States remain unknown.

With the positive relationship between no religious affiliation and higher education, but also religious involvement among Protestants and some post-secondary education, further research should examine the social mechanisms underlying these relationships. From the data, it seems this is a story of second-generation immigrants. For religious participation, is it religious involvement per se or a combination of good behaviors, perhaps motivated by religious devotion, that lead to good study habits and then to higher education? For Latino/as who have become religiously unaffiliated, does a lack of a religious identity open educational dreams otherwise blocked for Latino/as? Or, as the United States becomes more religiously unaffiliated, is the no religion effect for higher education among Latino/as simply the result of greater integration to a less religious America? In addition, how is immigrant social capital—often considered a positive force for immigrant integration in the United States—perhaps not occurring to the same extent for second-generation Latino/as? These questions, among others, remain unanswered.

Future research seeking to answer such questions would benefit greatly from panel data that would allow researchers to look at change over time and parse out the mechanisms behind these relationships. However, such studies that also include large, representative samples of Latino/as do not exist at this time and would require extensive resources to carry out.

Although religion is often considered a bridge for immigrant groups in the United States for their economic integration, the data in this chapter indicate that religion may not always be as important for socioeconomic success for all immigrant-based groups and future generations. This chapter sought to describe the basic religious identities of current-day Latino/as living in the United States and how these religious identities may be shaping their socio-economic success. In this way, it has broadened the discussion beyond the typical relationship between religious involvement and socioeconomic status. However, additional research opportunities remain as we work to more fully understand the relationship between religion and the Latino/a American Dream.

Notes

1. While the survey included respondents ages eighteen and older, we focus our analysis on those ages twenty-five and older (and exclude those who did not answer the question about their age). This restriction ensures that our sample is based on those who are of working age and have completed most of their education.

2. For more information on the methodology of this survey, see the Pew Research Center report "The Shifting Religious Identity of Latinos in the United States," May 2014.

3. Not included in our analyses are Latino/as of other religious affiliations, including 2 percent who identify as Jehovah's Witness, 1 percent as Mormon, and fewer than 1 percent each who identify as Orthodox Christian, Muslim, Jewish, Buddhist, Hindu, some other religion, or who did not report their religion. The sample sizes for these religious groups are too small to analyze separately, and are therefore excluded for the purposes of this chapter.

4. There are some respondents who have become Catholic after being raised in another religion, or in no religion, but this group is too small to analyze separately.

5. Interestingly, Catholic immigrants initially faced public opposition in the economic mainstream (Higham 2007 [1955]), but Catholics actually used the resources of the Catholic Church like parochial schools and universities as a vehicle for economic mobility (Alba, Raboteau, and DeWind 2009; Hirschman 2004).

6. Although Keister (2011) finds that black Protestants and Hispanic Catholics are at the bottom of the religious class structure in the United States, even after controlling for race, these ethno-religious groups include a racial component.

7. The cross-tabulation results presented in tables 4 through 8 are based on analyses that excluded responses of "don't know" or refusals to answer on questions being analyzed. Such responses are treated as missing data for this analysis.

References

Alba, Richard, Albert Raboteau, and Josh DeWind, eds. 2009. *Religion and Immigration in America: Comparative and Historical Perspectives.* New York: New York University Press.

Bankston, Carl L., and Min Zhou. 1995. "Religious Participation, Ethnic Identification, and Adaptation of Vietnamese Adolescents in an Immigrant Community." *Sociological Quarterly* 36: 523–34.

Cavalcanti, H. B., and Debra Schleef. 2005. "The Case for Secular Assimilation? The Latino Experience in Richmond, Virginia." *Journal for the Scientific Study of Religion* 44 (4): 473–83.

Connor, Phillip. 2011. "Religion as Resource: Religion and Immigrant Economic Incorporation." *Social Science Research* 40 (5): 1350–61.

———. 2012. "International Migration and Religious Selection." *Journal for the Scientific Study of Religion* 51 (1):1 84–94.

Connor, Phillip, and Matthias Koenig. 2013. "Bridges and Barriers: Religion and Immigrant Occupational Attainment across Integration Contexts." *International Migration Review* 47 (1): 3–38.

Davidson, James D. 2008. "Religious Stratification: Its Origins, Persistence, and Consequences." *Sociology of Religion* 69 (4): 371–95.

Eck, Diane L. 2001. *A New Religious America.* San Francisco: Harper San Francisco.

Foner, Nancy, and Richard Alba. 2008. "Immigrant Religion in the U.S. and Western Europe: Bridge or Barrier to Inclusion?" *International Migration Review* 42 (2): 360–92.

Fry, Richard, and Mark Hugo Lopez. 2012. "Hispanic Student Enrollments Reach New Heights in 2011: Now Largest Minority Group on Four-Year College Campuses." Washington, DC: Pew Research Center.

Greeley, Andrew M. 1988. "Defection among Hispanics." *America* 159: 61–62.

———. 1997. "Defection among Hispanics (Updated)." *America* 177: 12–13.

Herberg, Will. 1960. *Protestant-Catholic-Jew.* Garden City, NY: Anchor Books.

Higham, John. 2007 [1955]. *Strangers in the Land: Patterns of American Nativism, 1860–1925.* New Brunswick, NJ: Rutgers University Press.

Hirschman, Charles. 2004. "The Role of Religion in the Origins and Adaptation of Immigrant Groups in the United States." *International Migration Review* 28 (3): 1206–34.

Hunt, Larry. 1998. "The Spirit of Hispanic Protestantism in the United States: National Survey Comparisons of Catholics and Non-Catholics." *Social Science Quarterly* 79: 828–45.

———. 1999. "Hispanic Protestantism in the United States: Trends by Decade and Generation." *Social Forces* 77 (4): 1601–24.

Keister, Lisa. 2011. *Faith and Money: How Religious Belief Contributed to Wealth and Poverty.* New York: Cambridge University Press.

Kochhar, Rakesh, Richard Fry, and Paul Taylor. 2011. "Hispanic Household Wealth Fell by 66% from 2005 to 2009: The Toll of the Great Recession." Washington, DC: Pew Research Center.

Krogstad, Jens Manuel, and Mark Hugo Lopez. 2014. "Hispanic Nativity Shift: U.S. Births Drive Population Growth as Immigration Stalls." Washington, DC: Pew Research Center.

Kurien, Prema. 1998. "Becoming American by Becoming Hindu: Indian Americans Take Their Place at the Multi-Cultural Table." In *Gatherings in Diaspora: Religious Communities and the New Immigration,* edited by R. S. Warner and J. G. Wittner. Philadelphia: Temple University Press.

Lenski, Gerhard. 1961. *The Religious Factor.* Garden City, NY: Anchor Books.

Lin, Tony Tian-Ren. 2010. "Best of Both Worlds: How Word of Faith Pentecostalism Teaches Latino Immigrants to Become Americans." PhD diss., University of Virginia.

Liou, Daniel D., Rene Antrop-Gonzalez, and Robert Cooper. 2009. "Unveiling the Promise of Community Cultural Wealth to Sustaining Latina/o Students' College-Going Information Networks." *Educational Studies* 45: 532–55.

Lopez, Mark Hugo, and D'Vera Cohn. 2011. "Hispanic Poverty Rate Highest in New Supplemental Census Measure." Washington, DC: Pew Research Center.

Martin, David. 1990. *Tongues of Fire: The Explosion of Protestantism in Latin America*. Cambridge, MA: Blackwell.

Marx, Karl. 1978 [1844]. "Economic and Philosophic Manuscripts of 1844." In *The Marx-Engels Reader, Second Edition*, edited by Robert C. Tucker. New York: W. W. Norton.

Massengill, Rebekah Peeples. 2008. "Educational Attainment and Cohort Change among Conservative Protestants, 1972–2004." *Journal for the Scientific Study of Religion* 47 (4): 545–62.

Mooney, Margarita. 2009. *Faith Makes Us Live: Surviving and Thriving in the Haitian Diaspora*. Berkeley: University of California Press.

Motel, Seth, and Eileen Patten. 2013. "Statistical Portrait of Hispanics in the United States, 2011." Washington, DC: Pew Research Center.

Niebuhr, H. R. 1929. *The Social Sources of Denominationalism*. New York: Henry Holt.

Perl, Paul, Jennifer Z. Greely, and Mark M. Gray. 2006. "What Proportion of Adult Hispanics Are Catholic? A Review of Survey Data and Methodology." *Journal of the Scientific Study of Religion* 45 (3): 419–36.

Pew Forum. 2012. "Faith on the Move: The Religious Affiliation of International Migrants." Washington, DC: Pew Forum on Religion and Public Life.

Pew Forum on Religion and Public Life. 2012. "'Nones' on the Rise." Washington, DC: Pew Research Center.

Pew Hispanic Center and Pew Forum on Religion and Public Life. 2007. "Changing Faiths: Latinos and the Transformation of American Religion." Washington, DC: Pew Research Center.

Pew Research Center. 2014a. "The Shifting Religious Identity of Latinos in the United States: Nearly One-in-Four Latinos Are Former Catholics." Washington, DC: Pew Research Center.

———. 2014b. "Religion in Latin America: Widespread Change in a Historically Catholic Region." Washington, DC: Pew Research Center.

Portes, Alejandro, and Robert D. Manning. 1986. "The Immigrant Enclave: Theory and Empirical Examples." In *Competitive Ethnic Relations*, edited by S. Olzak and J. Nagel. Orlando, FL: Academic Press.

Sikkink, David, and Edwin I. Hernandez. 2003. "Religion Matters: Predicting School Success among Latino Youth." South Bend, IN: Institute for Latino Studies, University of Notre Dame.

Smilde, David. 2007. *Reason to Believe: Cultural Agency in Latin American Evangelicalism.* Berkeley: University of California Press.

Smith, Christian, and Robert Faris. 2005. "Socioeconomic Inequality in the American Religious System: An Update and Assessment." *Journal for the Scientific Study of Religion* 44 (1): 95–104.

Stoll, David. 1990. *Is Latin America Turning Protestant? The Politics of Evangelical Growth.* Berkeley: University of California Press.

Telles, Edward Eric, and Vilma Ortiz. 2008. *Generations of Exclusion.* New York: Russell Sage Foundation.

Warner, R. Stephen. 2007. "The Role of Religion in the Process of Segmented Assimilation." *ANNALS of the American Academy of Political and Social Science* 612: 102–14.

Warner, W. Lloyd. 1963. *Yankee City.* New Haven, CT: Yale University Press.

Weber, Max. 2003 [1904]. *Protestant Ethic and Spirit of Capitalism.* Translated by T. Parsons. Mineola, NY: Dover.

Wuthnow, Robert. 1994. "Religion and Economic Life." In *The Handbook of Economic Sociology,* edited by N. Smelser. Princeton, NJ: Princeton University Press.

———. 2005. *America and the Challenges of Religious Diversity.* Princeton, NJ: Princeton University Press.

Latino/a, American, Dream

Men, Women

Sandra L. Hanson

Rising streams of Latino/a immigrants and the reality of an American racial/ethnic demographic in which whites will no longer be the largest race/ethnic group later in the century have created considerable discussion about race, ethnicity, and the American Dream. These discussions often refer to Latino/as as a group, without attention to distinct experiences of Latino/a men and women (Gandara and Contreras 2009; Babco 2001). Both public opinion and social scientists have historically conceived of race/ethnicity and gender as distinct areas of inquiry. As with other race/ethnic groups, Latino/a men and women do share in many experiences and dreams. Latino/a men and women's experiences and dreams are not, however, interchangeable. Here we look at the concept of the American Dream for Latino/as from a perspective that acknowledges the intersection of race/ethnicity and gender.

In thinking about Latino/a men, women, and the American Dream, the general context of how sociologists think about race/ethnicity, gender, and achievement (as well as inequality) in the United States is important to consider. The discussion below will briefly highlight some of the key approaches to achievement, race/ethnicity, and gender. It will be argued that these are not separate processes, and an understanding of Latino/a gender systems and the American Dream requires an acknowledgment of the unique way in which race/ethnicity and gender interact to create experiences for Latino/as that cannot be understood by looking at race/ethnic and gender processes separately. Following this discussion of approaches to achievement, race/ethnicity, and gender, reports from a variety of sources (including census data and the Pew Hispanic Center) will be used to examine how Latino/a men and women are doing on objective measures of achievement related to the American Dream, including income, jobs, poverty, education, housing, and health care. Finally, the chapter will include an analysis of public opinion data from the General Social Survey and Pew Hispanic Center that will provide insight into the relationship between race/ethnicity, gender, and attitudes about the American Dream for Latino/as in the United States. Although our look at the American Dream is mostly focused on race/ethnicity and gender in affecting Dream-related outcomes for Latino/as, the discussion below is important for presenting where social scientists are today in understanding the race/ethnic and gender *processes* that are involved in creating these different outcomes.

Background

MODELS OF ACHIEVEMENT

What do sociologists know about achievement of education, occupation, income, and other factors related to the American Dream in the United States, and how do race/ethnicity and gender affect our conclusions about these processes? One of the first attempts at explaining success came out of the work of Blau and Duncan (1967) and the early research on achievement often referred to as the Wisconsin model (Sewell, Haller, and Portes 1969). Although early status attainment models were applied to white male samples, later status research acknowledged the role of ascribed statuses such as race/ethnicity and sex in the educational achievement process. Research on achievement processes of Latino/as suggests that this model also provides some insight into achievement for Latino/as (Barton 2003; Rochin and Mellow 2007). Status attainment scholars stress the role of resources obtained through the family and their influence on individual characteristics and eventual achievement. They propose that interactions and expectations within families also provide advantages (or disadvantages) in the educational system (Walberg 1984). The value of these family resources for achievement was further developed in Coleman's (1988) notion of social capital, stressing the role of family styles, interactions, and values in promoting the types of behaviors and interactions in children that affect their success in the educational system (for example, Kao and Rutherford 2007). Another important addition to models of attainment involved school factors (for example, neighborhoods, segregation, resources, teachers) (Peng, Wright, and Hill 1995; Hanson 2009; Rossiter 1982; Brown 2000). In sum, the classic model of status attainment stresses family characteristics and resources and their influence on individual characteristics and educational achievement. Although later status attainment models did include race/ethnicity and sex, these models are important in showing how family background and education can affect occupational outcomes. We will see that these processes are relevant to Latino/as as they work to achieve the American Dream. The status attainment models often do not go far enough, however, in realizing the complex ways in which race/ethnicity and gender are structured into achievement systems.

MODELS OF RACE/ETHNICITY AND GENDER

In thinking about the intersection of race/ethnicity, gender, and the American Dream for Latino/as it is also helpful to consider the approach that sociologists have taken to studying race/ethnicity and gender. Historically, race/ethnicity and gender were seen as distinct areas of inquiry. The *intersectionality approach* is a response to the tendency in social science theory and research to consider gender and race/ethnic effects as separate processes. Historically, the race/ethnic focus has been on men of color and the gender focus has been on white women. Intersectionality does not focus on gender alone, but on the intersection between race/ethnicity, class, and gender. The intersection between these three concepts is implicit in this chapter since our major focus is on the ways that race/ethnicity and gender combine to affect a major aspect of the American Dream—class mobility. Gender and race/ethnic effects are not additive or summative. Instead, socially and culturally created categories such as race/ethnicity, class, and gender interact simultaneously on multiple levels. A quick look at current sociological approaches to studying race/ethnicity and gender provides additional insight here.

Although sociologists have historically acknowledged *race/ethnic inequality* in the United States, different explanations have been provided. Some theories focus on cultural deficits of race/ethnic minorities. This approach received considerable support with Moynihan's report (1965) on female-headed households as a factor in African American poverty. Although it is not a major approach sociologists use today, some (for example, Small, Harding, and Lamont 2010; Wilson 2010) argue that cultural components of race/ethnic groups interact with structure to create inequality. Another approach to understanding race/ethnic inequity focuses on biased attitudes of whites and has received considerable support from sociologists, including Lawrence Bobo (2009). There is substantial evidence for lingering race prejudice in the United States. The approach to racism in America that a majority of sociologists agree on (as at least one component of ongoing race/ethnic inequality) involves institutional racism. This view sees race advantage as built into social structures—including education, occupations, housing, legal and health care. It is structured into culture, laws, religion, and customs (Higginbotham and Andersen 2009). The idea of inequality as a part of "business as usual" is stressed. Here, injustice becomes normal and taken for granted (Winant 2009). Finally, a more recent approach to understanding race inequity—critical race—comes out of a paradigm shift in sociology, in general. The critical race approach originated in law schools in the United States in the 1980s as a way to examine and question racism in the US legal system (Yosso 2005). It questions traditional approaches to studying race and describes them as part of the problem in perpetuating racism. An alternate approach is suggested that is grounded in the experiences and voices of people of color and that acknowledges the central role of race in all aspects of the research process. The intersection of race/ethnicity, gender, and class; the importance of interdisciplinary knowledge; and the bias of traditional pedagogies are acknowledged. Critical theorists acknowledge historical context. The historical context of Latino/a immigration is important for understanding their experiences here. The approach also argues for a view of the experiences of race/ethnic minorities as a source of strength and agency instead of deficit (Solórzano and Yosso 2002; Yosso 2005).

An extra note should be added on the issue of the intersection of race and ethnicity in the context of this research on Latino/as and the American Dream. In the introductory chapter the editors commented on the need for more research in this area (for example, overlaps involving white Latino/as and Afro Latino/as). Outside of a small group of researchers (especially involving qualitative work), there has been little done on the intersection of race and ethnicity. Some argue that Latino/as are a diverse category and don't fit into the race or ethnic categories often used. Further discussions suggest that it may not be appropriate to refer to Latino/as as a race or an ethnic group (see, for example, Feliciano and Robnett 2014; Hitlin, Brown, and Elder 2007; Perez 2008; Roth 2010).

Like current thinking on race/ethnicity, contemporary *theorizing about gender* has moved away from an individualist (sex roles) approach that primarily focused on women, their attitudes, and their abilities. Current thinking about gender considers the individual, but also takes a macrostructural approach that focuses on institutions and discrimination (Hanson 2009; Grant, Horan, and Watts-Warren 1994; Lorber 1994; Osmond and Thorne 1993). Structural theories of gender often appear deterministic, however. As in race/ethnic scholarship, gender frameworks that take a critical approach add complexity and avoid the determinism of structural theories, allowing for a dialectic between structure and agency.[1] Studies of gender that take a critical approach examine processes that challenge status quo gender structures as well as processes that create gender inequality.[2] For this reason, the critical perspective is sometimes referred to as resistance theory. Individuals don't absorb all messages (for example, about gender, race/ethnicity, and class) and obediently comply with educational and other structures without protest (Grant, Horan, and Watts-Warren 1994). Critical gender theory recognizes diversity in gender structures, but an explicit focus on the intersection of race/ethnic and gender categories is often lacking.

Historically, *race/ethnicity and gender* were seen as distinct areas of inquiry. Early feminist theory also homogenized women and focused on white, middle-class women (Glenn 1991). In the 1980s women of color began to question this limited approach and stress the intersection of race/ethnicity, class, and gender as well as the unique history and subcultures of minority women (Dill 1980; Ruiz 1987). It is impossible to talk about the American Dream without considering racial/ethnic and gender variation.

The *intersectionality approach* is a response to the tendency in social science theory and research to consider gender and race/ethnic effects as separate processes. The approach derives from work by women of color who have attempted to correct these biases in social science research (Hooks 1984; Zinn and Dill 1996; Collins 1990, 1999). Here the focus is not on gender alone, but on the intersection between race/ethnicity, class, and gender (Anderson and Collins 1995; Rothenberg 1992; Glenn 1985; West and Fenstermaker 1995). The term *intersectionality theory* was first coined by Kimberle Crenshaw in 1989 when describing gender and race/ethnic effects that are not additive or summative (DeFrancisco and Palczewski 2007). Instead, socially and culturally created categories such as race/ethnicity, class, and gender interact simultaneously on multiple levels. Collins (1990, 1999, 2010) has been particularly effective in describing this approach. It is ironic that early work on gender biases didn't see its own white, middle class bias (Collins 1999). Collins suggests that no one form of oppression is primary. Rather, there are layers of oppression within individual, community, and institutional contexts. Like critical gender theorists, she argues that each of these locations is a potential site of resistance. The approach also stresses the unique history and subcultures of minority women and the influence of these cultures on the structures that limit and direct women's lives as well as the agency that allows them to retain some control and influence within these structures (Collins 1999).

The above discussions of social science approaches to race/ethnicity and gender suggest that thinking has evolved in similar ways in each of these disciplines. Earlier thinking on both race/ethnicity and gender tended to isolate the topic and think in individual terms. Social science research in general (as well as that focusing on race/ethnicity and on gender) has become more structural and critical over time. The critical perspective stresses the centrality of these statuses, the intersection of race/ethnicity, gender, social class, challenges to dominant ideologies, a commitment to social justice, the import of experiential knowledge, and the import of an interdisciplinary approach. Additionally, the power of structures and the power of the individual through human agency are key assumptions (Yosso 2005; Hanson 2009; Agger 1998; Grant, Horan, and Watts-Warren 1994). The dialectic between structure and agency in the vision and accomplishment of the American Dream for Latino/a men and women in the United States is acknowledged in this chapter. Finally, although some scholars have looked at gender intersections across race and ethnic groups, there is little on the more complex issue of the intersection of gender, race, and ethnicity that acknowledges the overlap between race and ethnicity that was noted earlier. Research on the unique gender systems across diverse groups of Latino/as (for example, white Latino/as, Afro Latino/as) is needed.

Recent applications of intersectionality apply the framework to both men and women. Although the framework was first used to examine the intersection of race/ethnicity and gender for black women, it has been expanded to include all race/ethnic and gender groups (Mann and Huffman 2005) at both individual and institutional levels (Browne and Misra 2003). Insights from this discussion of emerging approaches to a sociological understanding of race/ethnicity, gender, and achievement will be used below, where we focus on Latino/a men and women and their progress toward achieving the American Dream.

Gender and Objective Measures of the American Dream among Latino/as

How are Latino/a women and men doing on objective measures of the American Dream? We begin with some gender comparisons on income, poverty, and education and then include a separate discussion of achievement-related issues for Latino/a men and women.[3] Data on earnings from the 2010 census show that Latina women's earnings are 91 percent of Latino men's earnings. This figure was 78 percent for white women, 90 percent for African American women, and 80 percent for Asian American women (Glynn and Powers 2012). It is interesting that the gender gap in earnings is the smallest among Latino/as. This might suggest gains made by Latina women but also educational and occupational difficulties for Latino men.

Data on poverty often ignore the fact that many more women live in poverty than men (Bennetts 2011). Organizations like the National Women's Law Center are critical in providing this data by race/ethnicity and gender (National Women's Law Center 2011). Poverty figures show that the highest poverty rates (of any race/ethnic/gender group) are among women of color. Latina women's poverty rate is 25 percent. This figure is 19 percent for Latino men. These figures are 10 percent and 8 percent for white (non-Hispanic) women and men. They are 26 percent and 19 percent for African American women and men. The figures on poverty help reveal the ways in which race/ethnicity and gender come together to affect the chance of living in poverty. The level of poverty is the lowest for white (non-Hispanic) men. It is lower for white women than for women of color. The poverty rate is very similar for women of color, with Latina women and African American women having similar rates. The same pattern holds for minority men. When considering the male advantage on chances of being in poverty, the data show that the gender gap is smallest among whites and largest among racial/ethnic minority groups.

How are Latino/a women and men doing in the US educational system? Reports on college enrollment show that the gender gap (with women more heavily represented than men) has leveled off for all race/ethnic groups except Latino/as. Reports by the Pew Hispanic Center provide more insight into educational issues for Latino/a women and men. Trends show an increase in the percent of young Latino/as working, going to school, or serving in the military. Much of this increase over time is due to the increased participation of Latina women. The rate of participation for this group of women remains relatively low, however. The percent of young Latina women who are not in school or the workforce exceeded that for young African American men in one of the Hispanic Center's reports (Fry 2009). Among men, figures show that Latino rate of labor-force participation is the same as for white men, and both are higher than for young African American men. The next two sections look separately at Latino/a women and men on a number of measures of the American Dream.

LATINA WOMEN AND THE DREAM

Latina women do not fare well on many objective measures of the American Dream. They have higher poverty rates and less education than do other women in the United States (Gonzales 2008). Data from the Pew Hispanic Center show that although they have similar rates of labor-force participation as non-Latina women, Latina women are more likely than other women to be employed in blue-collar occupations such as building, grounds cleaning and maintenance, food preparation and serving jobs, and personal care/service occupations. Full-time Latina female workers make less than other, non-Latina females (Gonzales 2008). Data from the 2010 census show that the wage ratio (earnings compared to white males) for Latina women is lower than that for men and women in any other major race/ethnic group at 60 percent. Latino men make 66 percent of white male earnings. White women make 81 percent of white male earnings (Pearson 2015).

Unlike Latino men, Latina women are a part of a rising success story in the US education system. The total number of master's degrees awarded to Latina women more than doubled during the past decade (Kim 2011). Latina women have high school graduation rates that are 7 percentage points higher than for Latino men. They earn 60 percent of the higher education degrees awarded to Latinos (Kim 2011).

Scholars who have taken an intersectionality approach acknowledge the gains for Latina women (in some areas they are doing better than Latino men), but the barriers remain in achieving the American Dream of opportunity and upward mobility. One of the struggles for Latina women (especially working-class Latina women) involves traditional gender ideologies and patriarchal family systems (De Los Rios 2007). Related to this is an experience of many Latina women that affects their educational and occupational opportunities—early motherhood. Twenty-six percent of Latina women are mothers by the age of nineteen. This figure is higher than for any other race/ethnic group. For example, 22 percent of African American women and 11 percent of white women are mothers by the age of nineteen (Pew 2009). Although immigration has some positive effect on gender roles for immigrant Latina women, researchers have found that additional barriers involving undocumented status and language are sometimes added to the challenges they face in achieving the Dream of mobility in the United States. Other work from a multicultural perspective on intersectionality shows that types of gender ideologies vary across Latino/a families by economic status, country of origin, and generational status (Halgunseth 2004). Additionally, research on gender and Latino/a culture increasingly reveals that stereotypes involving machismo and *marianismo* in Latino/a families are oversimplified, and Latino/a families are more egalitarian than these notions suggest (Lindsey 2011). Even successful Latina women run into these Latina stereotypes. During the hearings for her Supreme Court appointment, Sonia Sotomayor made a comment about being a "wise Latina." The backlash against the comment was immediate and implied gender and ethnic bias. In fact, many nominees over the years had referred to their own backgrounds (Felix 2010).

Transformations in thinking about Latina women and Latino/a families question past assumptions about pathology that typify much of the research on minority (and Latino/a) families (Anderson 2005; Lindsey 2011). Work on gender and migration has contributed to this transformation in thinking, with researchers showing women (and Latina women) are major actors in the migration process and experience it in a unique way (Brettel and Sargent 2012; Buijs 1993; Chant 1992). In spite of their significant family responsibilities and risk of poverty, Latina women sometimes have a more positive immigration experience than do Latino men (Pedraza 1991; Romero 2002; Pearce, Clifford, and Tandon 2011). Reflections on Latina women and their quest for equality of opportunity and access to education, jobs, and a good life need to consider the distinct gender cultures among these women and the ways in which their fight for equality here intersect with their larger ability to achieve the American Dream.

Latino Men and the Dream

Employment figures show that Latino men are more likely than Latina women to be in the labor market, but economic pressures have led to a rising employment rate for Latina women, and the gender gap is narrowing (Mather and Jacobsen 2010). Analysts looking at economic consequences of the US recession conclude that Latino men may be seeing more negative impact than any other demographic group. Although African American men have fared worse on unemployment, the low levels of education and concentration in states that have been hit hard by the recession makes Latino men more vulnerable economically than many other groups. Their youth, however, does provide an advantage (Mather and Jacobsen 2010). Part of the vulnerability of Latino men also comes from the concentration in construction jobs and the lag in new home building in some areas.

To some extent, the Dream of upward mobility and access to good jobs is affected by the relatively low levels of education of Latino men. Nearly twice as many Latino men (41 percent) as African American men (21 percent) have not graduated from high school (Mather and Jacobsen 2010). Compared to most other demographic groups (including Latina women), young Latino males are less likely to be attending college (Mather and Jacobsen 2010; Daniels 2010; American Council on Education 2011). A recent study conducted by the American Council on Education shows that college attendance rates are increasing for both Latino/a men and women, but rates of increase are much higher for women than men (70 percent versus 56 percent). This gender gap is decreasing for other race/ethnic groups but increasing for

Latino/as. Young men are overrepresented among young Latino/a immigrants, and recent reports show that limited English skills are a major factor in providing limitations on higher education (Pew 2010). Conclusions from the College Board Advocacy and Policy Center (2010) based on census data, academic research, and in-depth interviews with both Latino and African American men provide cause for alarm. Men in these groups are doing relatively less well than non-Hispanic white and Asian men (as well as minority women) on many indicators associated with the Dream—high school graduation, college attendance, unemployment, and incarceration. The trend causing the most alarm among educators and policy makers at a recent Latino Male Symposium was the rising underrepresentation of Latino males in US colleges. Some of the factors that might be impacting this trend involve gender issues such as "machismo" and a gender equity movement for Latina women (Mangan 2011).

The College Board Advocacy and Policy Center's report on the educational crisis facing young men of color raises the issue of two Americas and has implications for equality of access to the American Dream (College Board Advocacy and Policy Center 2010). Their reference to a "third America" made up of young minority men that are often ignored by larger society provides a wake-up call. Too often it is stereotyped, inaccurate, violent images of gangs and drugs that are presented to Americans (and young men of color). Social pressures on young Latino men by gangs and other nonacademically oriented subcultures are powerful. Latino/a subcultures of machismo often stress being tough, independent, and not asking for help. These subcultures are also part of the issue that educators must deal with in solving the problem of young Latino men in educational systems that are often described as "white." Some researchers have found that young Latina women use educational attainment and schools as a way to resist cultural stereotypes, but young Latino men avoid school as a way to escape negative judgments associated with stereotypes (College Board Advocacy and Policy Center 2010). Both young men and women of color have challenges in the US education and achievement system, but minority women are better off than minority men on most educational outcome measures. Most importantly, the authors suggest that this group of Americans is experiencing declines in educational attainment and well-being at the same time that other groups are advancing. Key to the solution to the problems for young minority men, according to the College Board, is creating access and opportunities for educational attainment across race/ethnic, class, and gender lines. If these young men do not have expectations for success, and if they do not have any hope in the American

Dream, then social problems involving crime, unemployment, and poverty will be the only part of the American experience that they will have access to. Researchers are in agreement that in addition to stereotypes and gender and race issues for young Latino men, poverty and issues of English language proficiency are also factors that create challenges for these young men. Cultural pressures involving *familismo*, which stress work to support families, are also an issue when considering challenges to continuing education among Latino males. The College Board makes a number of recommendations, including model programs, funding, research, partnerships, dialogue, and changes in educational policy for advancing the educational outcomes of young men of color. A report by the American Council on Education provides data that reveal young women (across race/ethnic groups) doing better than generations before them on postsecondary educational attainment (Kim 2011). Young minority men (except Asian Americans) have done less well than earlier generations. This is the American Dream in reverse, with each generation of males slipping further behind rather than moving further ahead.

The pages above are meant to provide a preliminary framework and empirical foundation for thinking about the American Dream as it converges with race/ethnicity and gender for Latino/as in the United States. When social scientists examine Latino/as they often focus on problems associated with poverty, immigration, language barriers, and cultural conflicts. In this book the American Dream is developed as one that has been historically grounded in the dreams of immigrants. This chapter proposes an approach to studying achievement, race/ethnicity, and gender in the context of this historical and cultural idea of an American Dream. Discussion in the introductory chapter shows considerable similarity in how Americans (across historical periods, race/ethnic groups, and gender) view the Dream. It also suggests—as does this chapter—diversity and complexity in the conditions, possibilities, and hopes for achievement of the Dream in the United States. The final portion of this chapter looks at the attitudes that Latino/as have toward the American Dream, with the goal of exploring this complexity through comparisons involving the intersection of race/ethnicity and gender.

Methods: Data Sets and Measures for Analysis of Gender and Attitudes about the American Dream for Latino/as

DATA SETS

GSS 2012. The General Social Survey (GSS) has been conducted twenty-nine times between 1972 and 2012 (GSS 2012). It provides information on the demographic characteristics and attitudes of probability samples of noninstitutionalized US residents aged eighteen years and older. The survey is conducted via face-to face interviews by the National Opinion Research Center (NORC) at the University of Chicago. The GSS includes race and ethnicity variables. In this analysis we compare Latino/as to non-Latino/a whites and non-Latino/a African Americans. Unfortunately, a more refined analysis is not possible given the small N for Latino/as within separate race statuses (especially Latino/as who identified as African American).

Pew National Survey of Latino/as 2011. Pew's National Survey of Latino/as was fielded in 2011 by Social Science Solutions to a nationally representative sample of 1,220 Latino/as aged eighteen and older (Pew 2013). The survey was conducted via telephone interviews by a staff of bilingual interviewers and focused on the 2012 presidential election, identity, attitudes regarding immigration and enforcement, and values. In this survey of Latino/as there was a question that asked for race or ethnicity. Given that they were combined in one question, it is difficult to analyze race groups for the Latino/as in the Pew survey—thus we focus on the general sample of Latino/as.

MEASURES

GSS 2012. A number of items from the GSS 2012 survey were used to examine attitudes about the American Dream for Latino/as. Items measure issues involving *standard of living* (compared to parents, kids will be better, standard of living will improve, and should government help improve standard of living for poor), *financial situation* (satisfaction with financial situation, change in financial situation, and opinion of family income), *social position and attitudes about getting ahead* (self-ranking, subjective class identification, how people get ahead, and confidence in education), and *race discrimination* (race differences due to discrimination and race differences due to lack of education). A few of the items were measured with "yes," "no" options but a majority were measured with Likert scales that operationalized level of agreement with the statement. See table 1 for detail on the variables and responses used to measure attitudes about the American Dream with the GSS 2012 data. Additional items measuring family income, education, and age were used in the multivariate analyses of the GSS data.

Pew 2011 National Survey of Latino/as. The Pew Hispanic Center collected similar items measuring attitudes about issues involving the American Dream in their 2011 National Survey of Latino/as. Items measure issues involving *standard of living/situation of Latino/as* (situation of Latino/as compared to one year ago, Latino/as' success relative to others, conditions for raising children, children's relative standard of living, and respondent's relative standard of living), *satisfaction with country* (with the way things are going), and *financial situation* (personal, family, and for Latino/as). Responses to these items were measured with Likert scales that operationalized level of agreement with the statement. See table 2 for detail on the variables and responses used to measure items about the American Dream with the Pew 2011 National Survey of Latino/as. Additional measures of family income, education, and age were used in the multivariate analyses of the Pew data.

Analyses

In order to examine the research questions about the intersection of race/ethnicity, gender, and attitudes about the American Dream for Latino/as we begin with bivariate analyses of the Dream attitudes for race/ethnic and gender subgroups. Given the categorical nature of the independent (race/ethnicity and gender) and dependent (attitudes about the American Dream) variables, we use cross tables and chi-squares to test for significant differences across groups. We look at the effect of sex within race/ethnic groups and the effect of race/ethnicity within sex groups in order to examine the intersections of interest here. Additionally, multivariate OLS regression models are used to examine the effects of sex within race/ethnic groups and race/ethnicity within sex groups when other factors affecting attitudes are taken into account. The control variables used in the OLS regression models include family income, education, and age. As with the bivariate analyses, the effect of sex is examined within race/ethnic groups (with models including controls) and the effect of race/ethnicity is examined within sex groups (with models including controls). Although the dependent variable is measured at the ordinal level in this research, the large probability sample makes OLS regression appropriate here.

Findings: Race/Ethnicity, Gender, and Attitudes about the American Dream for Latino/as

Bivariate: Effect of Gender within Race/Ethnic Groups

Figures presented in table 1 show opinions of men and women on the American Dream within each race/ethnic group using data from the 2012 General Social Survey. For the sake of parsimony, not all categories are shown in the results from the analysis of cross tables. Results are shown for the category representing the most extreme (usually positive) view of the American Dream. Virtually all of the differences between men and women in table 1 are

Table 1. Percentages from cross-tabulations between sex and attitudes about the American Dream for Latino/as, African Americans, and whites (GSS 2012)

	Latino/as		African Americans		Whites	
	Males (%)	Females (%)	Males (%)	Females (%)	Males (%)	Females (%)
Standard of Living						
Standard of Living compared to Parents— Much Better	53	37	37	35	28	30
Kids' Standard of Living compared to R— Much Better	47	47	44	56	21	23
R's Standard of Living will Improve— Strongly Agree	28	23	24	16	9	10
Government Improve Standard of Living for Poor?— Yes	11	13	9	6	18	15
Financial						
Satisfaction with Financial Situation— Satisfied	22	15	21	22	32	29
Change in Financial Situation— Better	27	32	29	29	27	29
Opinion of Family Income— Far Above Average	2*	1*	2	4	3	3
Position/Getting Ahead						
Self-Ranking Social Position—Top	3	7	11	13	3	6
Subjective Class ID—Upper	3	1	2	4	6	3
Opinion How People Get Ahead—Hard Work	79	74	67	69	64*	74*
Confidence in Education—Great Deal	35	43	36	35	17	21
Race Discrimination						
Race Differences due to Discrimination—Yes	42	47	49	45	28	32
Race Differences due to Lack of Education—Yes	34	43	46	48	39	43

* Chi-square for cross-tab between sex and attitude item significant at .05 level.

Table 2. Percentages from cross-tabulations between sex and attitudes about the American Dream for Latino/as (Pew 2011 National Survey of Latino/as)

Standard of Living/ Situation of Latino/as	Males (%)	Females (%)
Situation of Latino/as compared to one year ago—Better	16*	11*
Latino/as' success relative to other ethnic/minority groups— More Successful	18	17
Conditions for raising children better US or country of origin —Better US	76*	69*
Children's standard of living relative to R's when reach R's age—Much Better	41	42
Standard of living compared to parent's at same age— Much Better	33	39
Satisfaction with Things Country		
Satisfaction with way things going in country—Satisfied	43	38
Financial		
Personal financial situation— Excellent Shape	6	3
Family financial situation over next year—Improve a lot	12	10
Latino/as hurt more or less than other groups by economy last 4 years—More	57	54

*Chi-square for cross-tab between sex and attitude item significant at .05 level.

shown to be nonsignificant. The major exception is for whites on the question of how people get ahead. Significantly more white females than males believe that working hard is important for getting ahead.

Figures presented in table 2 show opinions of men and women on the American Dream within Latino/as using data from Pew National Surveys of Latino/as (2011). The questions are similar but not identical to the questions in the GSS. Data in table 2 from the representative sample of Latino/as (Pew) concur with the data on Latino/as and other race/ethnic groups in the 2012 GSS and show few gender differences among Latino/as on a majority of opinions regarding the American Dream. The major exception is on conditions for raising children in the United States. Latino males are more likely than Latina females to say that conditions are preferable in the United States relative to country of origin of family. Across items, both Latino/a men and women tend to be most optimistic on this item.

BIVARIATE: EFFECT OF RACE/ETHNICITY WITHIN SEX GROUPS

Figures in table 3 show the influence of race/ethnicity within the male and female subsamples of the GSS data. Race has a significant effect on attitudes related to the American Dream on a majority of items for both males and females. The race pattern does vary, however, between men and women. For example, the items measuring attitudes about standard of living show that among males, most race/ethnic contrasts are significant, and Latino males are consistently the most optimistic while white males are consistently the least optimistic. The figures for females also show that race/ethnicity has a significant effect on most of the items. When there is a significant effect, sometimes Latina women are the most optimistic ("standard of living improve"), sometimes African American women are the most optimistic ("kids' standard of living much better"), and sometimes white women are the most supportive ("government improve standard of living for poor").

There are fewer race/ethnic differences within sex groups on the items measuring financial aspects of the Dream. Results do show that both white men and women are more satisfied with their financial situation than are their counterparts from other race/ethnic groups. The items measuring position and getting ahead show a complex pattern of race/ethnic/sex effects. Contrasts across race groups are significant for most items for both males and females. Both African American men and women tend to report a higher social ranking than do their counterparts. On subjective class identification white male reports are the highest among males, but both African American and white females report higher subjective class identification than do Latina

Table 3. Percentages from cross-tabulations between race/ethnicity and attitudes about the American Dream for males and females (GSS 2012)

	Males			Females		
	Latino (%)	African American (%)	White (%)	Latino (%)	African American (%)	White (%)
Standard of Living						
Standard of Living compared to Parents—Much Better	53*	37*	28*	37	35	30
Kids' Standard of Living compared to R—Much Better	47*	44*	21*	47*	56*	23*
R's Standard of Living will Improve—Strongly Agree	28*	24*	9*	23*	16*	10*
Government Improve Standard of Living for Poor?—Yes	11	9	18	13*	6*	15*
Financial						
Satisfaction with Financial Situation—Satisfied	22*	21*	32*	15*	22*	29*
Change in Financial Situation—Better	27	29	27	32	29	29
Opinion of Family Income—Far Above Average	2	2	3	1*	4*	3*
Position/Getting Ahead						
Self-Ranking Social Position—Top	3*	11*	3*	7*	13*	6*
Subjective Class ID—Upper	3*	2*	6*	1*	4*	3*
Opinion How People Get Ahead—Hard Work	79*	67*	64*	74	69	74
Confidence in Education—Great Deal	35*	36*	17*	43*	35*	21*
Race Discrimination						
Race Differences due to Discrimination—Yes	42*	49*	28*	47*	45*	32*
Race Differences due to Lack of Education—Yes	34	46	39	43	48	43

*Chi-square for cross-tab between race/ethnicity and attitude item significant at .05 level.

females. Interestingly, it is minority males and females (relative to white males and females) who have the most confidence in education.

Finally, results in table 3 show figures on attitudes toward race discrimination as a component in thinking about the American Dream for Latino/as. As with the confidence in education item, Latino males are similar to African American males (and similarly for Latina females and African American females) on their attitudes about race differences being due to discrimination. In both cases, these respondents report higher support of this statement than do their white counterparts. However, Latina women give even more support to this statement than do African American women. The opposite trend can be observed for males.

MULTIVARIATE MODELS FOR RACE/ETHNIC GROUPS
The trends shown in tables 1 through 3 provide an interesting look at the Latino/a American Dream through the lens of sex and race/ethnicity. Another goal of the chapter is to consider these sex/race/ethnic patterns in a multivariate context. First we consider multivariate findings for the effect of sex within race/ethnic groups (tables 4 through 7). We then consider multivariate findings for the effect of race/ethnicity for males and for females (tables 8 and 9). Tables 4 through 6 report findings from multivariate regression models predicting attitudes about the American Dream for Latino/as (table 4), African Americans (table 5), and whites (table 6) in the GSS data. Here we can examine the effect of sex within each race/ethnic group when other factors affecting attitudes are controlled (for example, socioeconomic status and age). Interestingly, the pattern shown in table 1 where there were few effects of sex on attitudes within any of the race/ethnic groups persists in the multivariate results presented in tables 4 through 6. The effect of sex was not being suppressed by the absence of age and socioeconomic status in the equation. Thus the GSS data suggest that Latino/a men and women have very similar attitudes about issues related to the American Dream. The same is the case for African American men and women as well as white men and women.

Results in table 7 show similar multivariate models (including sex and control variables) for Latino/as in the Pew Latino/a sample. As in the GSS data for Latino/as, African Americans, and whites, the bivariate trends showing little relationship between sex and attitudes about the American Dream (table 2) are replicated in the multivariate results. Even when education, income, and age are controlled, Latino/a men and women do not differ in their attitudes about the American Dream. Note that the one item that varied between Latino/a men and women in table 2 (on conditions for raising

Table 4. Regression of attitude about American Dream items on sex, class, and age—Latino/as (GSS 2012)†

Independent Variables	STANDARD OF LIVING (SOL)				FINANCIAL		
	SOL Compared to Parents	Kids' SOL Compared to R	R's SOL will Improve	Government Improve SOL for Poor?	Satisfaction with Financial Situation	Change in Financial Situation	Opinion of Family Income
Sex (1 = female; 0 = male)	-.25(.17)	.20(.19)	-.39(.14)*	.08(.08)	-.08(.10)	.23(.12)	-.05(.12)
Education (in years)	-.03(.02)	.00(.03)	-.04(.02)*	-.03(.01)*	-.00(.01)	.02(.02)	.02(.02)
Family Income (1 = < 1,000; 25 = 150,000+)	.05(.02)*	.01(.02)	.01(.02)	.01(.00)	.02(.01)	.02(.01)	.07(.01)*
Age (in years)	-.01(.01)	-.02(.00)*	-.02(.00)*	.00(.00)	-.01(.00)	-.10(.00)*	-.01(.00)
Constant	4.22(.46)*	4.58(.50)*	.08(.37)*	.26(.21)	1.82(.27)*	1.71(.33)*	1.63(.32)*
R²	.07	.05	.10	.14	.03	.06	.21

Independent Variables	POSITION/GETTING AHEAD				RACE DISCRIMINATION	
	Self-Ranking Social Position	Subjective Class ID	Opinion Get Ahead—Work	Confidence in Education	Race Differences Due to Discrimination	Race Differences Due to Lack of Education
Sex (1 = female; 0 = male)	.00(.26)	.06(.10)	-.07(.07)	.18(.10)	.03(.12)	-.22(.11)
Education (in years)	.10(.04)*	-.02(.02)	-.01(.01)	-.02(.01)	-.02(.02)	.02(.02)
Family Income (1 = < 1,000; 25 = 150,000+)	.02(.03)	.04(.01)*	-.01(.01)	-.03(.01)*	-.00(.01)	-.01(.01)
Age (in years)	.03(.01)*	.01(.00)	-.00(.00)	.00(.00)	.00(.17)	.01(.00)*
Constant	3.32(.69)*	1.47(.24)*	1.14(.17)*	.80(.28)*	.50(.33)	.12(.32)
R²	.10	.14	.04	.21	.06	.10

* Regression coefficient significant at ≤ .05.
† Standard errors in parentheses.

Table 5. Regression of attitude about American Dream items on sex, class, and age—African Americans (GSS 2012)†

Independent Variables	STANDARD OF LIVING (SOL)				FINANCIAL		
	SOL Compared to Parents	Kids' SOL Compared to R	R's SOL will Improve	Government Improve SOL for Poor?	Satisfaction with Financial Situation	Change in Financial Situation	Opinion of Family Income
Sex (1 = female; 0 = male)	.20(.19)	.45(.22)*	-.10(.17)	.01(.01)	-.05(.13)	.13(.14)	.15(.15)
Education (in years)	-.04(.04)	-.02(.04)	-.00(.03)	-.02(.01)*	.00(.02)	.02(.03)	.02(.03)
Family Income (1 = < 1,000; 25 = 150,000+)	.07(.02)*	-.01(.02)	.02(.02)	.01(.00)	.01(.01)	.02(.01)	.05(.01)*
Age (in years)	.01(.00)	-.02(.00)*	-.01(.00)*	.00(.00)	.00(.00)	-.01(.00)*	-.01(.00)
Constant	3.05(.55)*	5.26(.64)*	3.92(.50)*	.12(.15)	1.53(.36)*	1.81(.40)*	1.92(.41)*

Independent Variables	POSITION/GETTING AHEAD				RACE DISCRIMINATION	
	Self-Ranking Social Position	Subjective Class ID	Opinion Get Ahead—Work	Confidence in Education	Race Differences Due to Discrimination	Race Differences Due to Lack of Education
Sex (1 = female; 0 = male)	.58(.32)	-.01(.12)	.02(.08)	-.02(.12)	-.01(.14)	-.03(.14)
Education (in years)	-.08(.06)	.02(.02)	.01(.02)	.01(.02)	.01(.02)	.00(.02)
Family Income (1 = < 1,000; 25 = 150,000+)	.07(.03)*	.02(.01)	-.01(.00)	-.02(.01)*	-.01(.01)	-.01(.01)
Age (in years)	.00(.01)	.01(.00)	.00(.00)	-.00(.00)	.00(.00)	.00(.00)
Constant	5.52(.88)*	1.51(.32)*	.63(.22)*	.48(.32)	.38(.37)	.30(.37)
R^2	.06	.06	.01	.06	.02	.01

.12

* Regression coefficient significant at ≤ .05.

Table 6. Regression of attitude about American Dream items on sex, class, and age—whites (GSS 2012)†

Independent Variables	STANDARD OF LIVING (SOL)				FINANCIAL		
	SOL Compared to Parents	Kids' SOL Compared to R	R's SOL will Improve	Government Improve SOL for Poor?	Satisfaction with Financial Situation	Change in Financial Situation	Opinion of Family Income
Sex (1 = female; 0 = male)	.08(.09)	.20(.10)*	-.12(.08)	-.04(.03)	-.04(.05)	.06(.06)	.02(.06)
Education (in years)	-.03(.02)	.00(.02)	-.02(.02)	-.00(.00)	.04(.01)*	-.02(.01)*	.05(.01)*
Family Income (1 = < 1,000; 25 = 150,000+)	.05(.01)*	-.01(.01)	.01(.01)	.01(.00)	.04(.00)*	.01(.00)*	.09(.01)*
Age (in years)	.00(.00)	-.01(.00)*	-.01(.00)*	.00(.00)*	.01(.00)*	-.01(.00)*	.00(.00)
Constant	2.94(.29)*	4.18(.30)*	3.89(.25)*	.02(.11)	.50(.16)*	2.36(.19)*	.57(.18)*

Independent Variables	POSITION/GETTING AHEAD				RACE DISCRIMINATION	
	Self-Ranking Social Position	Subjective Class ID	Opinion Get Ahead—Work	Confidence in Education	Race Differences Due to Discrimination	Race Differences Due to Lack of Education
Sex (1 = female; 0 = male)	.05(.12)	-.02(.05)	.08(.04)*	-.02(.04)	.04(.05)	.06(.05)
Education (in years)	.08(.03)*	.06(.01)*	-.02(.01)*	-.01(.01)	.01(.01)	.03(.01)*
Family Income (1 = < 1,000; 25 = 150,000+)	.06(.01)*	.04(.01)*	-.00(.00)	-.01(.00)	-.02(.00)*	-.00(.00)
Age (in years)	.01(.00)*	.00(.00)	-.00(.00)	-.00(.00)	.00(.00)*	.00(.00)
Constant	3.96(.39)*	.64(.15)*	.97(.11)*	.48(.12)*	.41(.14)*	.06(.16)
R²	.08	.25	.02	.03	.06	.03

R² (Standard of Living / Financial panel): .05

* Regression coefficient significant at ≤ .05
† Standard errors in parentheses.

Table 7. Regression of attitude about American Dream items on sex, class, and age—Latino/as (PEW 2011 National Survey of Latinos)†

STANDARD OF LIVING (SOL)/SITUATION OF LATINO/AS

Independent Variables	Situation Latino/as Compared to One Year Ago	Latino/a Success relative to other ethnic/minority groups	Conditions for raising children better U.S. or Country of Origin	Children's SOL relative to R's when reach R's age	SOL compared to parent's at same age
Sex (1 = female; 0 = male)	.02 (.05)	.03 (.06)	-.06 (.04)	.07 (.09)	.02 (.09)
Education (1 = HS degree or higher; 0 = less than HS degree)	.09 (.06)	-.02 (.07)	.07 (.05)	.22 (.11)*	.08 (.10)
Family Income (1 = < $10,000; 25 = > $150,000+)	.02 (.01)	.01 (.02)	.01 (.01)	.06 (.02)*	-.06 (.02)*
Age (in years)	.00 (.00)	.01 (.00)*	.00 (.00)	.01 (.00)*	.00 (.00)
R^2	.00	.02	.01	.04	.01

Independent Variables	SATISFACTION WITH THINGS COUNTRY Satisfaction with way things going in country	FINANCIAL Personal financial situation	Family financial situation next year	Latino/as hurt more or less than other groups by economy last 4 years
Sex (1 = female; 0 = male)	.05 (.04)	-.02 (.05)	.05 (.11)	-.01 (.04)
Education (1 = HS degree or higher; 0 = less than HS degree)	.02 (.04)	-.07 (.06)	-.08 (.12)	.03 (.05)
Family Income (1 = < $10,000; 25 = > $150,000+)	.01 (.01)	-.15 (.01)*	-.01 (.03)	.02 (.01)*
Age (in years)	.00 (.00)	.00 (.00)	.00 (.00)	.00 (.00)
R^2	.00	.19	.00	.01

* Regression coefficient significant at ≤.05.
† Standard errors in parentheses.

children in the United States) no longer varies by sex when other factors are controlled.

MULTIVARIATE MODELS FOR MALES AND FEMALES

Figures from multivariate regression models predicting attitudes about the American Dream for males (table 8) and for females (table 9) allow us to answer additional questions about the influence of race/ethnicity on attitudes about the American Dream for Latino/a males and females. More specifically, they allow us to examine whether the influence of race/ethnicity within sex groups exists when other factors that influence attitudes are taken into account (for example, age and socioeconomic status). Results in tables 8 and 9 also allow us to see which race/ethnic contrasts (here our interest is in comparisons between Latino/as and other race/ethnic groups) are significant in the attitude equations for males and for females.

Figures in table 8 show that there are few differences among Latino males and those from other race/ethnic groups on the American Dream items when age and socioeconomic status are controlled. In table 3 we saw a good number of differences between males across race/ethnic groups on the Dream items. The multivariate results that control for other potential causal variables and make contrasts between Latino men and African American men (as well as white men) show fewer significant effects of race/ethnicity. When there are differences they involve the standard of living items, and the contrasts tend to be significant in both the comparisons with African Americans and the comparisons with whites. For all contrasts, it is Latino men who have more positive attitudes (as in the bivariate analyses presented in table 2). Latino men are more optimistic than African American men and white men on standard of living compared to parents' and on kids' standard of living compared to self. They are also more positive than white men on whether their standard of living will improve.

Figures in table 9 show the effect of race/ethnicity on attitudes about the American Dream for women when age and socioeconomic status are controlled. There are slightly more significant contrasts between Latina women and other women than there were for Latino men in table 8. These contrasts go across areas of the American Dream (standard of living, financial, and position/getting ahead). It is the contrasts with white women that are more often significant. Latina women are more positive about standard of living items and the getting ahead item measuring confidence in education than white women. White women are, however, more positive than Latina

Table 8: Regression of attitude about American Dream items on race/ethnicity, class, and age—males (GSS 2012)†

	STANDARD OF LIVING (SOL)				FINANCIAL		
Independent Variables	SOL Compared to Parents	Kids' SOL Compared to R	R's SOL will Improve	Government Improve SOL fo: Poor?	Satisfaction with Financial Situation	Change in Financial Situation	Opinion of Family Income
African American (comparison is Latino)	-.55 (.20)*	-.48(.23)*	-.13(.18)	-.02(.10)	-.22(.12)	.18(.15)	-.10(.12)
White (comparison is Latino)	-.81(.15)*	-.92(.18)*	-.51(.14)*	.07(.07)	-.17(.09)	.18(.11)	-.05(.10)
Education (in years)	-.03(.02)	-.01(.02)	-.03(.02)*	-.01(.00)*	.03(.01)*	-.01(.00)	.04(.01)*
Family Income (1 = < 1,000; 25 = 150,000+)	.06(.01)*	-.01(.01)	.01(.01)	.01(.00)	.03(.00)*	.01(.00)	.08(.01)*
Age (in years)	-.01(.00)	-.02(.00)*	-.01(.00)*	.00(.00)	.00(.00)	-.01(.00)*	-.00(.00)
Constant	3.86(.29)*	5.32(.33)*	4.72(.26)*	.09(.14)	1.17(.18)*	2.13(.21)*	1.12(.19)*
R²	.12	.13	.10	.03	.09	.03	.32

	POSITION/GETTING AHEAD				RACE DISCRIMINATION	
Independent Variables	Self-Ranking Social Position	Subjective Class ID	Opinion Get Ahead—Work	Confidence in Education	Race Differences Due to Discrimination	Race Differences Due to Lack of Education
African American (comparison is Latino)	.04(.26)	.06(.10)	-.06(.08)	-.04(.13)	-.03(.13)	-.15(.14)
White (comparison is Latino)	.35(.21)	.08(.08)	-.00(.06)	-.06(.07)	-.14(.09)	-.14(.10)
Education (in years)	.07(.03)*	.04(.01)*	-.02(.01)*	-.03(.00)*	-.00(.00)	.01(.01)
Family Income (1 = < 1,000; 25 = 150,000+)	.06(.02)*	.05(.01)*	-.00(.00)	-.01(.00)*	-.02(.00)*	-.00(.00)
Age (in years)	.01(.00)	.00(.00)	.00(.00)	.00(.00)	.01(.00)*	.00(.00)
Constant	3.64(.40)*	.91(.15)*	1.01(.12)*	.81(.15)*	.63(.17)*	.38(.19)*
R²	.10	.25	.02	.09	.09	.01

* Regression coefficient significant at ≤ .05.
† Standard errors in parentheses.

Table 9. Regression of attitude about American Dream items on race/ethnicity, class, and age—females (GSS 2012)†

Independent Variables	STANDARD OF LIVING (SOL)				FINANCIAL		
	SOL Compared to Parents	Kids' SOL Compared to R	R's SOL will Improve	Government Improve SOL for Poor?	Satisfaction with Financial Situation	Change in Financial Situation	Opinion of Family Income
African American (comparison is Latina)	.05(.19)	.10(.19)	.01(.18)	-.11(.07)	-.16(.11)	.20(.13)	.24(.13)*
White (comparison is Latina)	-.38(.16)*	-.51(.16)*	-.43(.15)*	-.04(.06)	-.16(.10)	.25(.11)*	.11(.11)
Education (in years)	-.02(.02)	-.02(.02)	-.04(.02)*	-.01(.00)*	.02(.01)*	.00(.01)	.04(.01)*
Family Income (1 = < 1,000; 25 = 150,000+)	.05(.01)*	.00(.01)	.01(.01)	-.01(.00)*	.04(.00)*	.02(.00)*	.07(.01)*
Age (in years)	.00(.46)	-.02(.00)*	-.01(.00)*	.00(.00)	.00(.00)*	.01(.00)*	.00(.00)
Constant	3.31(.30)*	5.07(.30)*	4.52(.27)*	.07(.11)	.89(.18)*	1.77(.20)*	.93(.20)*
R^2	.07	.09	.07	.06	.12	.04	.27

Independent Variables	POSITION/GETTING AHEAD				RACE DISCRIMINATION	
	Self-Ranking Social Position	Subjective Class ID	Opinion Get Ahead—Work	Confidence in Education	Race Differences Due to Discrimination	Race Differences Due to Lack of Education
African American (comparison is Latina)	.68(.25)*	-.10(.09)	-.05(.06)	-.21(.08)*	.01(.10)	.06(.10)
White (comparison is Latina)	.06(.03)*	.04(.01)*	-.00(.00)	.00(.00)	-.01(.01)	.02(.01)*
Education (in years)	.05(.01)*	.03(.01)*	-.01(.00)*	-.01(.01)*	-.01(.01)	-.01(.01)
Family Income (1 = < 1,000; 25 = 150,000+)	.05(.01)*	.01(.00)*	-.00(.00)	-.00(.00)	-.01(.01)*	.00(.00)
Age (in years)	.01(.00)*	.01(.00)*	-.00(.00)	-.00(.00)	-.01(.01)*	.00(.00)
Constant	3.55(.43)*	1.10(.16)*	1.01(.12)*	.67(.15)*	.69(.17)*	.09(.18)
R^2	.08	.17	.02	.08	.05	.02

* Regression coefficient significant at ≤ .05.

† Standard errors in parentheses.

women on a financial item (change in financial situation) and a position item (self-ranking). African American women are also more positive than Latina women on these two items.

Our analysis of data from two large probability samples (GSS and Pew) has provided some insights into questions about the intersection between race/ethnicity, sex, and the American Dream for Latino/as. Analyses of the effects of sex within race/ethnic groups for the 2012 GSS data and the 2011 Pew data show few differences between Latino/a males and females on attitudes about the American Dream even when socioeconomic status and age are controlled. This pattern held for other race/ethnic groups as well (African Americans and whites). We also looked at the effect of race/ethnicity within gender groups using the GSS data. Here our results showed considerable differences across race/ethnic groups for both males and females. On a good number of items, Latino/a men and women were more positive about the Dream than their African American or white counterparts. The pattern did vary somewhat for men and for women. These findings on effects of sex and effects of race/ethnicity changed very little in our multivariate models that controlled for age and socioeconomic status.

Conclusions

SUMMARY

This chapter examines the American Dream for Latino/as from a perspective that stresses the intersection between race/ethnicity and gender. Early models of achievement in the social sciences tended to take an individualist approach and examined the influences of race/ethnicity and gender as separate processes. Increasingly, scholars across a wide array of disciplines are moving toward an acknowledgment of the fact that race/ethnicity and gender are embedded in social structures, and they intersect in ways that are not additive or cumulative. Our findings on the American Dream for Latino/a men and women confirm the ongoing race/ethnic and gender inequality in the United States through the perspective of the American Dream. We find that Latino/as have had lower success in achieving the American Dream than other race/ethnic groups on most measures. To some extent, Latino/a men and women are both struggling to achieve the Dream and have not experienced the success of other race/ethnic groups. On the other hand, Latino men are ahead of Latina women on some measures of the Dream, and Latina women are catching up to and surpassing Latino men on others. We also examined attitudes about the American Dream for Latino/a men and women. Here we find considerable optimism. On many items (for example, involving standard of living and getting ahead), Latino/a men and women are more optimistic than men and women in other race/ethnic groups. This is not the case for financial items, however. The race/ethnic pattern is not identical for Latino/a males and females; for example, on some items Latina females are the most positive among females but Latino males are not the most positive among males.

Discussion

One of the notes of optimism in this chapter involves the gains that Latina women are making in achieving the American Dream. Data from the 2010 census show that the wage ratio (earnings compared to white males) for Latina women is lower than that for men and women in any other major race/ethnic group at 60 percent (Pearson 2012). In spite of this wage disadvantage relative to Latino men and to other women, findings in this chapter show considerable gains for Latina women. In fact, unlike Latino men, Latina women are a part of a rising success story in the US education system. The total number of master's degrees awarded to Latina women more than doubled during the past decade (Kim 2011). Some researchers have found that young Latina women use educational attainment and schools as a way to resist cultural stereotypes, but young Latino men avoid school as a way to escape negative judgments associated with stereotypes (College Board Advocacy and Policy Center 2010). A recent report by the American Council on Education provides data that reveal young women (across race/ethnic groups) doing better than generations before them on postsecondary educational attainment (Kim 2011). The intersectionality approach and a critical perspective shed insight on these gains by suggesting the positive impact of immigration on some gender systems, the diversity of gender cultures among Latino/as, and the inaccuracy of simple stereotypes about traditional, passive Latinas.

Additionally, the acknowledgment of the power of structures as well as the power of the individual through human agency are key to understanding the experiences and hopes of Latino/as in achieving the American Dream (Yosso 2005; Hanson 2009; Agger 1998; Grant, Horan, and Watts-Warren 1994). It is through this lens that we can best understand the optimism of Latino/a men and women on their opportunity to get ahead and improve the standard of living for themselves and their children in spite of their low ranking on many objective measures of the American Dream. The hopefulness of these Latino/a men and women reflects (and revives) core values of the American Dream. It is also through this lens that we can understand the increased agency of Latina women in their optimism about education as a way to get ahead and in their rising educational achievements.

Our findings on the situation of young Latino men in their search for the American Dream are less optimistic. Here, structural arrangements involving a weak economy, poor educational systems, and peer gang cultures have had negative implications for these young men's dreams. Young minority men (except Asian Americans) have done less well than earlier generations. This is the American Dream in reverse with each generation of males slipping further behind rather than moving further ahead. The College Board Advocacy and Policy Center (2010) has suggested an educational crisis facing young men of color. They suggest that public and media images of young men of color are powerful tools that too often present stereotyped, inaccurate, violent images of gangs and drugs. The Center raises the issue of a "third America" made up of young minority men who are often ignored by larger society and the implications of this trend for equality of access to the American Dream (College Board Advocacy and Policy Center 2010).

We began this chapter with a statement about the current concern among Americans over the possibility of the American Dream. Contemporary trends involving immigrant streams and the Great Recession have colored the attitudes of Americans toward the Dream and who is most deserving of it. Both public opinion and the media seem most concerned with whether the American Dream will continue to be achievable by white, middle-class Americans. The nation's immigrant history and the contributions of contemporary immigrant groups to the US culture and economy are seldom noted in this discussion of the Dream. Charles Gonzales (former representative and chair of the Congressional Hispanic Caucus) argues that the fifty-million-strong Hispanic community in the United States has a vision, work ethic, and creativity that has helped America become a better and stronger nation (Gonzalez 2011). The examination of Latino/as and the American Dream in this chapter shows a belief in the Dream that has not been paralleled by equality of achievement. Our look at the way gender and race/ethnicity combine to affect the pursuit of and belief in the American Dream suggests that Latino/a men and women have much in common, but also distinct experiences on their path to the Dream. Research and policies aimed at reducing race/ethnic inequality in the United States need to consider the structures that limit Latino/as, their agency in sometimes surmounting the limits of these structures, the unique experiences of Latino/as (relative to other ethnic/minority groups), and the ways in which the American experience and Dream are not identical for Latino/a men and women.

Notes

1. *Agency* is a term often used by critical theorists to denote the degree of free will exerted by the individual in social actions. *Structure*, on the other hand, refers to recurring patterns of behavior in an area of life that put pressures on us to conform (James, Jenks, and Prout 1998).

2. Giddens's (1984) theory of structuration is very informative for multicultural gender scholars taking this critical perspective. Giddens argues the import of structure but the potential for human action to modify and change these structures.

3. Although we note the import of the intersection between race and ethnicity, data from Pew and other sources seldom provide information for different race groups among Latino/as.

References

Acs, G. 2012. "Downward Mobility from the Middle Class: Waking Up from the American Dream." A Research Report. Washington, DC: Pew Charitable Trusts.

Agger, B. 1998. *Critical Social Theories: An Introduction.* Boulder, CO: Westview.

Alba, R. 2005. "Bright vs. Blurred Boundaries: Second Generation Assimilation and Exclusion in France, Germany, and the United States." *Ethnic and Racial Studies* 28: 20–49.

American Council on Education. 2011. "By the Numbers: ACE Report Identifies Education Barriers for Hispanics." Accessed on July 11, 2012, at http://www.acenet.edu/the-presidency/columns-and-features/Pages/By-the-Numbers-ACE-Report-Identifies-Educational-Barriers-for-Hispanics.aspx.

Anderson, M. L. 2005. *Thinking about Women: Sociological Perspectives on Sex and Gender.* Boston: Allyn and Bacon.

Andersen, M. L., and P. H. Collins. 1995. *Race, Class, and Gender: An Anthology.* Belmont, CA: Wadsworth.

Babco, E. L. 2001. "Underrepresented Minorities in Engineering: A Progress Report." American Association for the Advancement of Science.

Barton, P. E. 2003. "Parsing the Achievement Gap: Baselines for Tracking Progress." Policy Information Report. Accessed on May 10, 2013, at http://eric.ed.gov/?id=ED482932.

Bennetts, L. 2011. "Women: The invisible Poor." Daily Beast, September 14. Accessed on June 20, 2012, at http://www.thedailybeast.com/articles/2011/9/14.

Blau, P. M., and O. D. Duncan. 1967. *The American Occupational Structure.* New York: John Wiley and Sons.

Bobo, L. D. 2009. "Race Attitudes and the Maintenance of Inequality: Do They Matter and Why?" Presentation at American Sociological Association, San Francisco, August.

Brettel, C. B., and C. F. Sargent. 2012. *Gender in Cross Cultural Perspective.* Upper Saddle River, NJ: Pearson.

Brown, A. H. 2000. "Creative Pedagogy to Enhance the Academic Achievement of Minority Students in Math." In *The Academic Achievement of Minority Students*, edited by S. T. Gregory, 365–90. New York: University Press of America.

Browne, I., and J. Misra. 2003. "The Intersection of Gender and Race in the Labor Market." *Annual Review of Sociology* 29: 487–513.

Buijs, G. 1993. *Migrant Women: Crossing Boundaries and Changing Identities.* Providence, RI: Berg.

Chant, S. 1992. *Gender and Migration in Developing Countries.* New York: Bellhaven Press.

Cobas, J. A., J. Duany, and J. R. Feagin. 2009. *How the United States Racializes Latinos: White Hegemony and Its Consequences.* Boulder, CO: Paradigm.

Coleman, J. S. 1988. "Social Capital in the Creation of Human Capital." *American Journal of Sociology* 94: S95–S120.

College Board Advocacy and Policy Center. 2010. "The Educational Crisis Facing Young Men of Color." Accessed on April 16, 2012, at http://www.advocacy.collegeboard.rog/sites/default/files/educational.

Collins, P. H. 1990. *Black Feminist Thought.* Boston: Unwin Hyman.

———. 1999. "Moving beyond Gender: Intersectionality and Scientific Knowledge." In *Revisioning Gender*, edited by M. M. Ferree, J. Lorber, and B. B. Hess, 261–84. Thousand Oaks, CA: Stanford University Press.

———. 2010. "Gender, Black Feminism, and Black Political Economy." *Annals of the American Academy of Political and Social Science* 568: 41–53.

Daniels, S. M. 2010. "Report: College Remains Elusive for Many Hispanic Men." Accessed on March 5, 2012, at http://articles.chicagotribune.com/2010-04-04/news/ct-met-latinos-college-20100316_1_hispanic-immigrants-latino-studies-chicana-and-chicano-studies.

DeFrancisco, V. P., and C. H. Palczewski. 2007. *Communicating Gender Diversity: A Critical Approach.* Los Angeles: Sage.

De Los Rios, C. 2007. "Gender and Identity in a Community of Working-Class Latina Mothers." PhD diss., University of Maryland–Baltimore.

Dill, B. T. 1980. "The Means to Put My Children Through: Childrearing Goals and Strategies among Black Female Domestic Servants." In *The Black Woman*, edited by L. F. R. Rose, 107–24. Beverly Hills, CA: Sage.

Feliciano, C., and B. Robnett. 2014. "How External Racial Classifications Shape Latino Dating Choices." *DuBois Review* 11 (2): 295–328.

Felix, Antonia. 2010. *Sonia Sotomayor: The True American Dream*. New York: Berkley Books.

Fry, Richard. 2009. "The Changing Pathways of Hispanic Youths into Adulthood." Pew Hispanic Research Center. http://www.pewhsiapnic.org/files/reports/114.pdf.

Gandara, P., and F. Contreras. 2009. *The Latino Education Crisis: The Consequences of Failed Social Policies*. Cambridge, MA: Harvard University Press.

GSS (General Social Survey). 2012. Accessed at http://publicdata.norc.org:41000/gss/documents/BOOK/GSS_Codebook.pdf.

Giddens, A. 1984. *The Constitution of Society: Outline of the Theory of Structuration*. Berkeley: University of California Press.

Glenn, E. N. 1985. "Racial Ethnic Women's Labor: The Intersection of Race, Gender, and Class Oppression." *Review of Radical Political Economics* 17: 8–108.

———. 1991. "Racial Ethnic Women's Labor: The Intersection of Race, Gender, and Class Oppression". In *Gender, Family, and the Economy: The Triple Overlap*, edited by R. L. Blumberg. Newbury Park, CA: Sage.

Glynn, J., and A. Powers. 2012. "The Top 10 Facts about the Wage Gap: Women Are Still Earning Less Than Men across the Board." Center for American Progress. http://americanpprogress.org/issues/2012/04/wage_gap_facts.html.

Gonzalez, C. 2011. "Renewing the American Dream: Hispanics' Share of the Dream." Accessed on January 10, 2011, at http://www.whitehouse.gov/blog/2011/10/11/renewing/american/dream/hispanics.

Gonzalez, F. 2008. "Hispanic Women in the United States, 2007." Pew Hispanic Research Center. Pew Research Center.

Grant, L., P. M. Horan, and B. Watts-Warren. 1994. "Theoretical Diversity in the Analysis of Gender and Education." *Research in Sociology of Education* 10: 71–109.

Halgunseth, L. C. 2004. "Continuing Research on Latino Families." In *Handbook of Contemporary Families*, edited by M. Coleman and L. H. Ganong. Thousand Oaks, CA: Sage.

Hanson, S. L. 2009. *Swimming against the Tide: African American Girls in Science Education*. Philadelphia: Temple University Press.

Higginbotham, E., and M. L. Andersen, eds. 2006. *Race and Ethnicity in Society: The Changing Landscape*. Belmont, CA: Wadsworth.

Hitlin, S. J., S. Brown, and G. H. Elder. 2007. "Measuring Latinos: Racial vs. Ethnic Classification and Self-Understandings." *Social Forces* 86: 587–600.

Hooks, B. 1984. *Feminist Theory: From Margin to Center.* Cambridge, MA: South End Press.

James, A., C. Jenks, and A. Prout. 1998. *Theorizing Childhood.* New York: Teachers College Press.

Jarvis, G. A., and M. Salomone. 1988. "Principles of Language Learning and Teaching, 2nd ed. H. Douglas Brown. Englewood Cliffs, NJ: Prentice-Hall, 1987. Pp. xvi + 285." *Studies in Second Language Acquisition* 10 (03): 400–402.

Kao, G., and L. T. Rutherford. 2007. "Does Social Capital Still Matter? Immigrant Minority Disadvantage in Social Capital and Its Effects on Academic Achievement." *Sociological Perspectives* 50: 27–52.

Kim, Y. M. 2011. "Minorities in Higher Education." Accessed on February 15, 2012, at http://diversity.ucsc.edu/resources/images/ace_report.pdf.

Lindsey, L. L. 2011. *Gender Roles: A Sociological Perspective.* Upper Saddle River, NJ: Pearson, Prentice Hall.

Lorber, J. 1994. *Paradoxes of Gender.* New Haven, CT: Yale University Press.

Mangan, K. 2011. "Educators Push Efforts to Get More Latino Men into College." *Chronicle of Higher Education* 58 (6): B4–B7.

Mann, S. A., and D. J. Huffman. 2005. "The Decentering of Second Wave Feminism and the Rise of the Third Wave." *Science and Society* 69: 56–91.

Mather, M., and L. A. Jacobsen. 2011. "Hard Times for Latino Men in the U.S." Accessed on February 10, 2012, at www.prb.org/Publications/Articles/latinomen.aspx.

Moynihan, D. P. 1965. "The Negro Family: The Case for National Action." Office of Policy Planning and Research, US Department of Labor. Washington, DC: Government Printing Office.

National Women's Law Center. 2011. "Poverty among Women and Families, 2000–2010." Washington, DC: National Women's Law Center.

Omi, M., and H. Winant. 2009. "Thinking through Race and Racism." *Contemporary Sociology* 38 (2): 121–25.

Osmond, M. W., and B. Thorne. 1993. "Feminist Theories: The Social Construction of Gender in Families and Society." In *Sourcebook of Family Theories and Methods: A Contextual Approach*, edited by P. G. Boss, W. J Doherty, R. LaRossa, W. R. Schumm, and S. K. Steinmetz, 591–623. New York: Plenum.

Pearce, S. C., E. J. Clifford, and R. Tandon. 2011. *Immigration and Women: Understanding the American Experience.* New York: New York University Press.

Pearson Education. 2015. "The Wage Gap, by Gender and Race." Accessed on August 14, 2015, at http://www.infoplease.com/ipa/A0882775.html.

Pedraza, S. 1991. "Women and Migration: The Social Consequences of Gender." *Annual Review of Sociology* 17: 303–25.

Peng, S. S., D. Wright, and S. Hill. 1995. "Understanding Racial-Ethnic Differences in Secondary School Science and Mathematics Achievement." Washington, DC: National Center for Education Statistics. February.

Perez, A. D. 2008. Who Is Hispanic? Shades of Ethnicity among Latino/a Youth." In *Racism in Post-Race America: New Theories, New Directions,* edited by C. A. Gallagher, 17–35. Chapel Hill, NC: Social Forces Publishing.

Pew Hispanic Center. 2009. "Between Two Worlds: How Young Latinos Come of Age in America." Accessed on January 12, 2010, at http://www.pewhispanic.org/2009/12/11/between-two-worlds.

———. 2010. "Statistical Portrait of Hispanics in the United States, 2008. Washington, DC: Pew Hispanic Center.

Pew. 2013. National Survey of Latinos. Accessed at http://www.pewhispanic.org/2013/09/25/2011-national-survey-of-latinos/.

Rochin, R. I., and S. F. Mello. 2007. "Latinos in Science: Trends and Opportunities." *Journal of Hispanic Higher Education* 6 (4): 305–55.

Romero, M. 2002. *Maid in the U.S.A.* New York: Routledge.

Rossiter, M. S. 1982. *Women Scientists in America: Struggles and Strategies to 1940.* Baltimore: Johns Hopkins University Press.

Roth, W. D. 2010. "Racial Mismatch: The Divergence between Form and Function in Data for Monitoring Racial Discrimination of Hispanics." *Social Science Quarterly* 91: 1288–311.

Rothenberg, P. S. 1992. *Race, Class, and Gender in the United States.* New York: St. Martins Press.

Ruiz, V. 1987. *Cannery Women, Cannery Lives: Mexican Women, Unionization, and the California Food Processing Industry, 1939–1950.* Albuquerque: University of New Mexico Press.

Sewell, W. H., A. O. Haller, and A. Portes. 1969. "The Educational and Early Occupational Attainment Process." *American Sociological Review* 34: 82–92.

Small, M. L., D. J. Harding, and M. Lamont. 2010. "Reconsidering Culture and Poverty." *Annals of the American Academy of Political and Social Science* 629 (1): 6–27.

Solórzano, D. G., and T. J. Yosso. 2002. "Critical Race Methodology: Counter-Storytelling as an Analytical Framework for Education Research." *Qualitative Inquiry* 8 (1): 23–44.

Walberg, H. 1984. "Improving the Productivity of America's Schools." *Educational Leadership* (May): 19–27.

West, C., and S. Fenstermaker. 1995. "Doing Difference." *Gender and Society* 9 (1): 8–37.

Wilson, W. J. 2010. "Why Both Social Structure and Culture Matter in a Holistic Analysis of Inner-City Poverty." *Annals of the American Academy of Political and Social Science* 629 (1): 200–219.

Wiborg, Ø. N., and M. N. Hansen. 2009. "Change over Time in the Intergenerational Transmission of Social Disadvantage." *European Sociological Review* 25 (3): 379–94.

Winant, H. 2009. "Just Do It: Notes on Politics and Race at the Dawn of the Obama Presidency." *DuBois Review* 6 (1): 49–70.

Yosso , T. J. 2005. "Whose Culture Has Capital? A Critical Race Theory Discussion of Community Cultural Wealth." *Race Ethnicity and Education* 8 (1): 69–91.

Yosso, T. J., and D. G. Solórzano. 2005. "Conceptualizing a Critical Race Theory in Sociology." *Blackwell Companion to Social Inequalities*, 117–26.

———. 2006. "Latino Policy and Issues Brief." UCLA Chicano Studies Research Center (13).

Zinn, M. B., and B. T. Dill. 1996. "Theorizing Difference from Multiracial Feminism." *Feminist Studies* 22 (2): 321–31.

Conclusion

SANDRA L. HANSON AND JOHN KENNETH WHITE

ome years ago, Richard M. Nixon declared, "People react to fear, not love. They don't teach that in Sunday school, but it's true" (Nixon 1992). Nixon's statement was uttered at the height of the Cold War—a time when Americans were attuned to fears about communism (both abroad and at home). The Cold War provided an easy paradigm political discussion: "us" were the good Americans and "them" were the bad communists behind the Iron Curtain. We espoused freedom, equality of opportunity, and individual rights, while the Soviet Union and its allies favored state control, an equality of result, and an emphasis on working class (supposedly).

While the Cold War has long since ended, Nixon's unfortunate aphorism still holds true. But today instead of American wrath being directed at communists, our fears are directed at one another. In both instances, the source of fear remains the same: Are those we classify as being "un-American" truly so, and are they in our midst? During the Cold War, the phrase *McCarthyism* became a kind of political shorthand for those who saw their fellow citizens as not sharing their fundamental values. Today a different kind of McCarthyism exists, as fears about the future are directed at newcomers to our homeland—whether they are here legally or illegally. Harry Truman once said, "Confident people do not become communists" (Truman 1948, 610). While Truman sought to allay fears about communists in our midst, his point about confidence is well taken. Today there is a lack of confidence in the nature of the American experiment, whether its continued success is assured, and what the future holds.

A key feature of our current politics is the willingness of so many Americans to be impervious to facts. Daniel Patrick Moynihan famously said, "Everyone is entitled to his own opinions, but not his own facts" ("An American Original" 2010). Ronald Reagan agreed, telling his fellow Republicans in 1988, "Facts are stubborn things" (Reagan 1988). While still stubborn, facts no longer seem to govern much of our highly charged partisan debates. This is especially true when it comes to immigration. Many longtime natives see today's newcomers as the "other." A new politics of "us" versus "them" is animated by Nixon's politics of fear, just as it was during the Cold War. Native-born Americans feel threatened by newly arrived Hispanics who speak a language other than English, have different cultural tastes, and often live in self-contained enclaves. This resentment is also fueled by a kind of perverse patriotism, as memories of a mostly all-white 1960s America fade into history, and whites are destined to become the nation's newest minority group by midcentury. This perverse patriotism longs for a simpler time, when cultural mores were set and values more clearly defined.

This book has demonstrated several incontrovertible facts about US Hispanics. Like their forebears, Hispanics dream in much the same way as the rest of American society. They want better lives for themselves and their children; they would like to live in a house they own; they pine for a good job; and they believe that their lives will be better in the U.S.—if not for themselves, then surely for their children. These sentiments form the core of the American Dream and may actually be helping to revive it. In many ways, Hispanics (and those of Hispanic descent) are better dreamers than native-born whites who, the data show, are losing faith in the American Dream. In addition, Hispanics, like their immigrant forebears, are moving into the political arena with alacrity, voting in ever larger numbers with each passing presidential election. In 2012, Hispanics accounted for 10 percent of the total vote in Barack Obama's successful reelection campaign, far more than the less than 1 percent of the vote in Ronald Reagan's 1980 landslide. Their numbers will surely rise in 2016 given another stubborn fact: with each passing month, 50,000 Hispanics turn eighteen years old in the United States (Navarrette 2011).

These incontrovertible facts should guide present-day debates. Logic dictates that the major political parties, interested in their survival, would take note of the changing demographics and plan accordingly. In 2012, Barack Obama received 71 percent of the Hispanic vote, leading fact-minded tacticians at the Republican National Committee to conclude: "[We] must embrace and champion comprehensive immigration reform. If we do not, our party's appeal will shrink to its core constituencies only" (Republican National Committee 2013, 8).

But facts have given way to emotion, as fear among Republican base voters about the Hispanic presence—and what kinds of changes might result from it—have served as an insurmountable roadblock (for the moment) to immigration reform. A sign posted on an abandoned army barracks in rural Maryland captures these fears: "NO ILLEAGLES HERE NO UNDOCUMENTED DEMOCRATS" [*sic*] (Associated Press 2014).

This book is unlikely to change the contemporary climate in which we find ourselves. Only strong, transforming leadership can do that. But this manuscript gives policy makers a guide to the "stubborn facts" and the complexities of race/ethnicity, mobility, and the American Dream that may help to guide the inevitable changes in public policy making that are sure to come. What are the facts and complexities that our authors from multiple disciplines note in areas of politics, history, religion, and sociology?

Politics is a major part of the landscape when considering the American Dream for Latino/as. The first two chapters in this volume deal with presidents and policy (respectively). In his chapter, "Whose Dream? US Presidents, Hispanics, and the Struggle for the American Future," John Kenneth White describes how presidents have used the American Dream to advance the idea of equality for immigrants. By telling their stories and immersing themselves in the mythology of the American Dream, presidents have sought to advance the immigrant's standing in US society. This historic truth has particular relevance in today's immigration debate.

Ever since James Truslow Adams first coined the term "American Dream," it is expected that US presidents pay homage to it by using their personal stories (and those of others) as illustrations of its success. Barack Obama is no different from his predecessors. But what makes today's articulation of the American Dream challenging for presidents is a ferocious debate as to whether Hispanics are entitled to share in the American Dream and whether their claims to it are legitimate. Polling data show Hispanics are fervent subscribers to the tenets of the American Dream: believing in its precepts of having the opportunity to do better than one's parents, owning a home and obtaining a college education as symbols of the Dream's success, having personal freedom to make individual choices, and hard work as the key to an individual's success.

However, the demographic changes that have come to the United States in the twenty-first century have produced an impassioned debate over immigration policy. It is expected that by 2050 whites will be a minority of the US population—a trend foreshadowed by the fact that Hispanics constitute today's leading minority group. Both George W. Bush and Barack Obama have been thrust into the midst of this debate, as both have advocated immigration reforms only to be thwarted by opponents. Most of the resistance has come from Republicans who are nostalgic for the past. This opposition often borders on fanaticism and is reminiscent of previous debates over immigration policy during the twentieth century. This chapter finds that Hispanics are thoroughly "American" when it comes to their identification with American values, including patriotism, hard work, freedom, and using their individual rights to make a better life for themselves.

In his chapter, "DREAM-ing the American Dream: The Struggle to Enact the DREAM Act," Matthew Green describes the ongoing legislative history of the DREAM Act, legislation that grants legal status and in-state tuition to young undocumented residents of the United States. For hundreds of thousands of young immigrants, the DREAM Act represents a powerful opportunity to achieve the American Dream. After a brief outline of the history of immigration reform since the late nineteenth century, Green describes the piecemeal successes of DREAM Act advocates at the state level starting in the 1990s, which have resulted in elements of the act (namely, the ability to attend state schools at in-state tuition rates) being adopted in nearly twenty states by mid-2014 and a potential consensus of support among leaders of both political parties for the DREAM Act, if not comprehensive immigration reform. Drawing upon the work of John Kingdon and other theorists of policy change and immigration policy, Green argues that the partial success to date of the DREAM Act at the state and national level illustrates the critical role that activists, public opinion, and political elites play—as well as widespread belief in the American Dream—in making immigration policy at the state and national level. It also underscores the status quo bias of policy at the national level and the frequent divisions that occur within national parties, which together discourage the passage of legislation like the DREAM Act—as well as the American system of federalism, which encourages its passage at the state level.

What about Latino/a migrants who are crossing our borders in large numbers? Is it the American Dream that lures them? In the chapter on "'The American Dream': Walking toward and Deporting It," Daniel Martínez, Jeremy Slack, Alex E. Chávez, and Scott Whiteford ask what role, if any, does the continued search for the "American Dream" play in explaining the reasons for Mexican deportees' future crossing intentions postdeportation? Does the search for the American Dream still seem to matter for people who have spent time living and working in the United States before being deported? Or do other more proximate social factors, such as the intimacy of one's home or family in the United States, help to explain repeat crossing intentions among this group? The authors address these questions by drawing on the second wave of the Migrant Border Crossing Study (MBCS), a new and unprecedented data set based on surveys and in-depth interviews with recently repatriated Mexican migrants. The data show how people have left Mexico looking for something that approximates the American Dream as the search for opportunity, but after they have been deported, this no longer figures as the predominate reason to go back. Rather a strong connection to the United States—one based largely on a sense of "home"—is what drives repeat migration after deportation. The authors conclude that the search for the American Dream is not simply driven by a sense of relative deprivation or an abstract search for "something better," but rather the "Latino/a American Dream" is increasingly connected to keeping one's family together and fostering an emerging sense of "place" and "home" in the United States.

How does race/ethnicity intersect with the American Dream for Latino/as? More specifically, does ethnic nationality make a difference for opportunities among Latino/as to achieve the Dream? And how do Latino/as fare relative to the other major race/ethnic minority group in the United States—African Americans? Two chapters in this volume explore these issues involving race/ethnicity and the American Dream. In his chapter "Hispanics and the American Dream: Lessons from the Experiences of Hispanics across Nationalities Residing in Washington, DC," Enrique S. Pumar uses both census data and recent interviews to explore the extent to which Hispanic residents in the District of Columbia have achieved the American Dream. The chapter reaches several critical conclusions. First, despite the troubles associated with the insertion into American society, Hispanics consume the ideals of the American Dream at a rate higher than most. Second, these ideals constitute one of the most powerful pulling factors attracting Hispanic immigrants to American shores. Most importantly, Pumar's research on the Hispanic experience demonstrates the need to disaggregate ethnic data by nationalities. He argues that this is necessary in revealing how particular stocks of knowledge, tied to levels of national development, impact the rate of success among immigrants even when they entered the United States around the same years and under similar conditions.

In his chapter "The Color of the Dream: Latino/as, African Americans, and the American Dream," Steven A. Tuch notes that a large increase in the Latino/a population in the United States since 1980 has dramatically changed the racial and ethnic terrain of twenty-first-century America. His chapter examines Latino/as' views of the American Dream and compares them to the views of African Americans. How hopeful are Latino/as about their prospects for attaining the Dream? Do Latino/as view themselves as competing with blacks over economic and other scarce resources? If so, do these perceptions dampen their views of the likelihood of success in realizing the Dream? An examination of nationally representative survey data from 2000 to 2012 reveals that both Latino/as and African Americans believe more strongly than non-Hispanic whites that their pursuit of the Dream will ultimately succeed. Tuch concludes that there are not two American Dreams—one for Latino/as and another for blacks—but one shared Dream.

Religion is of central importance to Latino/as, and two chapters in this volume consider its connection to the American Dream. In their chapter "From the Margins to the Center: The US Catholic Bishops, Latino/as, and the American Dream in the Twentieth Century," Maria Mazzenga and Todd Scribner focus on the bishops' engagement with Latino/a communities in the twentieth century. Viewed through the prism of the American Dream, the authors take a historical look at the US bishops' support for these communities and the extent to which this support enhanced the political and social standing of Latino/as in the United States. Did the actions of the bishops help this population move from the margins of American life to its center? Their examination of archival data suggests that this support was provided in different ways at different times. In the first half of the century the bishops affirmed a distinct form of Catholic Americanization, which included an embrace of American middle-class values centered on achievement of the American Dream: attaining middle-class status, acquiring citizenship, achieving English language proficiency, and practicing an officially approved Catholicism. Within a few short decades the bishops initiated efforts in the arena of Hispanic ministry, with the hope of providing for the material and, in particular, spiritual needs of these communities. With the emergence of illegal immigration as a problem in the 1970s, advocacy efforts in support of amnesty and, later, the more robust notion of comprehensive reform became central to the institutional church's activities. Throughout, the bishops had to navigate the needs of Latino/a populations, both spiritual and material, alongside resistance that native-born Americans often expressed toward these populations. The authors conclude that the Catholic bishops engaged Latino/a communities in different ways during the twentieth century in an attempt to empower these communities in the public square, and simultaneously nurture their commitment to the church. Efforts by the hierarchy aimed at helping Latino/as "make it" in America and better access the American Dream. These efforts have not been an unadulterated success; a variety of obstacles that originated both inside and outside the church hindered the bishops' ability to fully realize their broader objectives of empowering Latino/as living in the United States.

The chapter titled "Changing for the Dream? Latino/a Religious Change and Socioeconomic Success" by Jessica Hamar Martínez and Phillip Connor looks at another issue involving religion and the American Dream for Latino/as. They note that as the Latino/a population has grown in the United States some complex changes in religious affiliation have taken place. Although a majority of Latino/as have historically been and continue to be Catholic, there has also been religious change among Latino/as in recent years as increasing shares have become Protestant or have no religious affiliation. The authors ask, "Is this religious change associated with differential success in attaining the American Dream?" They use recently released data from a nationally representative survey of Latino/a adults collected by Pew Research Center to examine whether or not religious change is associated with varying levels of socioeconomic success. Findings suggest that neither religious affiliation nor religious switching is associated with higher or lower employment rates or income. However, religion is associated with educational outcomes among Latino/as. More specifically, Protestants and the unaffiliated are more likely to have some postsecondary education, particularly for second-generation Latino/as. Religiously active Protestants are even more likely to have a higher education. However, those who were raised in a religion but currently claim no religious affiliation have the highest likelihood of all groups to have some postsecondary education.

Social scientists have historically conceived of race/ethnicity and gender as distinct areas of inquiry. In her chapter "Latino/a, American, Dream: Men, Women," Sandra L. Hanson argues that although Latino/a men and women do share in many experiences and dreams, they are not interchangeable. The chapter examines the concept of the American Dream for Latino/as from a perspective that acknowledges the intersection of race/ethnicity and gender. Data from a number of sources (including Census and Pew Hispanic Center) are used to examine how Latino/a men and women are doing on objective measures of achievement related to the American Dream as well as attitudes about the American Dream. Latino/as have had lower success in achieving the American Dream on most objective measures such as education, occupation, and income relative to other race/ethnic groups, and to some extent both Latino/a men and women are struggling to achieve the Dream. On the other hand, Latino men are ahead of Latina women on some measures of the Dream (for example, poverty rates), and Latina women are catching up to and surpassing Latino men on others (for example, high school degrees). In spite of this objective situation, there is considerable optimism in attitudes (and hopes) about the American Dream for Latino/a men and women, and there are few gender gaps here. On many items (for example, involving standard of living and getting ahead), Latino/a men and women are more optimistic than men and women in other race/ethnic groups. This is not the case for financial items, however. The chapter concludes with a discussion of the rising success rates of Latina women on many measures of the American Dream and the difficulties being experienced by increasing numbers of young Latino men. Low levels of education and concentration in states that have been hit hard by the recession make Latino men economically vulnerable. Research and policies aimed at reducing race/ethnic inequality in the United States need to consider the structures that limit Latino/as, their agency in sometimes surmounting the limits of these structures, the unique experiences of Latino/as (relative to other ethnic/minority groups), and the ways in which the American experience and American Dream are not identical for Latino/a men and women.

The authors in this volume use multiple perspectives to examine the attitudes and experiences of Latino/as in their quest for the American Dream. The questions that motivated the research involve the intersections of race, ethnicity, and the American Dream in the context of politics, history, religion, immigration experience, country of origin, and gender. Although the answers to our questions about Latino/as and the American Dream are complex, a thread throughout is an optimism and focus on family, community, hard work, and religion that reflects and revitalizes some of the core values of the American Dream. The chapters will hopefully contribute to the ongoing dialogue on the complex historical and contemporary experiences with assimilation, multiculturalism, and the Dream for US Latino/as.

References

"An American Original." 2010. *Vanity Fair*, October 6.

Associated Press. 2014. "Maryland State Police Investigate Graffiti." *Washington Post*, July 15.

Navarrette, Ruben, Jr. 2011. "Solving Immigration Problems Requires Honest Debate." *Contra Costa Times*, September 28.

Nixon, Richard M. 1992. PBS, *The American Experience*. September 24.

Reagan, Ronald. 1988. "Remarks at the Republican National Convention. New Orleans, August 15.

Republican National Committee. 2013. *Growth and Opportunity Project.*

Truman, Harry S. 1948. "Address in Oklahoma City," September 28. In *Public Papers of the Presidents: Harry S. Truman*, 1949. Washington, DC: US Government Printing Office.

Index

Adams, James Truslow, ix, 19, 24, 59, 100, 103, 223
Adams, John Quincy, 19
African Americans: and American Dream, 13, 23, 119–23, 127–33, 192–98; in demographics, 4–6, 11, 19, 27, 72, 200, 202–204, 209, 212, 225–26; as a minority, ix, x, 189
age: college, 50; in demographics, 9–10, 75, 77–80, 121–22, 128, 130–31, 150, 168, 171–74, 176, 178, 194, 198–99, 201, 204, 209, 212; high school, 49
agenda setting, 34, 43–45, 158
Agendas, Alternatives, and Public Policies, 44
Alabama, 56, 91
Alba, Richard, 175
Alliance for Progress, 105
Alvarez, Alfredo, 30
American Council on Education, 195, 197, 213
American Creed, 20, 71
American Dream: and assimilation, 103–04, 113–15; and economy, 1, 31, 74–76, 102, 121–22, 127, 142, 196–99; history of, 18–22, 24, 59, 100, 191, 197; for immigrants, ix–x, 2–6, 23–25, 37, 42, 47, 69–70, 73–78, 81, 83–84, 86–90, 92–94, 99, 132, 187, 225–28; and Latino/a culture, 6–14, 119, 133, 146–47, 157–58, 181–82, 188–95, 202, 204, 209, 212–14, 222; in politics, 10, 12–13, 43, 51, 61, 154, 156, 223–24; and religion, 13–14, 137–39, 144–45, 152, 160, 167, 169, 174, 181–82; values of, 8–9, 25–26, 71–72, 105–108, 128, 157
American Exceptionalism, 26, 103
American Immigration Reform, 53
American Revolution, ix, 28

Americanization, 138–40, 142, 144, 157–58, 226
amnesty, 34, 47, 58, 153–54, 156–57, 226
Anderson, Benedict, 26
Anglo culture, 27, 73, 145, 157–58
Anticommunism. *See* communism
Argentina, 108
Arizona, 30, 32–33, 54–55, 88, 91
ASPIRA, 6

Bakhtin, Mikhail, 70
Bankston, Carl, 175
Barbados, 108
Barletta, Lou, 31–32
Belize, 107
Bernardin, Joseph, 152
Bishops' Conference of the United States, 13, 138–39, 146–47, 154
Blau, P. M., 188
Blumer, Herbert, 120
Bobo, Lawrence, 120, 132, 189
Boehner, John, 32, 58–59
Boone, Caroline, 142–43, 145
Boorstin, Daniel, 26
borders: and American immigration, 27, 29, 32, 54, 76, 104, 115, 137, 224; and drugs, 32; Mexico-US, 46, 55, 68–70, 77–94, 106, 139–40, 142–43, 145, 157; and security, 153. *See also* coyotes; US Border Patrol
Bracero guest-worker program, 46, 80, 139, 146–47, 155
Breen, Joseph I., 143–44
Buchanan, Patrick J., 30
Bureau of Immigration, 141, 143–45, 157. *See also* NCWC
Burke, John J., 141–42
Bush, George H.W., 21, 29

Bush, George W., 21, 31, 34, 37, 48–49, 53–55, 223
Bush, Jeb, 36

California, 28, 30, 32, 50, 54, 104; Baja, 77, 80; Los Angeles, 51, 73, 87, 92
Calles, Plutarco Elías, 145
Calleros, Cleofás, 145–46
Canada, 19, 46
Cantor, Eric, 32, 58, 59
Cantril, Hadley, 25
capabilities: social, 108; development and personal, 109–11, 113–14; deprivations, 109
capitalism, 74, 172
Carville, James, 31
Castro, Fidel, 47
Catholicism: Catholics, 27, 142, 150–51, 156–59, 167, 175, 180–81; clergy, 13, 56, 137–39, 148–49, 226; and immigrants, 13, 38, 139–41, 144–45; and Latino/a culture, 12, 14, 141, 143, 157, 166, 168–70, 172, 178–79, 226–27; social doctrines, 138; Vatican Council, 139, 159.
Cavalcanti, H.B., 166
census (US): 1920, 143; 2000, 7; 2010, 4–5, 100, 111–12, 192, 194, 213; Bureau and data, 30, 187, 196, 225, 227
Center for Immigration Studies, 53
Central America, 8, 107, 147
"chain migration", 148
Chasing the Dream: Different Paths, One Shared Future, 103
Chevalier, Michel, 21–22
Chesterton, G.K., 25
Chicago, 152
childhood religion, 169–71
Cicourel, Aaron, 110
citizenship: American, 93, 106; classes, 140, 142, 144–45; granting of US, 19, 25, 26, 30, 32–36, 42–3, 45, 49–51, 53–60, 71, 73, 99–100, 102, 106, 114, 146–48, 154, 157, 226
Civil Rights Act of 1964, 27–28
Clinton, Bill, 21, 28, 47
Cold War, 26–27, 46, 105, 221–22
College Board Advocacy and Policy Center, 196–97, 214
Colorado, 30, 53, 55, 57, 141
communism, 26, 46, 107, 221
community: and immigrants, 76–78, 80,

90, 94, 100, 102, 104, 140; and Latino/a culture, 3, 11–12, 35, 133, 138–39, 148, 151–52, 157–58, 214, 226; and religion, x, 149, 158–59; and values, 8, 10, 26–27, 71, 75, 144, 154, 191, 228; work, 6, 147
community college, 4
competition-threat, 128, 131–32
"concepts of personhood and agency", 70, 76, 87, 90, 93
Congress (US): and the American Dream, 26; and Bracero program, 155; and the DREAM Act, 42–44, 49, 51–57, 59–60; Hispanic Caucus, 215; and immigration, 27, 32, 35–36, 45–48, 50, 58–59, 61, 107, 147, 152–53; and the President (US), 34–35, 107
consequences delivery system (CDS), 69
conservatism, 56–58, 128, 131, 159
"consumer culture", 74
Coolidge, Calvin, 27
coyote, 68, 86, 88–89. See also borders
Crenshaw, Kimberle, 191
Cronbach's alpha reliability coefficient, 128
Cuba, 29, 47
Cuban National Forum, 6
cultural diplomacy, 105, 114, 116

Deferred Action for Childhood Arrivals (DACA), 56–57, 93
Deferred Action for Parents (DAP), 93
Democrats (US political party): and DREAM Act, 49, 54–56, 58, 60–61; and immigration reform, 57, 223; and Latino/as, 10, 12, 30–32 35–36
demography: ethnic, 2, 4, 6, 119, 187, 195, 198, 222–23; and immigration, 29, 36, 78; Latino/a, 3, 9, 101, 129, 172; and religion, 150–51, 157, 172; sociodemographic, 176
Department of Agriculture (US), 147
Department of Homeland Security (US), 69
Department of Justice (state—US), 30, 32
deportation: and the American Dream, 78, 81–84, 87–88, 224–25; Latino/a, 35, 69, 145; Romney, 20; in the US, 36, 51, 53–54, 56–57, 59, 70, 77, 90–91, 93–94, 145–46, 154
Development as Freedom, 108
Dick, Hilary Parsons, 70, 87